Java®
FOR
DUMMIES®
A Wiley Brand

*e*LEARNING KIT

Java® FOR DUMMIES®
A Wiley Brand
eLEARNING KIT

by John Paul Mueller

Java® eLearning Kit For Dummies®

Published by
John Wiley & Sons, Inc.
111 River Street
Hoboken, NJ 07030-5774
www.wiley.com

Contents at a Glance

Table of Contents

Introduction

If you've been thinking about taking a class online (it's all the rage these days), but you're concerned about getting lost in the electronic fray, worry no longer. *Java eLearning Kit For Dummies* is here to help you, providing you with an integrated learning experience that includes not only the book you hold in your hands but also an online version of the course at `http://learn.dummies.com`. Consider this introduction your primer.

About This Kit

Each piece of this eLearning Kit works in conjunction with the others, although you don't need them all to gain valuable understanding of the key concepts covered here. Whether you follow along with the book, go online to see the course, or some combination of the two, *Java eLearning Kit For Dummies* teaches you how to:

- ✔ Install a copy of Java on your particular platform. (Windows, Linux, and Macintosh instructions are all provided.)
- ✔ Obtain an Integrated Development Environment (IDE) for your copy of Java, should you wish to use one.
- ✔ Write a basic Java program.
- ✔ Obtain help using Java to write applications for your machine.
- ✔ Use variables to store information for use in your application.
- ✔ Create and use objects that model real world information.
- ✔ Employ the new date and time API for Java in your applications.
- ✔ Perform mathematical tasks using Java.
- ✔ Make decisions based on input that the application receives.
- ✔ Perform repetitive tasks.

 ✔ Decide what to do when an error occurs in your application.

 ✔ Use lambda expressions to make your code simpler and smaller.

 ✔ Work with collections of information.

 ✔ Make the output of your application look nice.

 ✔ Work with data that appears on your hard drive.

 ✔ Interact with the XML data that appears in so many different places (both on your local hard drive and online).

How This Book Is Organized

This book is split into the 13 chapters that are described in this section. You can find more information about using all the pieces of the multimedia kit together in the "Accessing the Java eCourse" section of this introduction.

Chapter 1: Starting with Java: Before you can begin doing anything with Java, you need a copy of Java on your system. More importantly, you need a copy of Java with all the current features. This chapter helps you obtain a current version of Java and install it on your Windows, Macintosh, or Linux system. You'll also learn how to obtain an Integrated Development Environment (IDE, for short) should you wish to use one with the book. (You can use any text editor that you like.) Of course, when you have Java installed, you'll want to create at least a basic program with it, so this chapter introduces you to Java programming techniques as well. Java is a rich language, so it's important to know how to obtain help when you need it (even the professionals use help) — this chapter ends by showing you how.

Chapter 2: Using Primitive Variables: Variables provide a kind of storage box that you use to hold information while your application works with it. This chapter introduces you to basic variables that Java developers call *primitives* because they don't require anything fancy to use them.

Chapter 3: Using Object Variables: Primitive variables have limitations. Yes, they're simple to use, fast, and don't require much memory, but they lack many of the features that developers want. This chapter introduces you to feature-rich object variables. The basic idea is the same as using primitive variables — variables are meant to hold data, after all — but object variables make it so much easier to perform special tasks that you'll wonder how you got along without them. This chapter also introduces you to the new date and time API that makes working with both date and time significantly easier.

Chapter 4: Formatting Variable Content: The output from your application is important. Sure, you can output that number in any old way, but your user may not understand what it means. Formatting is an essential part of writing applications. To an extent, creating a nice output simply makes your application easier on the eyes, but formatting also contributes to understanding what the output means.

Chapter 5: Working with Operators: Many applications are used to perform math-related tasks. Operators provide a means of telling Java what math tasks to perform and the order in which you want them performed. There are also operators that help the application make decisions, such as whether one number is greater than another. In fact, you'll use lots of operators in your application to tell Java how to view a particular variable, how to interact with it, or simply what task to perform with one or more variables.

Chapter 6: Working with Conditional Statements: Most applications have to make decisions based on the data they receive. For example, if a number is higher than the one you expected, then you need to tell the application what to do about it. Just as you make thousands of decisions every day, the applications you write must also make decisions to model the real world. This chapter helps you understand the methods that Java provides for making decisions.

Chapter 7: Repeating Tasks Using Loops: Writing an application that performs a task only one time doesn't make too much sense. The time required to write the application is almost always greater than the time required for you to perform the task once. This chapter helps you create applications that can perform tasks more than once. Repetition is one of the fortes of computer systems. A computer will perform the same task as many times as you want precisely the same way every time.

Chapter 8: Handling Errors: Everyone makes mistakes. Even if a human isn't involved, mistakes happen. A program can experience an error simply due to a hardware glitch or as the result of something that another application is doing on the host system. This chapter emphasizes the benefits of detecting errors and then doing something about them, rather than letting your application crash. If you've ever been upset because an application lost your data after a seemingly needless crash, then you'll definitely want to read this chapter to avoid those problems in your own application.

Chapter 9. Creating and Using Classes: You'll have seen objects used quite a bit by this point in the book. Java relies on classes to create objects. If you haven't seen the class of your dreams, Java may not provide it. Never fear! You can create your own classes that meet any need that you can imagine. This chapter shows how to create classes that you can then use as objects in your applications to perform amazing tasks. It also demonstrates the use of lambda expressions, which is a new Java feature that will make your code smaller, faster, and less prone to errors.

Chapter 10: Accessing Data Sets Using Arrays and Collections: You see collections of things all around you. If you have a bookshelf, then you have a collection of books. When you go to the closet, you see a collection of clothing. A collection is an assortment of like items that are placed in a single storage container. This chapter helps you understand what collections (and the related arrays) are and how using them can make your application work better.

Chapter 11: Performing Advanced String Manipulation: The string is the most common variable used in Java because a string models how humans think about information. Every sentence you've read so far in this Introduction is a string. When you read any other book, you read strings. Look at an advertisement with writing and you see strings. In short, strings are everywhere. This chapter helps you perform some advanced tasks using strings that you'll find helpful as your applications become more complex.

Chapter 12: Interacting with Files: Variables represent temporary storage of data in an application. When the application ends, the variables are destroyed and the data they contain is gone. Of course, you may want to store that information in some permanent form for later use. This chapter shows how to use files, which provide permanent storage for your data on the hard drive of your machine.

Chapter 13: Manipulating XML Data: Your machine contains a wealth of file types. Chapter 12 introduces you to text files, which provide a means of storing basic information as strings. Unfortunately, basic text files don't have any intelligence — meaning they can't communicate what the data they contain means. You can't save the context of the information so that the information is easy to understand later. The eXtensible Markup Language (XML) makes it possible to add intelligence to data storage so that it's possible to tell the difference between a name and a color later. This chapter provides a brief overview of working with XML in a Java application.

Conventions Used in This Book

A few style conventions will help you navigate the book part of this kit efficiently:

- ✔ Terms or words that I truly want to emphasize are defined in Lingo sections.
- ✔ Website addresses, or URLs, are shown like this: `http://www.dummies.com`.
- ✔ Numbered steps that you need to follow and characters you need to type (such as a user ID or password) are set in **bold**.

Foolish Assumptions

For starters, I assume you know what eLearning is, you need to find out how to build Java applications (and fast!), and you want to get a piece of this academic action the fun and easy way with *Java eLearning Kit For Dummies*.

I'm also assuming that you know the basics of working with your computer and the operating system installed on that computer. You need to know how to work with the input devices for your computer, perform basic tasks that require you to start applications, and how to perform tasks with those applications, such as using your browser to access information online. The first chapter provides instructions on how to install Java on your system, but it's a plus if you've installed applications on your system before.

There are a number of places in the book where you'll need to go online to perform tasks. For example, accessing basic Java help requires that you get online for the latest information. The Go Online icon (see the "Icons Used in This Kit" section) will also direct you to online resources that you'll want to access.

Icons Used in This Kit

The familiar and helpful *For Dummies* icons point you in the direction of really great information that's sure to help you as you work your way through assignments. Look for these icons throughout *Java eLearning Kit For Dummies*, in the book and in the electronic lessons.

The Tip icon points out helpful information that's likely to make your job easier.

This icon marks an interesting and useful fact — something you probably want to remember for later use.

The Warning icon highlights lurking danger. When you see this icon, pay attention and proceed with caution.

Some programming concepts are a little harder to understand than others are. This icon points out ways in which you can improve your knowledge of these harder areas by practicing with the examples provided in that section of the chapter.

In addition to the icons, the book includes these friendly study aids that bring your attention to certain pieces of information:

- ✔ **Lingo:** When you see the Lingo box, look for a definition of a key term or concept.

- ✔ **Go Online:** Serving as your call to action, this box sends you online to view web resources, complete activities, or find examples.

- ✔ **Extra Info:** This box highlights something to pay close attention to in a figure or points out other useful information related to the discussion at hand.

Accessing the Java eCourse

Your purchase of this For Dummies eLearning Kit includes access to the course online at the For Dummies eLearning Center. If you have purchased an electronic version of this book, please visit `http://www.dummies.com/go/getelearningcode` to gain your access code to the online course. If you purchased the paperback book, you find your access code inside the front cover of this book.

Dummies eCourses require an HTML5-capable browser. If you use the Firefox or Chrome browser, make sure you have the latest version. Internet Explorer 10 is also HTML5-capable.

Class Is In

Now that you're primed and ready, it's time to begin. Most readers will want to start with Chapter 1. This chapter provides essential information for getting Java installed, obtaining and installing an IDE, creating a simple first application, and obtaining help about Java features. If you're absolutely certain that you already know all of this information, then you can probably start with Chapter 2. If you feel like downloading the book's sample Java code, head on over to `http://www.dummies.com/go/javaelearning`, where you'll find the code nicely organized by chapter.

Chapter 1

Starting With Java

- ✔ Java's increasing popularity makes it *the most common language* used to develop cross-platform applications.

- ✔ Developers rely on the fact that Java is a *standards-based language.*

- ✔ Each platform that Java supports has its own version of the Java Software Development Kit (SDK) and Java Runtime Engine (JRE), *yet uses precisely the same language.*

- ✔ All Java applications share *common components.*

- ✔ Java applications rely on *a special application called a compiler* to change Java source code that the developer understands to an executable form that the JRE understands.

- ✔ Use comments *to make it easier to remember what tasks your application performs.*

- ✔ Java applications *rely on the Java Application Programming Interface (API)* to perform many tasks.

- ✔ Develop a better understanding of Java *by viewing the help files.*

*J*ava is an amazing language. Most programming languages are designed around a single operating system or environment. For example, when you work with the Microsoft .NET Framework languages, such as C# or Visual Basic, you're working with Windows unless you get a special third-party product to make these languages work elsewhere. Likewise, Macintosh developers commonly use Objective C to create their applications. Using PHP means that you're creating applications that appear in a browser, rather than applications that run within the host operating system. Java crosses all these boundaries. You can find Java running on just about every operating system, and Java applications can run both within the operating system environment and as part of a browser presentation.

It isn't hard to find a copy of Java. Some operating systems come with Java installed, or another application will install Java for you. Even if Java isn't installed on your system, a version of the language is available for most platforms. One of the first tasks that you perform in this chapter is to install your own copy of Java.

Java receives strong support in the developer community. You can find all sorts of tools, add-on products, and free source code. In fact, the number of choices can become overwhelming. This chapter starts out slowly and makes you aware of choices you need to make based on how you plan to use Java to create applications.

Programs contain standard basic parts that this chapter shows you how to construct. You can add to program functionality by using standardized features found in the Java *Application Programming Interface*

LINGO

Java programmers use the **Java Software Development Kit (SDK)** to gain access to Java features, such as the ability to display information on screen or to work with files. To make the process of writing applications as easy as possible, the programmer uses an **Integrated Development Environment (IDE)** to write code. The IDE provides special help, such as reminding you about the Java features you can access as you type and finding errors in your code. After the programmer finishes writing an application, the source code is compiled into a `.class` file, and you can run it using the **Java Runtime Engine (JRE)**.

(or Java API), a collection of code samples that lets you write Java applications with greater ease by reducing the amount of code you need to write. Code makes your application do something useful, but in order to understand the code, you need to add comments as a means of documentation. Adding comments to your code makes it easier to read.

An essential fact to remember about Java is that you can get lots of help using this language — you're never left to your own devices with Java, because help is always available. You don't need to know any sort of special handshake or rely on certain people to discover how Java works. This chapter provides you with basic information about getting help with Java. You'll also find more information on getting help as the book progresses.

LINGO

Lots of people talk about platforms, but most of them don't explain what the term means. It can mean different things to different people. When you see the term **platform** in this book, it means a combination of hardware and an associated operating system. It isn't enough to refer to the operating system alone. For example, some versions of Windows work across multiple kinds of hardware (everything from PCs to tablets and phones). The combination of hardware and operating system denotes a platform.

Considering Why You'd Use Java

Java, like all programming languages, has both positive and negative features. It's important to know why you're learning Java before you do anything else because having a good reason to do something is a motivator. The following sections describe some of the benefits of using Java as a programming language.

Using a popular language

Literally hundreds (perhaps thousands) of computer languages are available today. Some of these languages are definitely more popular than others. Precisely which language is most popular depends on who you ask. For example, many people trust the judgment of TIOBE — an organization that tracks programming language popularity (amongst other things) — when it comes to language popularity (http://www.tiobe.com/content/paperinfo/tpci/index.html). The TIOBE information is a little stark. If you prefer some commentary with your statistics, try a site such as Udemy/

blog (`https://www.udemy.com/blog/best-programming-language`).
Just about everyone agrees that Java is a popular language (and many
organizations view Java as the most popular language).

If you're learning a first programming language and you want to ensure
you have the best chance of success of getting a job based on your skills
using the language, Java is a great choice. Java's popularity also makes it a
good choice because you have better access to a wide range of third-party
tools, libraries, and add-ons. Using a popular language also means that your
chances of finding someone to help you with a problem are significantly
better. In fact, popularity makes Java an excellent choice as a language
even when learning a third or fourth language, just because it's used in
so many places.

However, popularity doesn't necessarily make Java the right language for
you to use to satisfy a particular application requirement — functionality
makes Java the right language to use. The reason you encounter so many
languages is that people often find something lacking in an existing language and try to create a better language that addresses the failure. Java
is great for satisfying business and user-oriented needs, but I wouldn't
use it to create a device driver for an operating system because Java
lacks low-level support. This book can't answer the question of whether
Java will precisely match your needs, but it will give you the knowledge
required to answer that question on your own. Always consider language
features when choosing a language for a particular application need. If
you still need help figuring out whether Java is the right programming
language for you, consider looking online at sites such as Java Pros
and Cons (`http://c2.com/cgi/wiki?JavaProsAndCons`).

Working with a standardized language

For Java to work in all the environments that
it does, it has to have a strong standardized
language. *Standardization* means that code
designed to perform a specific task on one platform performs that same task on every other
platform. Of course, each platform must run the
same version of the JRE to ensure compatibility.
You knew there was going to be a little gotcha,
didn't you? When you think about it, this is a
small gotcha and a reasonable requirement.

GO ONLINE

The technologies found in Java
are created, monitored, and con-
trolled by the Java Community
Process (JCP). The JCP ensures
that you can discover what features new versions of Java will
contain. Individuals can even join
the JCP for free and have a voice
in what will happen with Java.
You can learn more about the JCP
at `http://jcp.org/en/home/index`.

Creating applications for multiple platforms

At one time, writing an application for Windows running on a PC answered the needs of most businesses. Organizations simply didn't require many platforms to complete required tasks. Most organizations today, however, have to support a number of platforms. People want to access the same data using their PC, tablet, and smartphone, for example. An application has to be versatile enough to work well on all three pieces of hardware (as a minimum). Because tablet and smartphone operating systems vary considerably, an application must also work well across a number of operating systems and present the user with essentially the same interface to reduce support costs. Java makes it possible to support all these requirements.

Defining other reasons to use Java

When you start talking with people about Java, you'll find many reasons to make Java your next programming language. Many developers would argue that Java is a good choice because it's free or that, with Java, it's easy to leverage skills acquired from mastering other languages, such as JavaScript and C/C++. Whether these reasons make sense to you as a developer depends on your current skill set and the requirements of your next application. Java does have a lot to offer, and you should at least consider the following reasons to adopt it:

- Java provides a large, standardized library of functions that make it possible to write robust applications without relying on any third-party products.

- The people who created Java are constantly trying to simplify its syntax (language structure) to make it easier to learn.

- Relying on Object-Oriented Programming (OOP) techniques makes Java more robust and less susceptible to problems than other languages because OOP technologies have a great track record in that area. (See the discussion at `http://www.freetopessays.com/content/paper-outlining-various-concepts-found-object-oriented-programming-oop` for details.)

- All memory-related tasks are handled for you, so all you have to worry about is writing your code.

- The huge help facility means that you won't be left out in the cold trying to figure something out.

- Strong community support means that you can ask someone what the documentation means when you can't figure it out.

- Great performance on a wide variety of platforms.

Don't worry about understanding all these reasons now. Some of these reasons are emphasized later in the book, and some of them won't really matter unless you work with other languages. File these reasons away for now and think about them later as you work through this book and begin building applications of your own.

Obtaining and Installing the Java 8 JDK

The examples in this book rely on the Java Standard Edition (SE) Development Kit 8, which is the latest version of Java. At least some of the examples will work with older versions of Java, but you'll find that you get better results using Java 8. Oracle does create Java 8 in a number of other editions, but don't worry about them for this book. Yes, if you have Java Enterprise Edition (EE) Development Kit 8, the examples will work just fine, but you really don't require such a fancy version of the product to use this book. With that in mind, the following sections describe how to download and install the Java SE Development Kit 8.

Downloading Java 8

To create a Java application, you must have the Java Development Kit (JDK). If you want others to run your application, but these others don't need to write application code, then they must have the Java Runtime Environment (JRE). The version of the JRE must match the version of your JDK to ensure that the application will run as expected. You can download a copy of the JDK for your operating system from `https://jdk8.java.net`. The JDK currently supports the following:

- ✔ Windows 32-bit and 64-bit
- ✔ Macintosh OS X 64-bit
- ✔ Linux 32-bit and 64-bit
- ✔ Linux for the Acorn RISC Machine (ARM) 32-bit processor (ARM processors are typically used in tablets and smartphones.)
- ✔ Solaris 32-bit and 64-bit (You have to install the 32-bit version first and then the 64-bit version.)
- ✔ Solaris SPARC 32-bit and 64-bit (You have to install the 32-bit version first and then the 64-bit version.)

Simply follow the link for the version of Java 8 that you require. When you want to obtain a copy of the JRE for your users, you can get it from `https://jdk8.java.net` by clicking the JRE link rather than the JDK link. (You must use the JDK when working with a device equipped with an ARM processor.) The JDK also comes with a copy of the JRE as a subdirectory of the installation.

Performing the Windows installation

Files needed: The Java installation program you downloaded

The Windows version of Java comes as an executable file that installs much like any other executable file on your system. After you download the version of the JDK for your system, use the following steps to install it.

1. **Double-click the downloaded file.**

   You may see a User Account Control dialog box appear. This dialog box asks whether you want to allow the application to make changes to your system. Click Yes to allow system changes. If you click No, the application exits, and Java doesn't install.

   You see the Welcome page of the setup wizard.

2. **Click Next.**

   You see the Custom Setup page of the wizard, as shown in Figure 1-1. The three items you must install — Development Tools, Source Code, and Public JRE — are already selected in the figure.

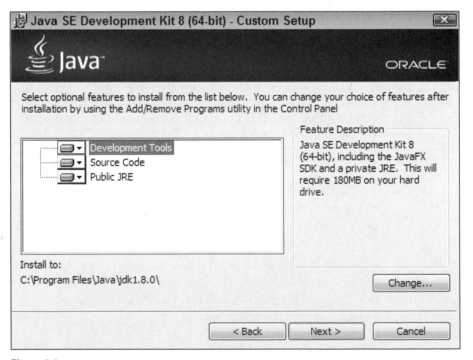

Figure 1-1

3. **(Optional) Click Change to select a location to store the Java files.**

   Normally, it's best to use the default installation location unless you have a special reason for storing the files somewhere else. Using the default location makes it easier for tools, such as an IDE, to find the files later.

4. **Click Next.**

   The setup wizard performs the installation.

   After the JDK installation is complete, you see a secondary setup dialog box appear for the JRE installation.

5. **(Optional) Click Change to select a location for the JRE installation.**

   In most cases, using the default installation location works fine.

6. **Click Next.**

   The JRE installation starts. After the JRE installation is complete, the secondary setup dialog box disappears, and you return to the initial setup dialog box.

7. **Click Close.**

   The setup is complete, and the setup wizard disappears.

GO ONLINE

The Java installation program used to include a Demos and Samples option. This option is no longer available in Java 8. To obtain this feature, you must perform a separate download from `https://jdk8.java.net`. The demos and samples come as a `.zip` file that you extract onto your hard drive. Separate versions of this file are available for the Windows, Mac, and Linux platforms.

Performing the Linux installation

Files needed: The Java installation program you downloaded

The precise steps you use to install Java on Linux depend on your Linux distribution. Installing Java by using the downloadable files means acting as the root user. Some versions of Linux (such as Fedora, Red Hat, and open-SuSE) enable the root user, but others (such as Ubuntu and Debian) don't. No matter which version of Linux you own, you generally have access to the super-user do (sudo) command. With this in mind, the easiest way to get Java on Linux is to execute the following command:

```
sudo apt-get install oracle-java8-installer
```

Performing the Mac installation

Files needed: The Java installation program you downloaded

After you download the version of the JDK for your system, extract the file on your hard drive, preferably to the `/System/Library/Java/java-8` folder. To use Java from an IDE, all you need to do is tell the IDE where to find the files. However, if you want to use Java for running applications normally, you must create a path to it by using the instructions found in the "Creating a path on the Mac" section, later in this chapter.

Accessing the Java executables

The location of the Java executable files on your system is important. The folder containing these files provides access to all the tools you require to use Java. When you install Java, the setup program tells you where these files will be stored. The following sections tell you the default location for storing the Java 8 files and provide some tips on accessing them.

Creating a path in Windows

If you're not using an IDE in Windows, you'll always have to create a path to the Java executable files. That's because Windows doesn't normally offer any Java support out of the box. The files you need will normally appear in one of two locations, unless you specifically store them somewhere else.

EXTRA INFO

One of the advantages of using an IDE is that you don't normally need to worry about the location of the Java executable files. Install the JDK first and then install the IDE. The IDE setup program will automatically locate the JDK files for you and configure the IDE to use these files when you need help, or compile, debug, or run an application.

- ✔ The `\Program Files\Java\jdk1.8.0\bin` folder is the standard storage location. (If you install a newer version of the JDK, you may find it stored in a slightly different folder. For example, if you install version 1.8.0.1, then you might see the JDK stored in the `\Program Files\ Java\jdk1.8.0.1\bin` folder.)

- ✔ When you install the 32-bit bit version of Java on a 64-bit version of Windows, the standard storage location is `\Program Files (x86)\ Java\jdk1.8.0\bin`.

You can use Windows Explorer to find the precise location of the JDK on your system. When you know this information, you can create a path to those files. In the following exercise, you create a path to the Java installation in Windows.

Files needed: None

1. **Right-click Computer and choose Properties from the contextual menu that appears, or open the System applet in the Control Panel.**

   You see the System window shown in Figure 1-2.

2. **Click Advanced System Settings in the Control Panel Home menu on the left.**

   You see the Advanced tab of the System Properties dialog box, as shown in Figure 1-3.

Figure 1-2

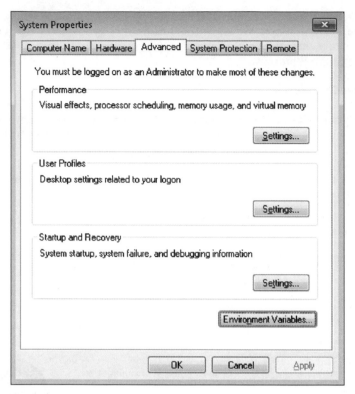

Figure 1-3

3. Click the Environment Variables button in the lower-right of the dialog box.

You see the Environment Variables dialog box shown in Figure 1-4. Notice that this dialog box is split into two sections. The upper section affects only the local user, whereas the lower section affects everyone who uses the system.

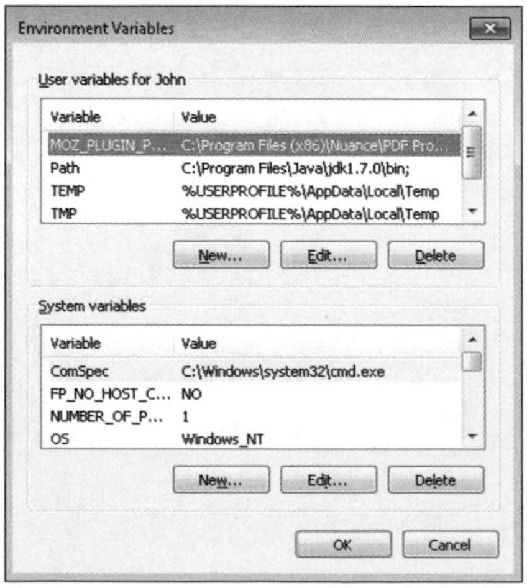

4. Highlight the Path entry for the user (if you want to use Java for just the current user's account) or the system (if everyone on the system will use Java) and click Edit.

a. If a Path entry doesn't exist, click New.

*b. Type **Path** in the Variable Name field.*

Figure 1-4

You see a variable dialog box similar to the one shown in Figure 1-5. The variable dialog box can have one of four names depending on which version you access: Add User Variable, Edit User Variable, Add System Variable, or Edit System Variable. All four versions differ in name only — they work precisely the same way.

Figure 1-5

5. **Type the path to the JDK in the Variable Value field, followed by a semicolon, without changing any of the existing content.**

   Figure 1-5 shows an example entry.

6. **Click OK three times to close the three dialog boxes you've opened.**

7. **Close the System window.**

   The environment variable is in place, and you can access Java at the command line.

Creating a path in Linux

To ensure that you can access Java 8 as needed, you must configure a path to the Java executable files by using this command:

```
sudo apt-get install oracle-java8-set-default
```

The techniques described for Solaris in the following section also work with Linux.

Creating a path in Solaris

When working with Solaris, it's likely that you already have a version of Java installed on your system. Most versions of Java will work with most of the examples in this book. However, to obtain the maximum benefit from these examples, you really do need Java 8. To determine whether you can access Java at the command line, type % **Java –Version** and press Enter. If you see a version number, you can access Java without trouble. When you see a version number older than Java 8, you'll need to think about installing a newer version of Java on your system.

In some cases, you may not be able to access Java from the command line on your system, even though Java is installed. Java 8 is normally installed in the /usr/local/jdk1.8.0/bin/ directory on your machine. (You can find other versions of Java in the appropriate version-specific directory.) If you find that Java is installed and you simply can't access it, use the appropriate procedure (depending on the shell you're using) in the following sections to provide access.

Working with the bash shell

The bash shell is one of two popular shells supplied with Solaris. (There are others, including the C shell described later in this chapter.) In the following exercise, you add a path to Java when you use the bash shell.

Files needed: None

1. **Open the ~/ `.bashrc` file for editing.**

2. **Modify the `Path` variable to include the path to your Java installation.**

    Your `Path` variable will look something like: `PATH=/usr/local/jdk1.8.0/bin`.

3. **Type** Export Path **and press Enter.**

    The shell exports the `Path` variable for you.

4. **Save the file and exit the editor.**

5. **Open a new terminal window when necessary.**

    Many versions of Linux open a terminal window immediately when you start the operating system. If you don't have an open terminal window, look for an application called Xterm, Terminal, Konsole, Console, or something similar.

6. **Type** % Java –Version **and press Enter.**

    You see the version number of the Java installation.

Working with the C shell

The C shell is one of two popular shells supplied with Solaris. (There are others, including the bash shell described earlier in this chapter.) In the following exercise, you add a path to Java when you use the C shell.

Files needed: None

1. **Open the ~/.`cshrc` file for editing.**

2. **Type** set path=(/usr/local/jdk1.8.0/bin) **and press Enter.**

3. **Save the file and exit the editor.**

4. **Open a new terminal window when necessary.**

    Again, many versions of Linux open a terminal window immediately when you start the operating system. If you don't have an open terminal window, look for an application called Xterm, Terminal, Konsole, Console, or something similar.

5. **Type** % Java –Version **and press Enter.**

    You see the version number of the Java installation.

Creating a path on the Mac

The Mac OS X Leopard setup includes several versions of Java as part of the base installation. So, you do have Java available, but you may not have the right version available. To use Java 8 as your default version of Java, you must open Terminal (by choosing the Applications⇨Utilities⇨Terminal command) and export a path to Java 8 by typing the following command:

```
$export JAVA_HOME=/System/Library/Java/java-8
```

After you export the path, you need to verify that you have the right version of Java selected. Test your installation by typing the following command in Terminal:

```
$java -version
```

You see the version number of Java that you have selected.

Choosing an IDE for Java

An IDE is simply a special kind of text editor. It provides a wealth of features that make your coding experience easier. However, you can just as easily use any text editor. For example, a Windows user could rely on Notepad to get the job done, whereas Linux users have vi and Mac users have TextEdit. The following sections discuss the use of an IDE for your projects. However, this book doesn't assume you're using any particular IDE and you won't have to worry about matching your output to the output of any particular IDE.

Working with a text editor

You can use any editor that produces pure text output to create Java applications. The most important consideration when working with a text editor is that it produces *pure text* output — text without any formatting information whatsoever. Bare-bones text editors (such as Notepad on Windows or vi on Linux) are great for producing the required pure text, but text editors that are just slightly more complicated (such as Wordpad for Windows and TextEdit

GO ONLINE

Windows users have Notepad, and it works fine for creating Java applications. If you really want something with more pizzazz, try Notepad++ (`http://notepad-plus-plus.org`). Linux developers will likely want something friendlier than vi to use. You can find a number of plain text editors at `http://www.yolinux.com/TUTORIALS/LinuxTextEditors.html`. Mac users may want to investigate Plain Text Editor for Mac, found at `http://download.cnet.com/Plain-Text-Editor/3000-2079_4-10138406.html`. Otherwise, check out the article at `http://mac.blorge.com/2009/07/14/mac-software-five-best-free-plain-text-editors-for-mac` for a description of other editors that will work on the Mac. If you work with multiple programming languages, you might want to try an editor that caters to them, such as PilotEdit (`http://www.pilotedit.com/About%20PilotEdit.htm`), a free editor that supports a host of programming languages.

on the Macintosh) will add formatting codes to the output, making the text useless to the compiler. (You can set up TextEdit as a plain text editor using the instructions at `http://support.apple.com/kb/ta20406`, but it's important that you remember to perform the task as needed.)

If you do use a plain text editor to create your applications, you'll also need to manually compile and execute the applications at the command line. It isn't difficult to perform these tasks, but it does involve extra work that an IDE would normally perform for you. This chapter tells you how to compile the application in the "Opening the command prompt" section as well as how to execute it in the "Using the Java command" section, so using a plain text editor or an IDE is completely up to you.

Finding an IDE

There are many Java-specific IDEs on the market and even more editors that will work with Java, even if they aren't specifically designed for Java. In fact, there are so many editors out there that it could (and possibly will) make your head spin, and no one wants that. If you're going to invest time and effort into learning how to work with an IDE, it's best to get a Java-specific product.

One of the fastest and most feature-complete Java editors on the market today is JCreator Pro. This IDE is written entirely in C++, a language that's valued for its high performance, which is the reason it runs so fast. It also provides a complete feature set that works well with all levels of Java development. However, this product has a few issues that make it unsuitable for this particular book. For one thing, it only runs on Windows. For another, it's not free. You can download a limited time demo version from `http://www.jcreator.com`, but you'll want to reserve this product for a time when you're working with some larger applications. You can download an older version called JCreator Standard for free from `http://download.cnet.com/JCreator/3000-2212_4-7956957.html`.

The editor that most Java developers start out with is called Eclipse (`http://www.eclipse.org/downloads`). It's a little less capable than higher end IDEs like JCreator — it doesn't provide simplified project management or version control support, for example — but it runs fine on Linux, Mac, and Windows systems. Best of all, Eclipse is community supported (you get peer help, amongst other things) and free. I used Eclipse while writing this book, but you don't have to have it. None of the chapters require you to have Eclipse, and none of the screenshots reference it in any way. It's entirely up to you whether or not you use this IDE.

Some developers don't want an IDE — they prefer an editor (a simple application that only provides basic functionality such as code editing). An editor is a product that provides features such as keyword highlighting and language help, but doesn't offer compiling and debugging. Editors are simple and small. An example of a good Java editor is JEdit (`http://www.jedit.org/index.php?page=download`). This product is free, and you can obtain Linux, Windows, and Mac versions.

Determining when to use a particular development environment

It's important to make a good choice when you decide on tools to use for your application. A tool that works for one person may not work for someone else. Experienced developers usually have multiple tools at their disposal for this very reason — it isn't possible for a single tool to meet every requirement. However, you're just starting out, so one of the tools described in the previous sections will work for now. When you do start creating more complex or larger applications, you'll want to consider these guidelines in choosing a tool.

GO ONLINE

You can find entire sites devoted to the topic of Java editors and IDEs. One of the more comprehensive offerings is at `http://apl.jhu.edu/~hall/java/IDEs.html`. If you don't like any of the products mentioned in this section and still feel that you'd like something better than Notepad to write your applications, check online for other offerings. There's an editor or IDE out there that will meet your needs.

- ✔ Does the tool match the complexity and size of your application? Large applications require a good debugger. Working with multiple programmers means that the tool must provide team support.

- ✔ Are you comfortable with the tool's user interface?

- ✔ What level of support does the tool's vendor supply? If this is a community-supported tool, look at the online forums to see how many people are actually providing support (versus those who are asking questions).

- ✔ What additional tools does the product support? For example, if you're working in a team environment, it's important that your tool provide *source control* — a method of tracking changes to your code, including recording who is currently making changes to a particular file, amongst other things.

- ✔ Can you find good reviews for the tool? A good review is unbiased and discusses both the pros and cons of the tool. If you find yourself believing that the tool is too good to be true, it probably is.

- ✔ How much does the tool cost? Some of the best tools in the world are free, but often free means *crippled* — software whose functionality has been intentionally limited — or lacking support. Then again, some costly tools are poorly written or overkill for the simple projects that you're likely to start working on at first. Make sure you question whether the tool will provide everything you need at a cost you can afford.

Creating a Simple Application

Unlike most programming languages, Java applications maintain a basic semblance of structure no matter how complex they become. For example, every Java application has at least one class, and there is no code outside of a class. To create an application, the class must have a method (a kind of code) named `main()`. Don't worry too much about how all this works just yet — the following sections fill you in on the details.

Writing the application code

This section shows how to write a simple application. This is the simplest application you can write and still have the application *do* something. You don't need anything fancy to work with this application — just an editor and your Java setup will do.

Defining the class

Every Java application begins with a class. In the following exercise, you create a class for your first Java application and discover the components that make up a class.

Files needed: `GetStarted.java`

1. **Open the editor or IDE that you've chosen to use for this book.**

2. **Type the following code into the editor screen.**

```
/* This is your first Java program.
   Author: John Mueller (John@JohnMuellerBooks.com)
   Written: 6 January 2014 */

class GetStarted
{
}
```

This is typically how you start any application, by creating a class code block. This application also starts with a comment that describes the program, who wrote it, and when it was written — another typical feature. The compiler doesn't see the comment — only you see the comment. Comments document your code so you can remember what it does later.

3. **Save the code you've written to disk using the name of the class and a
.java extension, which is GetStarted.java in this example.**

The name of the file must match the name of the class. Even though you
can put multiple classes in a single .java file, most developers put just
one top-level class in each file to make the classes easier to work with.
The application now has a class, and you could compile it if desired, but
it wouldn't run.

Leave the editor or IDE open for the next exercise.

Defining main ( )

If you want an application to perform a task, it must have a main() method.
You can write classes that don't have a main() method, but you can't run
them as applications. In the following exercise, you create a main() method
so that you can run this application.

Files needed: GetStarted.java

1. **In GetStarted.java, type the following method block (in bold) in
the class block (within the class curly brackets).**

```
class GetStarted
{
    public static void main(String args[])
    {
    }
}
```

Most programmers use a technique called *indention* to show the code
block levels. The method block is indented two or three spaces for each
line in the class block.

2. **Save the code you've written to disk.**

If you compiled the application at this point, it would run, but it
wouldn't do anything.

Leave the editor or IDE open for the next exercise.

Giving the application something to do

The main() method doesn't do anything except give the application a place
to start. To do something, the application must have a set of steps — a
procedure — to follow. In the following exercise, you give the main() method
a task to perform.

Files needed: `GetStarted.java`

1. **In `GetStarted.java`, type the following steps (in bold) in the method block (within the curly brackets).**

```
public static void main(String args[])
{
    // This is an executable statement with its
    // associated data.
    System.out.println("This is your first Java
        program!");
}
```

Each task consists of telling Java to do something, just as you do when someone gives you a set of steps to perform, as I'm doing in this exercise. In this case, the application is telling Java to print some text to the screen. The `println()` method accepts some data as input and then displays that input on screen so you can see it.

Notice that there is another comment here, but it uses a different technique to tell the compiler that it is a comment. Any line that starts out with two slashes (//) is a comment. You'll learn all about comments as the book progresses.

2. **Save the code you've written to disk.**

If you compiled the application at this point, it would run and display a simple message on screen, "This is your first Java program!" You see how all this works later in this chapter.

Leave the editor or IDE open for the next exercise.

Identifying the parts of the application

It's time to look at the sample application as a whole, rather than in pieces as you've done previously. In the following exercise, you review the pieces of the complete GetStarted sample application.

Files needed: `GetStarted.java`

1. **View the GetStarted application you created in the previous exercises.**

Your source code should look like the source code shown here:

```
/* This is your first Java program.
   Author: John Mueller (John@JohnMuellerBooks.com)
   Written: 6 January 2014 */

class GetStarted
{
    public static void main(String args[])
```

```
    {
        // This is an executable statement with its
        // associated data.
        System.out.println("This is your first Java
            program!");
    }
}
```

2. **Examine the `class` block.**

   The `class` block will always begin with the word class, followed by the class name, which is `GetStarted` in this case.

3. **Examine the method block.**

   A method block begins with a number of keywords — `public`, `static`, and `void` in this case — as discussed in future chapters. The name of the method — `main`, in this case — follows next. A method can require that you provide information to it. The `main()` method here requires just one argument, which is named `args` in this case. The `args` argument is of type `String`, which you'll discover in Chapter 3. In addition, `args []` is also an array — a topic you'll encounter in Chapter 10. So, it may all look mysterious now, but the mysteries will be explained as time goes on.

4. **Examine the single line of code used to perform a task.**

   The `main()` method calls the `println()` method to display information on screen. The `println()` method is located in the `out` subclass of the `System` class. The `println()` method requires at least one input — the data that you want displayed on screen.

5. **Save the file and close the IDE or editor.**

Compiling the Simple Application

Your IDE very likely has a means of *compiling* — turning the human-readable words you write into something the computer can understand — and running the application created earlier in this chapter. In fact, many editors also provide this feature. However, it's important to know how to compile this application at the command prompt to better understand how Java works. The following sections describe how to open a command prompt and compile the GetStarted source code into an application.

Opening the command prompt

The command prompt actually appears within a special window supported by your operating system. How you open the command prompt depends on which operating system you're using.

Working with the Linux command prompt

Some versions of Linux open a command prompt immediately when you start them. If you're using a shell that doesn't, you can always open a command prompt separately. The official name for the command prompt in most versions of Linux is the terminal. You can open it by looking for an application called Xterm, Terminal, Konsole, Console, or something similar. When the command prompt is open, you can type commands to compile and run your Java application. To access your application, type **CD *Full Application Path*** and press Enter, where *Full Application Path* is the path you used to save the source code that you created in the previous sections.

Working with the Mac command prompt

The command prompt on the Mac is called a *terminal.* Use the Applications⇨Utilities⇨Terminal command to open the terminal. (The Terminal icon looks just like an old television set.) When you open Terminal, you can type commands to gain access to your application, compile it, and run it. To access your application, type **cd *Application Directory*** and press Enter, where *Application Directory* is the relative path you use to save the source code to disk. Normally, the Mac saves everything to the /Users/Your User Name directory on the system, and the source code will appear in a subdirectory under this directory.

Working with the Windows command prompt

The output screenshots you see in this book rely on the Windows command prompt. That doesn't mean your application won't run on Linux, Solaris, or the Mac. The examples in this book run on any platform that Java supports. In fact, the beta readers for this book are testing these applications on a number of platforms. (See my blog post at http://blog. johnmuellerbooks.com/2011/03/18/errors-in-writing.aspx for a description of beta readers.) The use of Windows screenshots simplifies the book's presentation and makes it less confusing.

The command prompt on a Windows system is actually called "the command prompt," rather than something obscure like "terminal" or "konsole." Choose Start⇨All Programs⇨Accessories⇨Command Prompt to open a command prompt on a Windows system. The command prompt automatically opens to your user directory on the machine — for example, the command prompt opens to C:\Users\John on my machine. Type **CD *Application Directory*** and press Enter, where *Application Directory* is the relative path you use to save the source code to disk, to access your application when you save it in your personal user folder. However, you might have saved the data to some other location on the hard drive, in which case you must type **CD *Full Application Path*** and press Enter to access it. The example screenshots will use a folder of \Java eLearning Kit for Dummies as the starting point for each chapter, followed by a chapter-specific folder. So the examples for this chapter appear in \Java eLearning Kit for Dummies\Lesson 01.

Creating the compiled .class file

After you've opened a command prompt and have access to your application, you can compile it. Compiling takes the words that you've typed and changes them into byte codes that the JRE understands. The JRE reads these byte codes and turns them into something that the native machine can understand. Your application can run on all sorts of machines because of the JRE! In the following exercise, you compile the GetStarted application and check for its existence.

Files needed: GetStarted.java

1. **Open the command prompt for your operating system.**

   You see the command prompt or terminal window.

2. **Type** javac GetStarted.java **and press Enter.**

   The javac utility used here calls up the Java Compiler (JavaC), which creates a .class file for your application. Note that all this activity takes place under the hood, as it were; you won't see anything happen onscreen.

Make absolutely certain that you include the .java file extension when you execute the javac utility. Otherwise, the compiler won't be able to find the file it's supposed to compile, and you'll see an error message.

3. **Type** Dir **(or type** ls **when working with a Mac or Linux computer) and press Enter.**

   You see both the original .java file and the new .class file. The .class file is the one you'll execute in the next exercise.

Leave the command prompt open for the next exercise.

Executing the Simple Application

Compiling an application makes it possible to execute it. When you run, or execute, an application, you get to see what task the application performs. In the case of GetStarted, the application displays a message. The following sections describe two main methods for executing applications.

Using the Java command

An IDE normally provides some way to execute a Java application. Some editors also provide this functionality. However, it's important to know how to execute a Java application without using the IDE or editor because your users won't have this software — they need to execute the application in some other way. In the following exercise, you execute the GetStarted application to see what it does.

Files needed: `GetStarted.java`

1. Type java GetStarted **and press Enter.**

You see the message shown in Figure 1-6.

The name of the application is case sensitive. If you don't type the name correctly, Java will complain. Notice that you don't include a file extension when using the `java` utility. You only provide the name of the `.class` file.

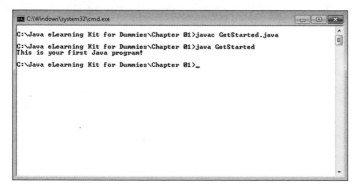

C:\Windows\system32\cmd.exe

```
C:\Java eLearning Kit for Dummies\Chapter 01>javac GetStarted.java

C:\Java eLearning Kit for Dummies\Chapter 01>java GetStarted
This is your first Java program!

C:\Java eLearning Kit for Dummies\Chapter 01>_
```

Figure 1-6

2. To test the case-sensitive nature of Java, type java getstarted **and press Enter.**

Java 8 displays an error message this time like the one shown in Figure 1-7.

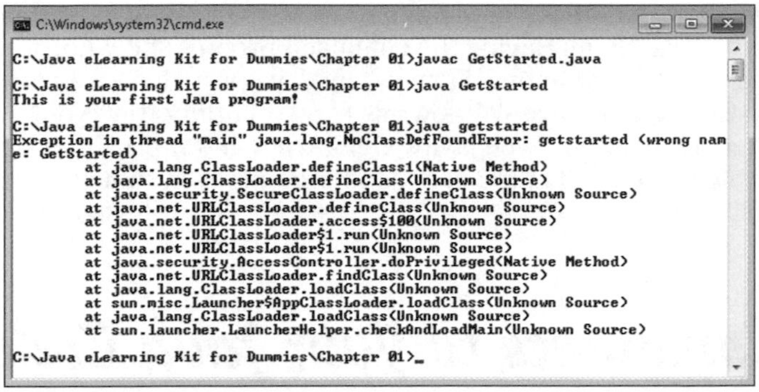

Figure 1-7

Leave the command prompt open for the next exercise.

EXTRA INFO

Earlier versions of Java displayed really complex looking error messages that looked like this:

```
Exception in thread "main" java.lang.
    UnsupportedClassVersionError: getstarted :
Unsupported major.minor version 52.0
at java.lang.ClassLoader.defineClass1(Native Method)
at java.lang.ClassLoader.defineClass(Unknown Source)
at java.security.SecureClassLoader.defineClass
    (Unknown Source)
at java.net.URLClassLoader.defineClass(Unknown Source)
at java.net.URLClassLoader.access$100(Unknown Source)
at java.net.URLClassLoader$1.run(Unknown Source)
at java.net.URLClassLoader$1.run(Unknown Source)
at java.security.AccessController.doPrivileged(Native
    Method)
at java.net.URLClassLoader.findClass(Unknown Source)
at java.lang.ClassLoader.loadClass(Unknown Source)
at sun.misc.Launcher$AppClassLoader.loadClass(Unknown
    Source)
at java.lang.ClassLoader.loadClass(Unknown Source)
at sun.launcher.LauncherHelper.checkAndLoadMain(Unknown
    Source)
```

Understanding the JavaW command difference

If you were to execute the `GetStarted.class` file using the `java` utility from something other than the command prompt, you'd see a command prompt appear for a moment, the message would display, and then the command prompt would disappear. Some Java applications (such as IDEs) are designed to work in the background, or they're designed to wait on other programs to call them. Having the command prompt show up, and then disappear can be distracting. Fortunately, Java provides a way around this problem through the Java Windowless (JavaW) utility. Try it out now with the GetStarted application. Type **javaw GetStarted** and press Enter. You won't see anything displayed at the command prompt, even though the application does run.

Adding Comments to Your Java Code

One of the most important tasks you can perform when writing code is to document it using comments. No matter how simple, you'll find that you forget what an application does later if you leave out the comments. Even the GetStarted program includes comments. The following sections describe comments and tell you how to use them.

Grasping the importance of comments

Many developers leave comments out of their programs because they think that comments are too difficult to write. However, comments are in fact quite easy to write. Trying to figure out what your code is doing six months after you've written it — *that's* hard. Most experienced programmers use copious comments because they've run into too many situations where a weekend was ruined due to the lack of comments. Comments provide many benefits, but these benefits are most important to the beginning programmer:

- ✔ Comments make it easier to remember what tasks your code performs.

- ✔ You use comments to document who makes changes, when, and for what purpose.

- ✔ Good comments make it easier to debug your application because they document how the code is supposed to work.

- ✔ Some IDEs make it possible to create the documentation for an application directly from the application comments.

- ✔ A comment can define specifics of an application, such as why a developer used a specific technique.

- ✔ It's possible to use comments to document resources that the application needs to run properly.

Creating single-line comments

A single-line comment can appear anywhere on the line. It begins with a double slash (//) and contains any text you want to include. The compiler ignores anything after the //, so the text can be anything you want. In the following exercise, you add a single-line comment to the GetStarted application.

Files needed: `GetStarted.java`

1. **Open the `GetStarted.java` file using your favorite editor or IDE.**

   You see the source code that you previously wrote.

2. **Use the description of the `main()` method earlier in the chapter to create a single line comment for it.**

   The comment you create can contain any information you find helpful. The text in bold shows a suggested series of single-line comments for this method.

   ```
   // This is the first method that Java calls when it
   // starts the application. This method is public, so
   // every other class can see the method. The method is
   // static, so it isn't used as part of an object, but
   // rather, called directly. The result is void, so this
   // method doesn't return any data to the caller. The
   // only argument, args, is a list of strings.
   public static void main(String args[])
   ```

   Notice that each single-line comment begins with a //. You'll discover more about what precisely this comment means as the book progresses. For now, this is an informational comment telling you everything there is to know about the `main()` method.

3. **Save the file to disk.**

4. **Use the steps in the "Creating the compiled `.class` file" section to compile the file.**

   The `javac` utility compiles the file without error.

5. **Use the steps in the "Using the Java command" section to execute the file.**

   Notice that the output of the application hasn't changed due to the comment you've provided. Compilers ignore any comments you may have added — they're included in the source code only for your benefit.

Leave the editor or IDE open for the next exercise.

Creating multiline comments

Multiline comments can start anywhere on a line, but they normally appear at the beginning of the line. The comment continues over multiple lines until the compiler reaches an End of Comment symbol. Multiline comments always begin with a /* and end with */. In the following exercise, you add a multiline comment to the GetStarted application.

Files needed: `GetStarted.java`

1. **Create a new multiline comment at the beginning of the file to document the change you've made to the application.**

   As with the single-line comment, the comment you create can contain any information you might find helpful. The text in bold shows a suggested multiline comment for this example:

   ```
   /* Add a comment to the main() method.
      Author: Your Name
      Written: Today's Date

   /* This is your first Java program.
      Author: John Mueller (John@JohnMuellerBooks.com)
      Written: 6 January 2014 */
   ```

   Every change you make to the application should receive a header comment at the beginning of the file so that others can see an application history. Application histories make it easier to discover which techniques have (and haven't) worked with the application.

2. **Save the file to disk and close the editor or IDE.**

3. **Use the steps in the "Creating the compiled `.class` file" section to compile the file.**

   The `javac` utility compiles the file without error.

4. **Use the steps in the "Using the Java command" section to execute the file.**

   Notice that the output of the application hasn't changed due to the comment you've provided.

5. **Save the file and close the IDE or editor.**

Importing Other Classes

The Java API is huge. It's unlikely that any developer can memorize even a small portion of it. Developers commonly memorize the portions of the API that they use often and then use the API help (http://docs.oracle.com/

javase/7/docs/api/help-doc.html) to locate the information
for a particular application. The following sections describe the Java
more detail and show you how to use it.

Introducing the Java API

The Java API is made up of a whole series of classes. The topmost class is
the java class, which isn't usable by itself. You'll always deal with a subclass, such as java.lang, which contains all the language elements for Java.
However, to perform any really useful work, you have to choose a subclass of
the java.lang class, such as String, which provides the means for working with text. So, the first usable class is actually java.lang.String. Every
API feature you use depends on a hierarchy such as java.lang.String.

The Java API has thousands of classes. Naturally, trying to access a particular
class would be hard if you didn't have some means of locating it quickly. Java
uses packages to hold groups of classes. The java.lang package holds all of the
classes that appear as subclasses to the java.lang class. Think of a package as
a means of wrapping classes up so that they're bundled together. You can find a
listing of packages and the classes they contain at http://download.java.
net/jdk8/docs/api/index.html. This site shows the packages in the upper-
left pane, elements of the package you select in the lower-left pane, and the documentation for the element you select in the right pane, as shown in Figure 1-8.

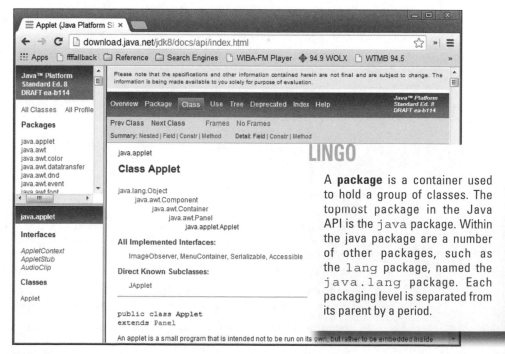

LINGO

A **package** is a container used
to hold a group of classes. The
topmost package in the Java
API is the java package. Within
the java package are a number
of other packages, such as
the lang package, named the
java.lang package. Each
packaging level is separated from
its parent by a period.

Figure 1-8

Importing single classes

Before you use a class in the Java API, you normally import it. The import keyword adds a class or an entire package to your application so that you can use it. In the following exercise, you create a new application that lets you interact with Java in a new way. You can type something at the command line, and Java will use a special class to import that information into the application.

Files needed: SayHello.java

1. **Open the editor or IDE that you've chosen to use for this book.**

2. **Type the following code into the editor screen.**

```java
// Import the required API classes.
import java.util.Scanner;
import java.lang.String;

class SayHello
{
    public static void main(String args[])
    {
        // Create an instance of the Scanner class to
        // use for keyboard access.
        Scanner getName = new Scanner(System.in);

        // Create a variable to hold the user's name.
        // This variable is designed to hold text.
        String userName;

        // Ask the user's name and place this name in
        // userName.
        System.out.print("What is your name?");
        userName = getName.nextLine();

        // Display a message to the user with the user's
        // name in view.
        System.out.println("Hello" + userName + "!");
    }
}
```

In this example, getName is a Scanner object. The Scanner object provides access to the keyboard so that you can store what the user types to a variable. A variable is a sort of box used to store information. To save what the user types, the application must grab the keystrokes from the keyboard and place them in the variable. When the application detects that the user has pressed Enter, it stops gathering keystrokes.

3. **Save the code you've written to disk using the name of the class and a .java extension, which is SayHello.java in this example.**

The name of the file must match the name of the class exactly, or the application won't compile.

4. **Open a command prompt to the directory for this example.**

5. **Type** javac SayHello.java **and press Enter.**

   The Java compiler creates a `.class` file for you.

6. **Type** java SayHello **and press Enter.**

   The application asks you to type your name.

7. **Type your name and press Enter.**

   You see a hello message that includes your name. Figure 1-9 shows a typical example of the output from this application.

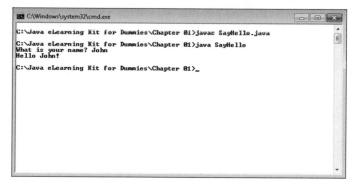

Figure 1-9

Save the file and close the IDE or editor.

Importing an entire package

When you find yourself using more than one class of a particular package, it's often more convenient to import the entire package. In this case, you follow the package name with an asterisk (*). For example, suppose you want to use multiple types from the `java.lang` package, such as `java.lang.String` and `java.lang.Integer`. In this case, you can import the entire package by using import `java.lang.*`. In the following exercise, you create a new application that uses multiple members of the `java.lang` package.

Files needed: `SayHello.java`

1. **Open the editor or IDE that you've chosen to use for this book.**

2. **Type the following code into the editor screen.**

```
// Import the required API classes.
import java.util.Scanner;

// Import the required API packages.
import java.lang.*;

class SayHello2
{
    public static void main(String args[])
    {
        // Create an instance of the Scanner class to
        // use for keyboard access.
        Scanner getName = new Scanner(System.in);

        // Create a variable to hold the user's name.
        // This variable is designed to hold text.
        String userName;

        // Ask the user's name and place this name in
        // userName.
        System.out.print("What is your name?");
        userName = getName.nextLine();

        // Create a variable to hold the number of letters
        // in the user's name.
        Integer letterCount;

        // Get the number of letters in the user's name.
        letterCount = userName.length();

        // Display a message to the user with the user's
        // name in view.
        System.out.println("Hello" + userName +
            "your name has" + letterCount + "letters in
            it!");
    }
}
```

This example extends the SayHello example to include a count of the number of letters in the user's name. Imagine that! Java can count letters and tell you how many there are.

3. **Save the code you've written to `SayHello2.java`.**

4. **Open a command prompt to the directory for this example.**

5. **Type** javac SayHello2.java **and press Enter.**

   The Java compiler creates a `.class` file for you.

6. **Type** java SayHello2 **and press Enter.**

   The application asks you to type your name.

7. **Type your name and press Enter.**

   You see a hello message that includes your name and the number of letters in your name. Figure 1-10 shows a typical example of the output from this application.

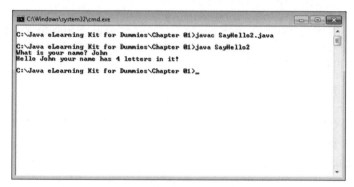

Figure 1-10

Save the file and close the IDE or editor.

Obtaining Help for Java

Java could be a little scary for someone who's just starting out. Don't worry about memorizing everything (or anything for that matter) or making mistakes. You can find help for using the Java API, all the utilities supplied with the JDK, and the various utilities output error messages when something is incorrect in your code. No one is expecting you to remember anything or to code perfectly. The following sections tell you how to obtain help when you need it.

Getting local help

The advantage of using local help, rather than online help, is that local help is always available — even when your Internet connection isn't working. A lot of people find that local help also provides faster access because you aren't using a network connection. However, local help does have a disadvantage — it's current as of the moment you download it. When an update appears to the Java help system, you won't see it unless you download a new copy of help. Often, the help on your hard drive simply continues to get outdated because there isn't any system in place to remind you to apply updates (or even tell you that they're available).

Even with its limitations, having a local copy of help comes in handy. In the following exercise, you download and install local help for your Java installation.

Files needed: None

1. **Open the page at** `https://jdk8.java.net` **in your browser.**

   You see the options for working with Java.

2. **Click the JDK 8 Release link.**

   You see a new page with download options for the JDK.

3. **Locate the Additional Resources section of this page. (Scroll down if necessary to find it.)**

4. **Click the Download icon next to the Java SE 8 Documentation entry.**

   You see a new page with a licensing agreement.

5. **Click Accept.**

   The JDK documentation download link becomes active.

6. **Click the download link.**

   Your browser downloads the documentation, which is in a `.zip` file.

7. **Open the** `.zip` **file in a directory on your local hard drive.**

   Use a folder related to the Java installation on your machine. For example, on a Windows system, you may want to create a `\Program Files\ Java\docs` folder and place the help file there.

8. **Open the** `index.html` **file in your browser.**

   You see an introductory page with a conceptual diagram. You can choose the help topic you want to use. For example, if you want to read about the `java.lang` package, you click the lang and util link. Figure 1-11 shows the conceptual diagram, which is part of a much larger page.

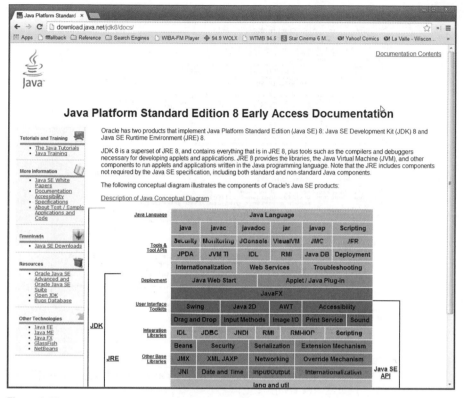

Figure 1-11

Getting local utility help

All the utilities supplied with the JDK provide their own help, so you don't
need to memorize their usage. To gain access to the help information, you
type the name of the utility followed by **–help**. For example, to access help
information about the java utility, you type **java –help**. Figure 1-12 shows a
typical utility help screen.

```
C:\Windows\system32\cmd.exe

C:\0266 - Source Code\Chapter 01>java -help
Usage: java [-options] class [args...]
           (to execute a class)
   or  java [-options] -jar jarfile [args...]
           (to execute a jar file)
where options include:
    -d32          use a 32-bit data model if available
    -d64          use a 64-bit data model if available
    -server       to select the "server" VM
                  The default VM is server.

    -cp <class search path of directories and zip/jar files>
    -classpath <class search path of directories and zip/jar files>
                  A ; separated list of directories, JAR archives,
                  and ZIP archives to search for class files.
    -D<name>=<value>
                  set a system property
    -verbose:[class|gc|jni]
                  enable verbose output
    -version      print product version and exit
    -version:<value>
                  require the specified version to run
    -showversion  print product version and continue
    -jre-restrict-search | -no-jre-restrict-search
                  include/exclude user private JREs in the version search
    -? -help      print this help message
    -X            print help on non-standard options
    -ea[:<packagename>...|:<classname>]
    -enableassertions[:<packagename>...|:<classname>]
                  enable assertions with specified granularity
    -da[:<packagename>...|:<classname>]
    -disableassertions[:<packagename>...|:<classname>]
                  disable assertions with specified granularity
    -esa | -enablesystemassertions
                  enable system assertions
    -dsa | -disablesystemassertions
                  disable system assertions
    -agentlib:<libname>[=<options>]
                  load native agent library <libname>, e.g. -agentlib:hprof
                  see also, -agentlib:jdwp=help and -agentlib:hprof=help
    -agentpath:<pathname>[=<options>]
                  load native agent library by full pathname
    -javaagent:<jarpath>[=<options>]
                  load Java programming language agent, see java.lang.instrument

    -splash:<imagepath>
                  show splash screen with specified image
See http://www.oracle.com/technetwork/java/javase/documentation/index.html for m
ore details.

C:\0266 - Source Code\Chapter 01>_
```

Figure 1-12

Locating Java information online

The advantage of using online help is that the information is always up-to-date. You don't have to ever worry about getting old information that could cause problems with your application. You'll always access the online help starting at http://download.java.net/jdk8/docs/api/index.html. As mentioned in the earlier "Introducing the Java API" section of the chapter, you begin by selecting a package, and then you select a class within a package to obtain help about that class.

 **Summing Up**

Here are the key points you learned about in this chapter:

- ✔ Java is one of the most popular languages available because it works well on so many platforms.
- ✔ Standardization is a key reason why Java is able to work in so many different environments.

✔ The JCP provides input on how Java should continue to change as a language.

✔ You can use any text editor to write Java applications, but using an IDE provides some significant advantages in the form of color coding, help, and convenience.

✔ Installing either the JDK or the JRE will let you run Java applications on your machine.

✔ To obtain the best functionality, the version of Java supported by your JRE must match the version of Java supported by the JDK used to write the application.

✔ When manually creating applications for Java, especially on Windows systems, you must ensure that your system has a path configured to find the Java executable files.

✔ An IDE will normally locate and configure the Java executable file path automatically for you.

✔ Classes can contain both methods and other classes.

✔ The `javac` command compiles your application from the source code you provide.

✔ The `java` command runs an application in a command window, whereas the `javaw` command runs an application without a command window.

✔ Java supports both single-line and multiline comments, both of which document your application so you can remember what it does later.

✔ The Java API is so huge that you can't memorize it all, but you can memorize the parts you use most often.

✔ When you use the Java API, you normally access a class hierarchy, such as `java.lang.String`.

✔ Import an entire package when you need to use more than one class from it.

✔ Local help has the advantages of being more reliable and faster than remote help.

✔ Remote help has the advantage of providing updates that could make it easier to write an application.

Try-it-yourself lab

For more practice with the features covered in this chapter, try the following exercise on your own:

1. **Open the GetStarted application.**
2. **Change the text that the application outputs.**

   For example, you might change it to read, "This text has been updated!"
3. **Compile the application.**
4. **Run the application.**

   You should see the new text you've provided on screen.
5. **Repeat Steps 1 through 4 for any other strings you'd like to see the application output.**

Know this tech talk

Application Programming Interface (API): Software consisting of classes contained in packages that come with the JDK. This software lets you write Java application with greater ease and reduces the amount of code you need to write.

argument: Information provided to a method so that the method has data to manipulate.

byte code: The compiled form of a Java application. Byte code normally appears within a `.class` file.

class: A method of combining code and data. Classes are the basis of OOP techniques. Using classes means that Java applications are self-contained and easier to work with.

code block: Any code that appears within a starting curly bracket ({) and an ending curly bracket (}).

compile: To turn source code into executable byte code. The compiled application resides in a `.class` file.

cross-platform: Software that can run on more than one platform.

Integrated Development Environment (IDE): A special kind of editor used by developers to write application code. An IDE normally provides features such as color coding and access to various forms of help. It also lets you provide special configurations to make compiling, running, and debugging applications significantly easier.

Java Community Process (JCP): A group dedicated to making Java a better language. Members of this group help improve standardization, discuss language additions, and work on fixes for language errors (bugs).

Java Development Kit (JDK): A special kind of SDK used specifically to write and test Java applications.

Java Runtime Engine (JRE): The special piece of software used to run Java applications.

object-oriented programming (OOP): A form of programming that makes development simpler by packaging data and code together in a way that makes it easier to access and manage. OOP relies on the use of objects that correspond to real world entities. As with real world objects, OOP relies on properties to describe the object, methods to interact with the object, and events to let the object communicate with the outside world.

package: A container used to combine a number of classes into an easily accessible whole. A package wraps up the classes so that you can find them with greater ease.

platform: A combination of hardware and operating software that creates a specific environment in which to run Java applications.

Software Development Kit (SDK): A combination of tools and software used to provide an application development environment.

variable: A kind of box used to hold information in an application.

Chapter 2
Using Primitive Variables

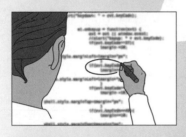

- ✔ Different variable types make it possible to *store specific kinds of information*.

- ✔ Each variable type *requires a different amount of storage space in computer memory*.

- ✔ Constant values *store a specific value for the life of the application*.

*T*his chapter discusses variables because you can't write most applications without using variables. In fact, you've already worked with variables in the SayHello and SayHello2 applications described in Chapter 1. A *variable* is a sort of box that holds information as data. When you want to store information in Java, you create a variable to hold it. The variable is actually a piece of computer memory that stores the information as binary data for you. The way in which your application interprets the data at a memory location gives it value and changes it from simply a number into information you can use.

Variables are categorized by the kind of information they store. The computer sees the information only as 1s and 0s. The letter A is actually the number 65 to the computer. As far as the computer is concerned, your data is simply a set of numbers stored in specific memory locations. It's the application that determines the sort of data stored in that memory location. Making data into a specific kind of information is called assigning a *type* to that data. Assigning a type to a variable helps the application interpret the data it contains.

This chapter looks specifically at *primitive types*. A primitive type is one that consists of data only. The information contained within a variable of a primitive type is one of the following:

- ✔ An *integer* number — numbers that can be written without a fractional or decimal component (byte, short, int, or long)

- ✔ A floating point number, which has an integer and a decimal part (float or double)

- ✔ A true or false value (boolean)

- ✔ A single character (char)

LINGO

Data is numbers assigned to specific memory locations on a computer. The data is actually stored as sequential 1s and 0s. A computer has no understanding of the data and doesn't do anything with it other than store it in the required memory location. An application can give the data a type, which defines the 1s and 0s as a specific kind of information. Information is an interpretation of the 1s and 0s. For example, the computer may see the number 65 (actually, the binary form of 1000001, which equates to 65 decimal) stored in a specific location, but the application may interpret that data as the letter A.

You'll also discover *constants* in this chapter. Constants are a special kind of variable that hold the same value throughout application execution. Constants are useful for a number of reasons:

- ✔ They use less memory
- ✔ They improve application execution speed
- ✔ They are more secure because no one can change them

Working with the Primitive Types

It's important to use the right type for a particular purpose. Otherwise, your application won't know how to interpret the data it creates and provide the user with the correct output.

Besides the way in which the application interprets the data as information, the main difference between these types is their size (measured in bits). Each bit is one little piece of memory — it can be either a 1 or a 0. Combining bits makes it possible to create larger numbers or more complex information. Table 2-1 shows the primitive types that Java supports.

EXTRA INFO

Oracle currently has plans for creating a unified type system for Java 10. This means that there would no longer be primitive types in Java — everything would be an object. Just how Oracle plans to implement this change isn't clear at the moment and it may not even happen, but it's always a good idea to keep track of changes that could occur to the language. For now, primitive types offer clear advantages and you should use them as appropriate, but keep in mind that future versions of Java may not support them.

Table 2-1		Java Primitive Types
Type Name	**Number of Bits**	**Range of Values**
byte	8	−128 to 127
short	16	−32,768 to 32,767
int	32	−2,147,483,648 to 2,147,483,647
long	64	−9,223,372,036,854,775,808 to 9,223,372,036,854,775,807

Type Name	Number of Bits	Range of Values
float	32	$1.40129846432481707^{-45}$ to $3.40282346638528860^{+38}$ (positive or negative)
double	64	$4.94065645841246544^{-324}$ to $1.79769313486231570^{+308}$ (positive or negative)
boolean	1	true or false
char	16	Any single 16-bit Unicode character including common letters such as A, the numbers 0 through 9, and common symbols such as !

Table 2-1 demonstrates something important. As the number of bits consumed by a variable increases, the range of values it can contain also increases. The type tells how to interpret the memory used by the variable. The same memory can hold one `long`, two `int`, four `short`, or eight `byte` variables. Only the type tells the application how to look at that memory.

Use smaller variables to improve application memory usage and execution speed. Larger variables allow your application to process greater values. It's important to choose the correct variable size for a specific use to ensure your application works as fast and efficiently as possible.

Now that you have an overview of the primitive types, it's time to look at them in detail. The following sections demonstrate how each of the primitive types work.

byte

The `byte` type consumes eight bits — one byte of the computer's memory. Each bit can be either a 1 or a 0. The combination of 1s and 0s determines the value of the `byte`. A `byte`-sized variable can hold any value between –128 and 127 or 256 different values (including 0).

In the following exercise, you create an application that interacts with a variable of type `byte`.

LINGO

A **bit** is a single memory location containing either a 0 or a 1. A byte consists of eight bits. The most significant bit determines whether a byte is positive or negative. So, a binary value (a group of bits) with a value of 10000001 has a decimal value of –127, while a binary value of 00000001 has a decimal value of 1. When the leftmost bit is a 1, the value is negative.

Files needed: `ShowByte.java`

1. Open the editor or IDE that you've chosen to use for this book.

2. Type the following code into the editor screen.

```java
// Import the required API classes.
import java.util.Scanner;

public class ShowByte
{
   public static void main(String[] args)
   {
      // Create the scanner.
      Scanner GetByte = new Scanner(System.in);

      // Obtain a byte value.
      System.out.print("Type any number: ");
      byte MyByte = GetByte.nextByte();

      // Display the value on screen.
      System.out.println("The value of MyByte is: " +
         MyByte);
   }
}
```

In this example, `GetByte` is a `Scanner` object that obtains (gets) the user's input from the keyboard. The `GetByte.nextByte()` method scans the next byte input from the keyboard and places it in `MyByte`, of type `byte`. The application then outputs the value of `MyByte` to screen.

3. Save the code to disk using the filename `ShowByte.java`.

4. In your command prompt, type javac ShowByte.java **and press Enter.**

The compiler compiles your application and creates a `.class` file from it.

5. Type java ShowByte **and press Enter.**

The application asks you to type any number. As mentioned in Table 2-1, a `byte` is limited to a range of –128 to 127.

6. Type 3 **and press Enter.**

The application outputs the expected value of 3 as shown in Figure 2-1. So, what happens if you try a negative value?

LINGO

It's important to remember that `GetByte` is an object of type `Scanner`. (`Scanner` is part of the Java API, so you don't need to worry too much about it now, except that it helps you obtain input from the user.) On the other hand, `MyByte` is simply a number — not an object — of type `byte`. A `byte` value is a number, an actual data location in memory, not an object.

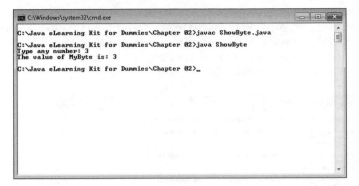

Figure 2-1

7. Type java ShowByte **and press Enter, then type** –15 **and press Enter.**

The application outputs the expected value of –15 as shown in Figure 2-2. Now it's time to have a little fun. When creating any application, you must assume that someone will enter the wrong information. Users could easily type a value that's too large.

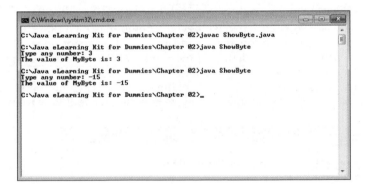

Figure 2-2

LINGO

8. Type java ShowByte **and press Enter, then type** 128 **and press Enter.**

The value you just typed is one larger than byte can support. The application doesn't output the value you typed. Instead, the application outputs a whole bunch of text as shown in Figure 2-3.

If you read the first line of output, you'll see the source of the problem. Java tells you that the number you typed is out of range. It then tells you what you typed (128).

An **exception** occurs whenever the application experiences something unexpected, such as incorrect user input. The exception output tells you what went wrong, provides the incorrect input (when appropriate), and shows you where the error occurred in your source code. All of this information helps you understand the exception and do something about it.

The last line tells you precisely where the error occurred in the source file. For now, you don't need to worry about the remaining information because you seldom need it. All of this information is called an exception. An *exception* occurs any time your application experiences a problem, such as incorrect input from the user.

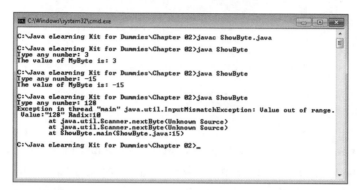

Figure 2-3

9. **Type** java ShowByte **and press Enter, then type** C **and press Enter.**

The value you just typed isn't even a number. Notice that the application provides an exception again, but this time the exception is different. The exception shown in Figure 2-4 tells you that the type of the input — a letter in this case — doesn't match the expected input, which would be a byte. (Just another example of how Java helps you understand when applications go wrong, why they've gone wrong, and how to fix them.)

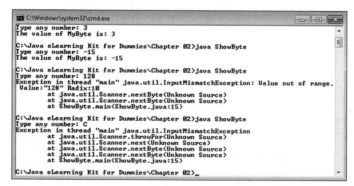

Figure 2-4

short

The short type consumes 16 bits, two bytes, or one word. A short-sized variable can hold any value between –32,768 and 32,767 or 65,536 different values (including 0).

In the following exercise, you create an application that interacts with a variable of type short.

Files needed: ShowShort.java

1. **Open the editor or IDE that you've chosen to use for this book.**

2. **Type the following code into the editor screen.**

```java
public class ShowShort
{
    public static void
        main(String[] args)
    {
        // Create a variable to hold a result.
        short MyVar = 1;

        // Display the initial value.
        System.out.println("The MyVar starting value
          equals: "
                + MyVar);

        // Add 5 to MyVar.
        MyVar += 5;

        // Display the result.
        System.out.println("Add 5 to MyVar equals: " +
          MyVar);

        // Subtract 4 from MyVar.
        MyVar -= 4;

        // Display the result.
        System.out.println("Subtract 4 from MyVar
          equals: "
                + MyVar);

        // Increment MyVar.
        MyVar++;
```

LINGO

You may hear two bytes of information referred to as a **word**, which in this context means a unit of computer memory that corresponds to 16-bits of information. The use of specific terms to describe memory units makes it possible to talk with other developers to exchange ideas without ambiguity. Other interesting memory units are the nibble (4-bits), DWORD, or double-word (32-bits), and QWORD, or quad-word (64-bits).

```
      // Display the result.
      System.out.println("Increment MyVar equals: " +
        MyVar);

      // Decrement MyVar.
      MyVar--;

      // Display the result.
      System.out.println("Decrement MyVar equals: " +
        MyVar);

      // Multiply MyVar by 6.
      MyVar *= 6;

      // Display the result.
      System.out.println("Multiply MyVar by 6 equals:
        " + MyVar);

      // Divide MyVar by 3.
      MyVar /= 3;

      // Display the result.
      System.out.println("Divide MyVar by 3 equals: "
        + MyVar);
    }
  }
```

This application performs a number of math operations. Of course, you know from school that the four basic math operations are add, subtract, multiply, and divide. However, this example also shows two special math operations: increment and decrement. You use these special math operations to add one or subtract one from the variable. Later chapters will demonstrate just how useful this feature is.

3. **Save the code to disk using the filename** ShowShort.java.

4. **In your command prompt, type** javac ShowShort.java **and press Enter.**

The compiler compiles your application and creates a .class file from it.

5. **Type** java ShowShort **and press Enter.**

You see the results of the various math operations as shown in Figure 2-5.

LINGO

Incrementing a variable means adding a value of 1 to it. **Decrementing** a variable means subtracting a value of 1 from it. You use incrementing and decrementing to perform special tasks within an application. For example, every time an event happens, you could increment a variable to keep track of the number of times the event has happened while the application is running.

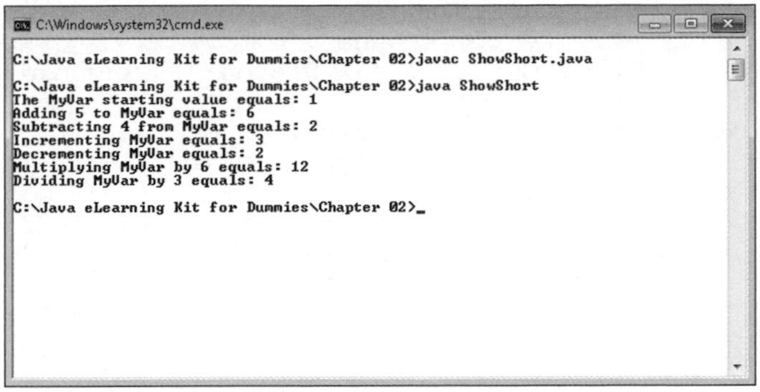

```
C:\Windows\system32\cmd.exe

C:\Java eLearning Kit for Dummies\Chapter 02>javac ShowShort.java

C:\Java eLearning Kit for Dummies\Chapter 02>java ShowShort
The MyVar starting value equals: 1
Adding 5 to MyVar equals: 6
Subtracting 4 from MyVar equals: 2
Incrementing MyVar equals: 3
Decrementing MyVar equals: 2
Multiplying MyVar by 6 equals: 12
Dividing MyVar by 3 equals: 4

C:\Java eLearning Kit for Dummies\Chapter 02>_
```

Figure 2-5

Change the code in the example shown in the "byte" section to use a `short` instead of a `byte`. What you need to do is change the line of code that reads, `byte MyByte = GetByte.nextByte();` to `short MyByte = GetByte.nextShort();`. Go through the exercise again and note the changes that occur.

int

The `int` type consumes 32 bits — 4 bytes, two words, or one DWORD. An `int`-sized variable can hold any value between –2,147,483,648 and 2,147,483,647 or 4,294,967,296 different values (including 0).

In the following exercise you create an application that interacts with a variable of type `int`. The result of this interaction is a guessing game where you try to guess the number that the computer has chosen.

Files needed: ShowInt.java

1. **Open the editor or IDE that you've chosen to use for this book.**

2. **Type the following code into the editor screen.**

```java
// Import the required API classes.
import java.util.Scanner;
import java.util.Random;
import java.util.Calendar;

public class ShowInt
{
    public static void main(String args[])
```

```
{
    // Create the scanner.
    Scanner GetInt = new Scanner(System.in);

    // Obtain an int value.
    System.out.print("Type a number between 1 and
        10: ");
    int YourGuess = GetInt.nextInt();

    // Get the current time.
    Calendar MyCal = Calendar.getInstance();

    // Create a random number generator.
    Random MyRandom = new Random();

    // Set the seed value for the random number using
    // the current number of milliseconds in the time.
    MyRandom.setSeed(MyCal.getTimeInMillis());

    // Obtain a random number between 1 and 10.
    int MyGuess = MyRandom.nextInt(10) + 1;

    // Display the value on screen.
    System.out.print("Your guess was: " +
        YourGuess);
    System.out.println(" My guess was: " + MyGuess);
}
}
```

This application performs a few new tasks. First, it gets an `int`, which is the same process as getting a `byte` or a `short` (see the examples in the "byte" and "short" sections of the chapter), but it relies on the `nextInt()` method. The first new task is obtaining an instance of a `Calendar` object, which you could use to discover the current date or time. In this case, the application uses the time as a means of ensuring that a random number is actually random. The next new task is creating a random number between 1 and 10, which consists of three subtasks:

- Create the `Random` object, `MyRandom`.

- Set the seed value, which is used to determine the starting point for random numbers generated by `MyRandom`. Imagine a seed value as you would a seed that you physically plant in the ground — the seed you choose determines the plant that grows (the output from the randomization process). Otherwise, you'll always get the same output — it won't be random at all.

- Get the random number between 1 and 10. The `MyRandom. nextInt()` method actually returns a value between 0 and 9, so you must add 1 to this output to obtain a number between 1 and 10. The output shows your guess and the application's guess side-by-side.

3. **Save the code to disk using the filename** ShowInt.java.

4. **In your command prompt, type** javac ShowInt.java **and press Enter.**

   The compiler compiles your application and creates a .class file from it.

5. **Type** java ShowInt **and press Enter.**

6. **Type any number between 1 and 10 and press Enter.**

   You see your guess and the application's guess as shown in Figure 2-6.

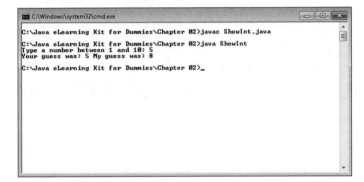

Figure 2-6

Try commenting out the MyRandom.setSeed(MyCal.getTimeIn Millis()) line of code in the application by typing // in front of the line of code. Perform steps 3 and 4 again to see what happens. Notice that the output is the same every time you run the application because the random number output is no longer random. Setting a seed value is an essential part of creating a random number.

long

The long type consumes 64 bits — 8 bytes, four words, two DWORDs, or one QWORD. It's the largest non-decimal variable type that Java supports. A long-sized variable can hold any value between –9,223,372,036,854,775,808 and 9,223,372,036,854,775,807 or 18,446,744,073,709,551,616 different values (including 0).

In the following exercise you create an application that interacts with a variable of type long.

Files needed: ShowLong.java

1. **Open the editor or IDE that you've chosen to use for this book.**

2. **Type the following code into the editor screen.**

```java
// Import the required API classes.
import java.util.Scanner;

public class ShowLong
{
    public static void main(String[] args)
    {
        // Create the scanner.
        Scanner GetLong = new Scanner(System.in);

        // Obtain the dividend (the first number in the
            division).
        System.out.print("Type a number for the
            dividend: ");
        long Dividend = GetLong.nextLong();

        // Obtain the divisor (the part used to divide the
        // dividend).
        System.out.print("Type a number for the divisor: ");
        long Divisor = GetLong.nextLong();

        // Perform the division.
        System.out.print(Dividend + " divided by ");
        System.out.print(Divisor + " equals ");
        System.out.print(Dividend / Divisor);
        System.out.print(" with a remainder of ");
        System.out.println(Dividend % Divisor);
    }
}
```

This application performs division of two numbers of any size that a long can support (a considerable range). The output can't contain a decimal portion, however, so the result also includes the remainder, which you obtain using the modulus (%) operator. In short, division with integer numbers includes a quotient and a remainder.

3. **Save the code to disk using the filename** ShowLong.java.

4. **In your command prompt, type** javac ShowLong.java **and press Enter.**

The compiler compiles your application and creates a .class file from it.

5. **Type** java ShowLong **and press Enter.**

The application asks you to enter the dividend, which is the number that gets divided.

6. **Type** 22 **and press Enter.**

   The application asks you to enter the divisor, which is the number used to divide the dividend.

7. **Type** 5 **and press Enter.**

   You see the results of the division (the quotient) as shown in Figure 2-7.

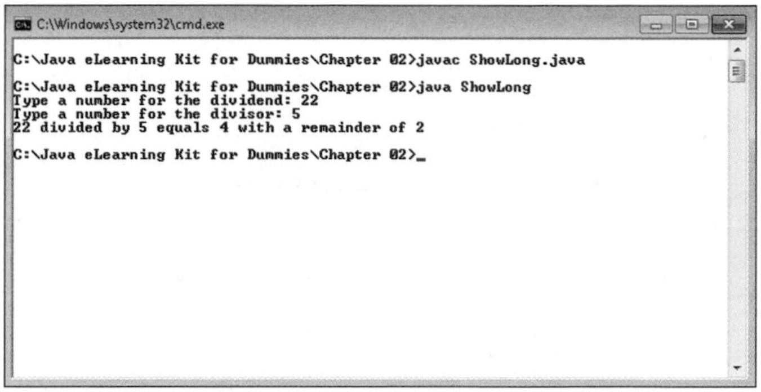

```
C:\Windows\system32\cmd.exe

C:\Java eLearning Kit for Dummies\Chapter 02>javac ShowLong.java

C:\Java eLearning Kit for Dummies\Chapter 02>java ShowLong
Type a number for the dividend: 22
Type a number for the divisor: 5
22 divided by 5 equals 4 with a remainder of 2

C:\Java eLearning Kit for Dummies\Chapter 02>_
```

Figure 2-7

float

Up to this point, all of the variable types have supported a specific number of bytes that directly correlate to a numeric range. None of these types have supported decimals — they have contained only the integer portion of the number. A float includes both an integer and a decimal portion. The float is 32-bits long. Precisely how the float supports numbers with a decimal portion is unimportant for the purposes of understanding Java, only the fact that it does so is important. A float can support numbers between $1.40129846432481707^{-45}$ to $3.40282346638528860^{+38}$ (positive or negative).

LINGO

Floating point numbers are those that contain both an integer and a decimal portion, such as 1.25. In this case, 1 is the integer portion and 25 is the decimal portion. A computer uses an entirely different set of circuits to work with floating point numbers, and the procedure for working with them is entirely different as well. Some people call floating point numbers real numbers. Strictly speaking, these people are incorrect because floating point numbers on a computer only approximate real numbers (the numbers as they actually are in the real world).

In the following exercise you create an application that interacts with a variable of type `float`.

Files needed: `ShowFloat.java`

1. **Open the editor or IDE that you've chosen to use for this book.**

2. **Type the following code into the editor screen.**

```
// Import the required API classes.
import java.util.Scanner;

public class ShowFloat
{
    public static void main(String[] args)
    {
        // Create the scanner.
        Scanner GetFloat = new Scanner(System.in);

        // Obtain the dividend (the first number in the
        // division).
        System.out.print("Type a number for the dividend: ");
        float Dividend = GetFloat.nextFloat();

        // Obtain the divisor (the part used to divide the
        // dividend).
        System.out.print("Type a number for the divisor: ");
        float Divisor = GetFloat.nextFloat();

        // Perform the division.
        System.out.print(Dividend + " divided by ");
        System.out.print(Divisor + " equals ");
        System.out.println(Dividend / Divisor);
    }
}
```

This application closely mirrors the ShowLong application found in the preceding "long" section of the chapter. The major difference here is that this version doesn't calculate a remainder — the use of a floating point number makes it possible to output a result that shows both an integer and a decimal portion.

3. **Save the code to disk using the filename `ShowFloat.java`.**

4. **In your command prompt, type** javac ShowFloat.java **and press Enter.**

The compiler compiles your application and creates a `.class` file from it.

GO ONLINE

For the purposes of this book, you really don't need to know the difference between floating point numbers and real numbers. However, there is a definite difference between the two. If you want to know more, you can find out about the details at http://ugweb. cs.ualberta.ca/~c229/ F07/resources/IEEE- reals.html.

5. Type java ShowFloat **and press Enter.**

The application asks you to enter the dividend, which is the number that gets divided.

6. Type 22 **and press Enter.**

The application asks you to enter the divisor, which is the number used to divide the dividend.

7. Type 5 **and press Enter.**

You see the results of the division (quotient) as shown in Figure 2-8. Notice that the input numbers are converted to floating point format. Even though you typed 22, the application outputs 22.0. The same thing happens when you type 5; the application converts the output to 5.0.

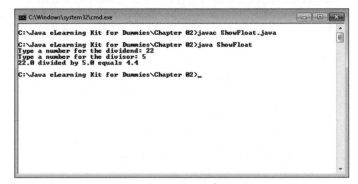

Figure 2-8

Repeat Steps 5 through 7. However, type **125.5** instead of 22 and **9.316** instead of 5. You should see 13.471447 as the output value. More importantly, you couldn't use 125.5 and 9.316 as inputs to the ShowLong application. Try these inputs with the ShowLong application to see what happens (the output should show an `InputMismatchException` error after you try to enter the dividend).

double

The double works precisely the same as the float, but it uses 64-bits instead of 32-bits to hold information. The larger memory space means that a double can hold larger numbers — a range from $4.94065645841246544^{-324}$ to $1.79769313486231570^{+308}$ (positive or negative). However, it also means that the double can add precision to inexact floating point values. For example, if you want to calculate the circumference of a circle, a double that contains the value of pi will offer more precision than an equivalent float.

In the following exercise you create an application that interacts with a variable of type `double`. This application will help you find the squares and square root of any number.

Files needed: `ShowDouble.java`

1. Open the editor or IDE that you've chosen to use for this book.

2. Type the following code into the editor screen.

```
// Import the required API classes.
import java.util.Scanner;
import java.lang.Math;

public class ShowDouble
{
    public static void main(String[] args)
    {
        // Create the scanner.
        Scanner GetDouble = new Scanner(System.in);

        // Obtain a number to manipulate.
        System.out.print("Type any number: ");
        double Calc = GetDouble.nextDouble();

        // Output the square and the square root
        // of this number.
        System.out.print("The square of " + Calc + " is:
          ");
        System.out.println(Calc * Calc);
        System.out.print("The square root of " + Calc +
          " is: ");
        System.out.println(Math.sqrt(Calc));
    }
}
```

This application relies on a new class, `java.lang.Math`, to perform some variable manipulation. Although you can find the square of any number simply by multiplying the number by itself, you need a special function to obtain the square root. The `Math.sqrt()` method performs this task.

3. Save the code to disk using the filename `ShowDouble.java`.

4. In your command prompt, type javac ShowDouble.java **and press Enter.**

The compiler compiles your application and creates a `.class` file from it.

5. Type java ShowDouble **and press Enter.**

The application asks you to type a number.

6. **Type** 121 **and press Enter.**

You see the square and square root of the input as shown in Figure 2-9.

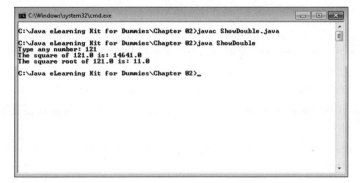

Figure 2-9

boolean

A boolean value is either true or false. It doesn't contain any other information. However, boolean variables are really important in Java because they help the application make decisions. Imagine what would happen if an application couldn't make up its mind!

In the following exercise you create an application that interacts with a variable of type boolean.

Files needed: ShowBoolean.java

1. **Open the editor or IDE that you've chosen to use for this book.**

2. **Type the following code into the editor screen.**

```
// Import the required API classes.
import java.util.Scanner;

public class ShowBoolean
{
    public static void main(String[] args)
    {
        // Create the scanner.
        Scanner GetBoolean = new Scanner(System.in);

        // Obtain input from the user.
        System.out.print("Do you like oranges? ");
        boolean TheTruth = GetBoolean.nextBoolean();
```

```
                    // Show the result.
                    System.out.print("It's " + TheTruth);
                    System.out.println(" that you like oranges.");
                }
            }
```

boolean values are always `true` or `false`. This application accepts a `boolean` value in response to a simple question and displays it on screen.

3. Save the code to disk using the filename `ShowBoolean.java`.

4. In your command prompt, type javac ShowBoolean.java **and press Enter.**

The compiler compiles your application and creates a `.class` file from it.

5. Type java ShowBoolean **and press Enter.**

The application asks whether you like oranges.

6. Type true **and press Enter.**

You see the result of answering the question as shown in Figure 2-10.

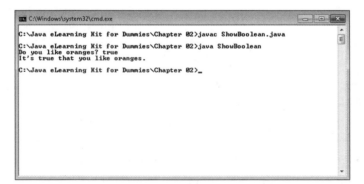

Figure 2-10

7. Repeat Steps 5 and 6, but this time type yes.

The application displays an `InputMismatchException` error message. Boolean values are really a number — either 0 (`false`) or 1 (`true`) as far as the computer is concerned. Of course, it's interesting to see how the application views the numeric status of a Boolean value.

8. Repeat Steps 5 and 6, but this time answer 1.

The application displays an `InputMismatchException` error message.

A type enforces not only a certain type of output, such as `true` or `false` for a `boolean` value, but also a certain type of input. You've seen that this holds true for numbers and now `boolean` values as well. It's essential to choose the correct variable type when you write an application.

char

Of all of the data types, the `char` is the one that your computer understands least. As far as the computer is concerned, a `char` is simply a 16-bit number that can contain any of 65,536 values. Java turns this number into a specific character. For example, the number 65 equates to the letter A. It's important to realize, though, that *Java* assigns the letter A to 65 — the computer sees just the number.

In the following exercise you create an application that interacts with a variable of type `char`.

Files needed: `ShowChar.java`

1. Open the editor or IDE that you've chosen to use for this book.

2. Type the following code into the editor screen.

```
// Import the required API classes.
import java.util.Scanner;

public class ShowChar
{
    public static void main(String[] args)
    {
        // Create the scanner.
        Scanner GetChar = new Scanner(System.in);

        // Obtain input from the user.
        System.out.print("Type any single letter or
          number: ");
        char AChar = GetChar.findInLine(".").charAt(0);

        // Display the input.
        System.out.println ("You typed: " + AChar);
    }
}
```

The `Scanner` class doesn't provide any means of obtaining a `char` directly, so this example shows a new way to work with `Scanner` input. In this case, the example retrieves any string because the period (.) represents any character. However, you don't need a string (a series of characters as in a sentence) — you need a `char`. The `charAt(0)` part of the code selects just the first character from any string that the user types and returns it as a `char`.

3. **Save the code to disk using the filename `ShowChar.java`.**

4. **In your command prompt, type** javac ShowChar.java **and press Enter.**

   The compiler compiles your application and creates a `.class` file from it.

5. **Type** java ShowChar **and press Enter.**

   The application asks you to type any character at all.

6. **Type** b **and press Enter.**

   You see the letter you typed as output. The fact that the pattern relies on a period may have you worried that you can't type a period as input.

7. **Repeat Steps 5 and 6, but type** . (a period) **instead of the b.**

   You see a period displayed on screen. So, you can type letters and special characters. It may be interesting to see whether numbers present a problem.

8. **Repeat Steps 5 and 6, but type** 123 **instead of the b.**

   The application doesn't display any sort of error, but it also displays only the 1. The input isn't treated as a number; it's treated as a series of characters. This input consists of three characters: 1, 2, and 3. You can probably guess what would happen if you typed a `boolean` value.

9. **Repeat Steps 5 and 6, but type** true **instead of the b.**

   This time you see just the t. Every input you provide is turned into a single character, as shown in Figure 2-11.

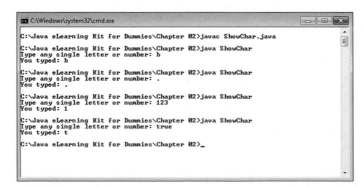

Figure 2-11

Change the code in the example shown in the earlier "byte" section to use a `char` instead of a `byte`. What you need to do is change the line of code that reads, `byte MyByte = GetByte.nextByte();` to `char MyByte = GetByte.findInLine(".").charAt(0);`. Go through the exercise again and note the changes that occur. For example, you'll notice that you don't see any errors from the application. However, instead of the intended output, you see 3, then –, then 1, and finally C, instead of 3, –15, 128, and C as intended.

Creating and Using Constants

Every variable you've worked with so far is a container that can hold anything. In addition, you can change the content as needed. *Constants* make it possible to create variables that can't change value during application execution.

Constants have a lot of uses, which you'll see as the book progresses. However, it's a good idea to get started with constants early because they can make your application more stable. For example, because you can't change a constant, using one can make your application more resistant to outside interference.

In this exercise, you create a constant and interact with it in various ways to see how it works. In this case, you also see the effect of errors in your application code.

Files needed: `CreateConst.java`

1. **Open the editor or IDE that you've chosen to use for this book.**

2. **Type the following code into the editor screen.**

```java
// Import the required API classes.
import java.util.Scanner;

public class CreateConst
{
    public static void main(String[] args)
    {
        // Create a constant.
        final int MyConst = 345;
```

```
// Display the constant on screen.
System.out.println("The current value of MyConst
   is: "
       + MyConst);

// Create the scanner.
Scanner GetConst = new Scanner(System.in);

// Try to change the value.
System.out.print("Enter a new value for MyConst:
   ");
MyConst = GetConst.nextInt();
   }
}
```

This application begins by creating a constant. Whenever you see a `final` variable, you know that it's a constant. `MyConst` is assigned the value of `345` and that value can't change as long as the application is running. The application displays the value of `MyConst` and then invites you to try changing the value of `MyConst` to a new value.

3. **Save the code to disk using the filename `CreateConst.java`.**

4. **In your command prompt, type** javac CreateConst.java **and press Enter.**

   You see an error message like the one shown in Figure 2-12 instead of the compiled `.class` file you expected. This has never happened with any of the other examples. You can expect to see an error message like this for any application that has a coding error in it of the sort we've created for this example.

The compiler will catch all of your syntax errors for you. It's illegal to assign a value to a constant in any location but the definition, so the compiler tells you about the error. The compiler will also normally tell you precisely which line has an error in it so that you can fix it easily.

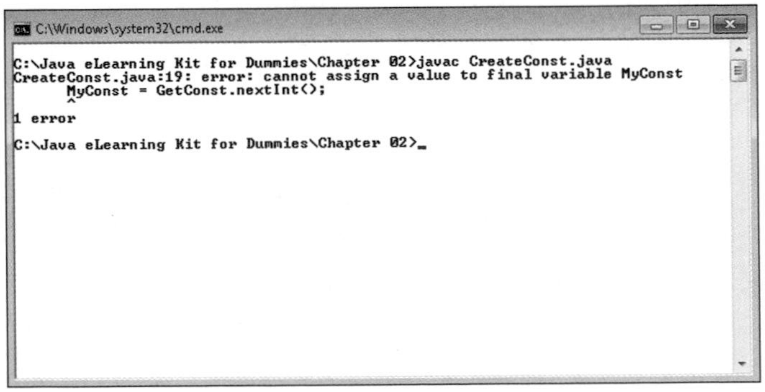

```
C:\Windows\system32\cmd.exe

C:\Java eLearning Kit for Dummies\Chapter 02>javac CreateConst.java
CreateConst.java:19: error: cannot assign a value to final variable MyConst
        MyConst = GetConst.nextInt();
        ^
1 error

C:\Java eLearning Kit for Dummies\Chapter 02>_
```

Figure 2-12

5. **Type // in front of the line of code that reads** `MyConst = GetConst.nextInt();`**.**

   This change will fix the error. Removing the `//` will change the line from a comment into code that the compiler will compile.

6. **Type** javac CreateConst.java **and press Enter.**

   The compiler compiles your application and creates a `.class` file from it.

7. **Type** java CreateConst **and press Enter.**

   You see the current value of `MyConst`, as shown in Figure 2-13. Ignore the request to type a new value because the line for accepting a new value is commented out.

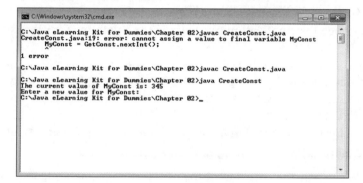

Figure 2-13

Constants can have any type. The only difference is that you can't change a constant. So, if you want to create a `final char`, feel free to do so.

Summing Up

Here are the key points you learned about in this chapter:

- ✔ Computers see only 1s and 0s on memory and don't understand the concept of information.

- ✔ Data types determine how an application interprets the 1s and 0s stored in computer memory.

✔ Primitive data types exist as pure numbers. They have the advantage of performing tasks faster using less memory.

✔ The primitive data types are: `byte`, `short`, `int`, `long`, `float`, `double`, `boolean`, and `char`.

✔ Constants make it possible to create secure, high performance variables that contain the same value throughout application execution.

Try-it-yourself lab

For more practice with the features covered in this chapter, try the following exercise on your own.

1. **Open the ShowByte application.**

2. **Change this application to use the `float` data type, rather than the `byte` data type.**

   You may want to rename the resulting application and its associated class to show the change in data type. For example, you could rename the application to FloatVersionOfShowByte, if you wanted, but something shorter would probably work better.

3. **Perform Steps 3 through 7 in the "byte" section of the chapter.**

4. **Note how the application behavior changes.**

   One change that you'll want to note is how the input affects the application. In addition, how does the output from the application appear? Different data types do indeed work differently, so this exercise points out the need to use the right type.

Know this tech talk

data: A series of 1s and 0s assigned to a specific location in memory.

decrement: Subtracting a value of 1 from a variable.

exception: A condition that occurs when the application experiences something unexpected, such as incorrect user input. An exception occurs during exceptional conditions — conditions that no one expected to happen. Every exception tells you the exception type, the incorrect condition (when known), and the place where the exception happened in the source file.

floating point number: An approximation of a real number, which is a number that has both an integer and a decimal portion, such as 5.1.

increment: Adding a value of 1 to a variable.

information: Data that has been assigned a type in order to give it meaning and make it possible to interpret what the data means.

overflow: An overflow occurs when an application attempts to create a value larger than the type is designed to hold. Java gets rid of the extra information and keeps just the bits that the type can successfully hold. Unfortunately, Java doesn't display an error message when this happens, so your application blissfully continues to run with the error in place. Use the `BigInteger` data type to prevent errors from occurring when performing integer math.

real number: A number that has both an integer and a decimal portion, such as 5.1. Some developers also call real numbers floating point numbers, but this isn't precisely true. A floating point number is merely an approximation of a real number.

Chapter 3
Using Object Variables

- Object data types make it possible to *create complex data storage variables*.

- Java makes it possible to process information that appears along with the application as *command line arguments*.

- It's possible to convert primitive variables into object variables to *use the additional features that objects provide for manipulating data*.

- Using scope makes it possible to hide information from parts of the application that *don't need to see it*.

- The new date and time API makes it possible to *interact with date and time values with less code and effort*.

- Using enumerations *reduces the chance of someone providing an incorrect value to your code*.

An object is different from a primitive type in that an object is actually a class, just like the many classes you've been creating throughout this book. An object has methods, properties, and events associated with it. Objects can also contain a wealth of variable types that you *can't* create using the primitive types described in the "Working with the Primitive Types" section of Chapter 2. The number of object types you can create is limited only by need and imagination. Objects can also contain complex data and have special behaviors.

Every application you create has at least one variable — the `args` variable — which is provided as an argument to `main()`. This chapter tells how to use `args` to perform useful tasks in an application. Using `args` to change application behavior is called processing *command line arguments* because the changes are made as part of what the user types after the application name at the command line.

It's also possible to tell Java to make some variables accessible by everyone and to hide other variables from view. The visibility of a variable is its *scope*. A public variable is visible to everyone, while a private variable is hidden from view. (Scope also applies to methods, which can be hid from view as well.) This chapter discusses scope so you know how to give variables the right level of visibility.

You want to store data in a primitive type most of the time to gain the speed and memory savings that primitive types provide. However, at some point you might need to convert that primitive type to an object in order to more

LINGO

Every Java class produces an **object,** even the classes you've created throughout this book. An object can have methods that define how the object interacts with data. For example, an `Add()` method might define how an object can add information to existing data. In addition to methods, objects can have properties and events. A **property** is a characteristic of the data that the object contains. For example, an object that represents a car could have a `color` property. An **event** is Java's way of allowing the object to listen to outside activities and react to them. For example, a pushbutton object in an application window could have a `click` event that occurs when the user presses the pushbutton using the keyboard or mouse. You've already used object methods, such as `System.out.print()` in the applications you created earlier in the book.

easily change the information it contains using the methods the object form provides. Fortunately, Java makes it possible to convert primitive types to specific kinds of objects and specific kinds of objects back to primitive types. This chapter describes the process so that you can use this technique in the applications you create.

LINGO

Scope determines which part of an application can see specific variables. You use scope to hide some kinds of information, but to make other sorts of information visible.

Java used to have problems with dates and times. In Java 8, you gain access to all sorts of interesting new date and time functionality. The new date and time objects are so numerous that it would actually take several chapters to cover them all. This chapter provides a good overview of some of the most commonly used date and time functionality.

This chapter also demonstrates the basic use of a special object — the enumeration. An enumeration is an object that provides access to a fixed set of values, such as the days of the week. Humans use enumerations all the time without thinking about it. Computers require a lot more help in the form of a special enumeration object. (Chapter 7 introduces you to some more advanced uses of enumerations.)

Working with Common Objects

Java places thousands of objects at your disposal, all of which manage data in some way. The number of available objects can be overwhelming at first. However, you'll use some common objects quite often and it's best to get introduced to the whole idea of objects by using them. The following sections describe the most common objects that you'll work with when writing Java applications.

String

A `String` is essentially text. Think of it as a list of `char` variables placed in a class that treats them as a unit. Most applications have a multitude of `String` objects in them — perhaps because humans tend to communicate using text and are most comfortable using text. Of course, the computer sees numbers — it doesn't understand text, but the `String` object lets you manipulate the text in a way that puts a computer at ease. Nearly every example in the book so far has had a string or two in it. You didn't create the object, but merely sent the string directly to the `System.out.print()` method.

The String data type is extremely flexible so I can't demonstrate everything it can do in a single chapter. The example in this section does show something important. You've tried several incarnations of the example in the "byte" section of Chapter 2, but in this exercise you finally see a version that works!

Files needed: `StringObject.java`

1. **Open the editor or IDE that you've chosen to use for this book.**

2. **Type the following code into the editor screen.**

```
// Import the required API classes.
import java.util.Scanner;
import java.lang.String;

public class StringObject
{
    public static void main(String[] args)
    {
        // Create the scanner.
        Scanner GetString = new Scanner(System.in);

        // Obtain a byte value.
        System.out.print("Type any string: ");
        String MyString = GetString.nextLine();

        // Display the value on screen.
        System.out.println("The value of MyString is: "
          + MyString);
    }
}
```

This example works much like the example in the "byte" section of the Chapter 2. The difference is that you're working with a String object this time. String objects are exceptionally flexible, so there isn't just one Scanner object method for working with them. This example shows how to use the nextLine() method to fill the String object (labeled MyString here) with data, but you'll see other methods as the book progresses.

3. **Save the code to disk using the filename StringObject.java.**

4. **In your command prompt, type** javac StringObject.java **and press Enter.**

   The compiler compiles your application and creates a .class file from it.

5. **Type** java StringObject **and press Enter.**

   The application asks you to type any string. A string can consist of just about anything.

6. **Type** 3 **and press Enter.**

The application outputs the expected value of 3.

7. **Type** java StringObject **and press Enter, then type** −15 **and press Enter.**

The application outputs the expected value of −15.

8. **Type** java StringObject **and press Enter, then type** 128 **and press Enter.**

The application outputs the expected value of 128.

9. **Type** java StringObject **and press Enter, then type** C **and press Enter.**

The application outputs the expected value of C. The ShowByte version of the program stops here, but let's try one last entry.

10. **Type** java StringObject **and press Enter, then type** Strings Work Great! **and press Enter.**

Not surprisingly, you see the expected output. Figure 3-1 shows that this amazing program can handle all the input you've provided to it! Strings aren't the best object in the world for everything, but they're extremely versatile and indispensable for most application development.

```
C:\Windows\system32\cmd.exe

C:\Java eLearning Kit for Dummies\Chapter 03>javac StringObject.java

C:\Java eLearning Kit for Dummies\Chapter 03>java StringObject
Type any string: 3
The value of MyString is: 3

C:\Java eLearning Kit for Dummies\Chapter 03>java StringObject
Type any string: -15
The value of MyString is: -15

C:\Java eLearning Kit for Dummies\Chapter 03>java StringObject
Type any string: 128
The value of MyString is: 128

C:\Java eLearning Kit for Dummies\Chapter 03>java StringObject
Type any string: C
The value of MyString is: C

C:\Java eLearning Kit for Dummies\Chapter 03>java StringObject
Type any string: Strings Work Great!
The value of MyString is: Strings Work Great!

C:\Java eLearning Kit for Dummies\Chapter 03>_
```

Figure 3-1

Calendar

Believe it or not, you've already worked with the Calendar type. The example appears in the "int" section of Chapter 2. A Calendar provides access to both time and date values. You can obtain the current time and date, manipulate them for any time zone in the world, create new times and dates as needed, and generally perform any task that you might need to create a calendar within an application.

Java 8 provides access to new date and time classes. You can read about these classes in the "Using the New Date and Time API" section of this chapter. These classes will eventually replace the functionality provided by the `Calendar` type. However, for now you need to know about the `Calendar` type because it appears in a large number of existing applications. When you create new applications, rather than change existing applications, try to use the new date and time classes so that your application will continue to work well into the future.

GO ONLINE

Java has an even older class than `Calendar` called `Date` that you can also use to work with time and date values. `Date` objects work similarly to `Calendar` objects, but with less functionality. Generally, you're better off using the `Calendar` object when working with date and time in existing applications. However, it's helpful to know about both classes. You can read about the `Date` class at `http://docs.oracle.com/javase/7/docs/api/java/util/Date.html`. The site at `http://www.java-forums.org/java-tutorials/2775-java-date.html` provides some simple examples you can try.

BigDecimal

Creating a decimal number in Java is an approximation. I could give you a really long and complex explanation of what happens, but the simple answer is that the `float` and `double` data types are using base 2 values, which is what a computer understands. (We humans rely on base 10 values.) Some numbers simply don't translate very well between the two bases. To overcome this problem, you can tell Java to use a special class called `BigDecimal` to represent decimal values in base 10, rather than base 2. The benefit of using `BigDecimal` is that your application becomes significantly more accurate — a requirement when performing financial calculations or a trip to Mars. The down side is that `BigDecimal` requires more processing cycles (making your program slower) and uses more memory. So, you use `BigDecimal` only when needed.

EXTRA INFO

The inability of Java to represent floating point numbers accurately doesn't stem from some problem inherent to Java, so no amount of work you perform in Java will fix this problem. The problem exists in the way the processor in your machine works — which means every computer language has precisely the same problem. Just about every computer language in existence has a decimal type of some sort to handle situations where absolute accuracy is required and the decimal type has precisely the same benefits and limitations as its Java counterpart in every case. To see the actual math behind this inaccuracy, check out the article at `http://en.wikipedia.org/wiki/Floating_point`. You can find a Java-specific article about floating point numbers at `http://www.ibm.com/developerworks/java/library/j-math2/index.html`.

It's hard to understand precisely how inaccurate float and double are unless you see them in action for yourself. In the following exercise, you first create an application that demonstrates the inaccuracy of double and you then compare the inaccuracy of double to the accuracy of BigDecimal.

Files needed: DecimalObject.java

1. **Open the editor or IDE that you've chosen to use for this book.**

2. **Type the following code into the editor screen.**

```java
// Import the required API classes.
import java.math.BigDecimal;

public class DecimalObject
{
    public static void main(String[] args)
    {
        // Create a decimal type from a float.
        BigDecimal Value1 = new BigDecimal(4.395f);

        // Because float relies on a base 2
        // representation of the number,
        // the output isn't what you'd expect.
        System.out.print("Using a float is inaccurate:
          ");
        System.out.println(Value1);

        // Create a decimal type from a double.
        BigDecimal Value2 = new BigDecimal(4.395);

        // Using a double is slightly more accurate.
        System.out.print("Using a double is inaccurate:
          ");
        System.out.println(Value2);

        // Create a decimal using a String instead.
        BigDecimal Value3 = new BigDecimal("4.395");

        // The output is what you'd expect this time.
        System.out.print("Using a String is accurate: ");
        System.out.println(Value3);
    }
}
```

This application answers the important question of just how accurate the float and double data types are. It converts these variables to the BigDecimal type to show what happens during the conversion. You'll be surprised at the result.

Notice that the application creates `Value1` by calling `new Big Decimal(4.395f)`. The `f` after `4.395` tells the compiler to use a `float`, rather than a `double`. You can use the same notation any time you want to use a `float`, rather than a `double`, in your own applications.

3. **Save the code to disk using the filename `DecimalObject.java`.**

4. **In your command prompt, type** `javac DecimalObject.java` **and press Enter.**

   The compiler compiles your application and creates a `.class` file from it.

5. **Type** `java DecimalObject` **and press Enter.**

   The application outputs the actual result of converting a `float`, and then a `double` to a `BigDecimal` (and the accompanying inaccuracy) as shown in Figure 3-2. Compare this to the `BigDecimal` output created using a `String` input (where no conversion between numeric types occurs). The difference is tiny between a `float` and a `double` — about 0.0000001907348590179935854439398. The difference between a `double` and `BigDecimal` is even smaller — about 0.000000000000000426325641 4560602. Even so, such incredibly small differences can quickly become a problem when working with really large numbers, such as those used by financial institutions and the space program.

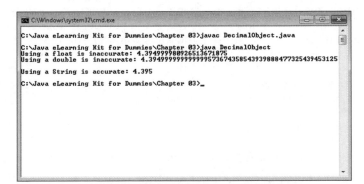

Figure 3-2

You have one way to avoid using `BigDecimal` to perform accurate math operations. You can use an integer type, such as `short`, `int`, or `long`, to perform the math operations, convert the result to a string, and artificially place the decimal point in the right place. For example, let's suppose you need to add 1.01 to 4.395. You'd convert 1.01 to 1010 and 4.395 to 4395, then you'd add the numbers together to produce 5405. Change the result to a string and then add a decimal point at the right place to produce a displayed output of 5.405. Using integer math is a time honored way to avoid decimals on a computer altogether. However, this solution can prove tricky at times and even with 64-bits of accuracy, some numbers are simply too large or too small for the `long` data type to represent. The "BigInteger" section has a solution to this problem.

BigInteger

Sometimes you need an integer value that can have more than 64-bits of accuracy. Programmers often need to create extremely large numbers. When that time comes for you, you can use a `BigInteger` to perform the required math. A `BigInteger` doesn't have a boundary — you can make it as large as needed to hold any value (assuming you have the required computer memory). Of course, `BigInteger` also comes with speed and memory usage penalties, so you don't want to use it all of the time — every choice you make when writing code has consequences, so you must make these choices carefully.

When a number grows too large for the variable container used to hold it, the container overflows. For example, if you try to store 33-bits of data in an `int` container, Java will retain 32-bits worth of data and let the remaining bit overflow without displaying an error. As with any container that overflows, you lose something when your number overflows — the number is no longer the same and it doesn't accurately represent the value you want to save. Of course, you could always move up to a `long` to overcome problems with an `int`.

In this exercise, you see what happens when a long variable overflows and how you can correct the problem by using `BigInteger`.

Files needed: `BigIntegerObject.java`

1. **Open the editor or IDE that you've chosen to use for this book.**

2. **Type the following code into the editor screen.**

```java
// Import the required API classes.
import java.math.BigInteger;

public class BigIntegerObject
{
    public static void main(String[] args)
    {
        // Create a long that contains the maximum value.
        long Overflow = 9223372036854775807;
```

```
        // Display the value so you can see
        // it works fine.
        System.out.println("Initial Overflow value: "
                + Overflow);

        // Create an overflow condition and display it.
        Overflow = Overflow + 1;
        System.out.println("Overflow + 1 value: " +
          Overflow);

        // Create a BigInteger that contains a maximum
        // long value.
        BigInteger NoOverflow =
                BigInteger.valueOf(9223372036854775807l);

        // Display the value so you can see
        // it works fine.
        System.out.println("Initial NoOverflow value: "
                + NoOverflow);

        // Add 1 and see what happens.
        NoOverflow = NoOverflow.add(BigInteger.ONE);
        System.out.println("NoOverflow + 1 value: "
                + NoOverflow);

        // Multiply the result by 3 to see what happens.
        NoOverflow =
                NoOverflow.multiply(BigInteger.valueOf(3));
        System.out.println("NoOverflow * 3 value: "
                + NoOverflow);
    }
}
```

This example begins with the largest long that you can create and then adds 1 to it. The variable overflows. It'll be interesting to see what happens. The BigInteger type is supposed to overcome this limitation, so the example does precisely the same thing to a BigInteger variable. In fact, it then multiplies this result by 3. If BigInteger lives up to its billing, NoOverflow shouldn't overflow despite the really large number it holds.

As with the float and double, you can control whether Java creates an int or a long. This example creates a long by adding l to the end of the number. Otherwise, the compiler could assume that you meant to create an int and raise an error.

Because BigInteger is an object, it has special methods for performing math tasks. Assign values to a BigInteger by calling the valueOf() method with the desired value. This example shows two math operations: addition and multiplication. To add 1 to a variable, you must use the `BigInteger.ONE` constant, rather than add 1 directly. In addition, you can't use the + sign. You must call the `add()` method instead. Likewise, multiplication is performed using the `multiply()` method.

3. **Save the code to disk using the filename `BigIntegerObject.java`.**

4. **In your command prompt, type** javac BigIntegerObject.java **and press Enter.**

   The compiler compiles your application and creates a `.class` file from it.

5. **Type** java BigIntegerObject **and press Enter.**

   The application outputs the initial value of `Overflow` without any problem as shown in Figure 3-3. However, adding 1 to `Overflow` creates a problem — the number is now negative! In fact, it's the maximum negative value that a `long` can contain — it's not possible to go any more wrong than that. Imagine that you're performing integer math on a large financial calculation. The huge deposit made by your favorite contributor becomes an equally huge withdrawal. Now look at the results for `NoOverflow`. Adding 1 to `NoOverflow` produces the correct value, as does multiplying it by 3. It's theoretically possible to create a `BigInteger` object the size of available memory in your machine, but you probably wouldn't ever need a number that huge.

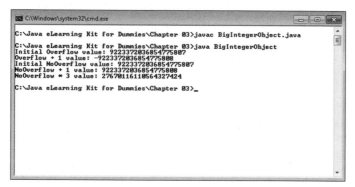

Figure 3-3

Changing Primitive Types into Objects

As described in Chapter 2, primitive types are simply containers that hold data. There is nothing else associated with them. Primitive types are small and fast. However, primitive types are also limited. You have to write a lot of code sometimes to get the simplest things done with primitive types because they don't contain any sort of logic to perform tasks for you.

An object has intelligence that helps you perform tasks. Some objects have more intelligence than others do, but all objects have some level of functionality that you won't find when working with a primitive type. So, when it comes to choosing between the two, what you're really deciding is whether you need the smaller size and faster speed of primitive types or the greater flexibility of objects. Each primitive type has an object version, as described in the following sections.

Automatic boxing and unboxing

It's important to understand that a primitive type is a pure value, whereas an object is a value plus code used to work with that value. The act of placing a value into an object is called *boxing*. The object acts as a box that holds the value and lets you perform tasks with it. When you need to access the value, you remove it from the box. This is called *unboxing* the value. Java automatically boxes and unboxes variables for you as needed; you don't really have to think about it. However, it's important to know that boxing and unboxing occurs.

LINGO

Boxing a primitive type places its value inside an object. **Unboxing** a value removes it from the object and places it in a primitive type. You box a value to gain access to the functionality that the object can provide and unbox a value to examine it.

Byte versus byte

The `Byte` object contains a `byte` primitive type. It also provides access to a number of interesting methods for working with `byte` values. Along with these methods, the `Byte` class provides a number of static methods. (A *static* method is a method that you can use without creating an instance of the class.) Many classes provide access to static methods that you use to work with the class in some way. It's important to differentiate between the class (the set of instructions used to build an object) and the object (an instance of the constructed class).

In this exercise, you work with both static and object methods to interact with the `Byte` type.

LINGO

A **static method** lets you perform a task with a class, such as discovering the minimum value that the class supports. Static methods are part of the class and you can access them at any time without first creating an instance of the class. In fact, some static methods are used to create objects.

Files needed: `ByteVersusByte.java`

1. **Open the editor or IDE that you've chosen to use for this book.**

2. **Type the following code into the editor screen.**

```java
// Import the required API classes.
import java.lang.Byte;

public class ByteVersusByte
{
    public static void main(String[] args)
    {
        // Display some Byte object statistics.
        System.out.println("Byte Statistics:");
        System.out.println("Size: " + Byte.SIZE);
        System.out.println("Minimum value: "
                + Byte.MIN_VALUE);
        System.out.println("Maximum value: "
                + Byte.MAX_VALUE);
        System.out.println("Type: " + Byte.TYPE);

        // Create a few Byte variables.
        Byte Value1 = Byte.valueOf("15");
        Byte Value2 = Byte.valueOf((byte)15);
        Byte Value3 = Byte.valueOf("15", 16);

        // Display their values.
        System.out.println();
        System.out.println("Byte Values:");
        System.out.println("Value1 = " + Value1);
        System.out.println("Value2 = " + Value2);
        System.out.println("Value3 = " + Value3);

        // Compare two values.
        System.out.println("\nByte Related Tasks:");
        System.out.println("Value1 compared to Value2? "
                + Value1.compareTo(Value2));
        System.out.println("Value1 compared to Value3? "
                + Value1.compareTo(Value3));

        // Convert Value1 to a float.
        System.out.println("Value1 float value: "
                + Value1.floatValue());
    }
}
```

This example begins by showing a number of static methods. Most data types provide methods to discover the size of the value contained within the object, the minimum and maximum value supported by the object, and the object's *unboxed type* — the primitive type you'd end up with if you unboxed the object.

The static methods also include several different methods of creating the object. This example shows how to use the `valueOf()` method. In this case, you can create the object using a `String` or a `byte` value. When working with a String, you can provide a *radix* — the base of the value. The last `valueOf()` method call creates a Byte object with a value of 15, base 16 (hexadecimal). If you don't provide a radix, Java assumes you want to use base 10 (decimal) numbers.

REMEMBER

When you create a `Byte` using a numeric value, you must add `(byte)` in front of the number. This is called *casting* — the process of converting an entity of one data type into another. Java assumes an `int` type whenever you provide numeric input. Casting tells Java that you really want to provide a `byte` type. Because `valueOf()` requires a `byte` as input, you must cast the `int` value that Java assumes you mean to a `byte` value.

You can use objects directly as shown in the example. Java automatically unboxes the object to obtain the value and display it on screen. Objects also include special object-related methods, such as `compareTo()`, which lets you compare one value to another. The `floatValue()` method outputs the `byte` value in the `Byte` as a `float`. So you can also cast between types using a method call when such a method is provided.

This particular example also shows how to add a blank space between lines. You can either use `System.out.println();` or add `\n` in front of the text that should appear with a space before it. The second form, `\n`, is called an *escape character*. When you use more than one pair of these characters, it's called an *escape sequence*. The "Using Escape Sequences" section of Chapter 4 tells you a lot more about working with escape sequences.

LINGO

Casting converts one data type to another. For example, you can change an `int` into a `byte` when necessary. A cast is an important Java feature because it tells Java that it's acceptable to perform a conversion. If you cast incorrectly, the result could be data loss and incorrect output from your application. For example, if you cast an `int` value of 200 to a `byte` value, the resulting `byte` value of –56 will be incorrect because a `byte` can't hold a value of 200.

3. **Save the code to disk using the filename** `ByteVersusByte.java`.

4. **In your command prompt, type** javac ByteVersusByte.java **and press Enter.**

   The compiler compiles your application and creates a `.class` file from it.

5. **Type** java ByteVersusByte **and press Enter.**

   You see the application output shown in Figure 3-4. As you might expect, the `byte` value consumes 8 bits, it has a minimum value of –128 and a maximum value of 127, and it has a type of byte. Notice that `Value3` actually contains 21. That's because the application creates it as a hexadecimal value of 15, which equates to a decimal value of 21. Value1 and Value2 are equal, so there is a 0 difference between them. However, there is a -6 difference between Value1 and Value3. Finally, notice that the floatValue() method actually does output Value1 as a float.

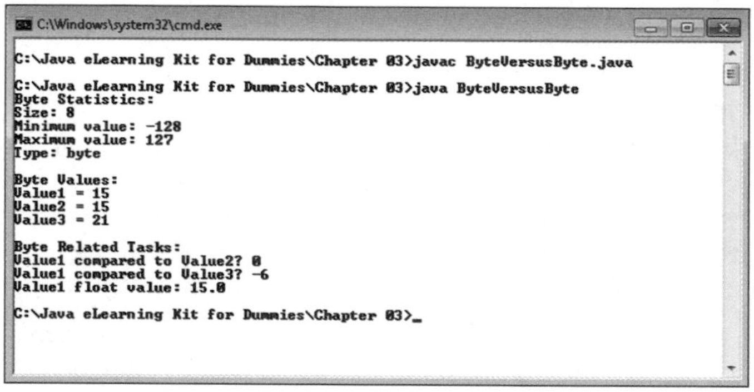

Figure 3-4

Short versus short

The Short object contains all the same features that the Byte object does, so you can perform tasks such as obtaining the size, minimum value, and maximum value of the type. It also includes the same valueOf() methods.

In the following exercise, you discover a method for letting users enter numbers in octal (base 8), decimal (base 10), or hexadecimal (base 16) format.

Files needed: ShortVersusShort.java

1. **Open the editor or IDE that you've chosen to use for this book.**

2. **Type the following code into the editor screen.**

```java
// Import the required API classes.
import java.lang.Short;

public class ShortVersusShort
{
    public static void main(String[] args)
    {
        // Obtain a Short value from the command line.
        Short MyShort = Short.decode(args[0]);
```

```
    // Display the value on screen.
    System.out.println("The value of MyShort is: "
        + MyShort);
  }
}
```

The code for this example looks and acts the same as the ShowByte example that you worked with in Chapter 2, but with a couple of important differences. Because this example works with a Short, you can use the Short.decode() method to obtain user input in octal, decimal, or hexadecimal format using specially formatted strings (as you'll discover later in the exercise). After the user types a numeric value, the code decodes it into a Short object (labeled MyShort) and then displays the value of MyShort on screen.

In addition to the ability to work with multiple bases, this application also accepts input from the command line, rather than using a Scanner object. The difference means that you type the value you want to use at the command line, rather than separately after the program provides a prompt. This form of input is used when you need to automate an application in some way. Automation makes it possible to include the application in a script or use it in some other way that requires the application to work without user interaction.

3. **Save the code to disk using the filename ShortVersusShort.java.**

4. **In your command prompt, type** javac ShortVersusShort.java **and press Enter.**

   The compiler compiles your application and creates a .class file from it.

5. **Type** java ShortVersusShort 15 **and press Enter.**

   The application outputs a value of 15 as expected. Notice that you don't have to wait for a prompt. The application processes the information directly from the command line.

6. **Repeat Step 5, but type a value of 015 (with a leading zero) this time.**

   The application outputs a value of 13. When you type a value of 015, the application sees it as octal input. In this case, octal means that the usual tens position actually equals 8. So, 8 + 5 = 13 (15 octal equals 13 decimal).

7. **Repeat Step 5, but type a value of 0x15 this time.**

   The application outputs a value of 21, which is the decimal equivalent of the hexadecimal 15. Figure 3-5 shows the outputs of this example.

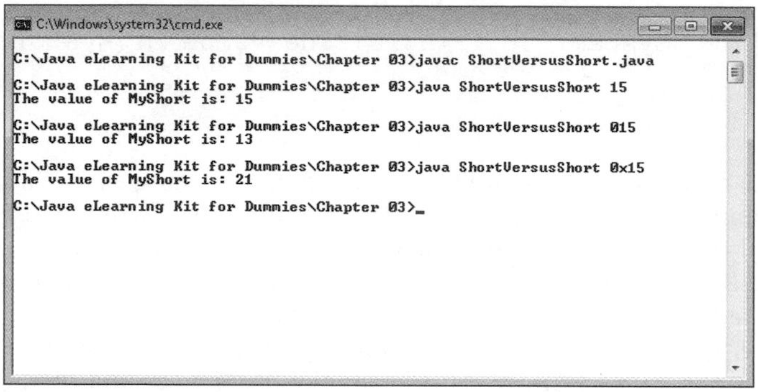

Figure 3-5

Try performing Step 5 with a value of 019. The application displays an error in this case because 9 doesn't exist in octal — the highest value is 7. Perform Step 5 again with a value of 0x1A. You should see an output of 26. Hexadecimal values use the letters A through F to represent the decimal numbers 10 through 15. That's right: A hexadecimal number can range from 0 through F. (That's 0 through 15 decimal.) Try performing Step 5 with other values, both positive and negative. For example, what do you see when you type –022? Playing with this application helps you understand how different bases of numbers work on the computer.

Integer versus int

The Integer class is one of the most flexible used for data types. It includes more methods than either Byte or Short for interacting with values.

In the following example, you try out a few of the special Integer methods.

Files needed: IntegerVersusInt.java

1. **Open the editor or IDE that you've chosen to use for this book.**

2. **Type the following code into the editor screen.**

```java
// Import the required API classes.
import java.util.Scanner;
import java.lang.Integer;

public class IntegerVersusInt
{
    public static void main(String[] args)
    {
```

```
// Create the scanner.
Scanner GetInteger = new Scanner(System.in);

// Obtain an Integer value.
System.out.print("Type any number: ");
Integer MyInteger = Integer.valueOf(GetInteger.
  nextLine());

// Display some of the Integer outputs.
System.out.println("\nVarious Base Output:");
System.out.println("Binary MyInteger: "
      + Integer.toBinaryString(MyInteger));
System.out.println("Octal MyInteger: "
      + Integer.toOctalString(MyInteger));
System.out.println("Decimal MyInteger: "
      + MyInteger);
System.out.println("Hexadecimal MyInteger: "
      + Integer.toHexString(MyInteger));

// Display the bit information.
System.out.println("\nBit Information:");
System.out.println("Bit Count (1's): "
      + Integer.bitCount(MyInteger));
System.out.println("Highest 1 Bit: "
      + Integer.highestOneBit(MyInteger));
System.out.println("Lowest 1 Bit: "
      + Integer.lowestOneBit(MyInteger));
System.out.println("Number of Leading 0s: "
      + Integer.numberOfLeadingZeros(MyInte
   ger));
System.out.println("Number of Trailing 0s: "
      + Integer.numberOfTrailingZeros(MyInte
   ger));
   }
}
```

As with some of the other examples in this chapter, this example asks the user for some numeric input and then manipulates that input in various ways. In this case, you get to see the output using various bases, and then you see some information about the actual bits used to create the value.

Integer provides a number of other methods, but the methods shown in this example are the most useful for right now. You can also use Integer to change the position of the bits in the value. Programmers sometimes need to perform some odd tasks with numeric values and Integer is one of the most flexible classes for accomplishing such tasks.

3. **Save the code to disk using the filename IntegerVersusInt.java.**

4. **In your command prompt, type** javac IntegerVersusInt.java **and press Enter.**

The compiler compiles your application and creates a `.class` file from it.

5. **Type** java IntegerVersusInt **and press Enter.**

The application asks you to type any number, but note that an `int` is limited to a range of –2,147,483,648 to 2,147,483,647.

6. **Type** 85 **and press Enter.**

You see the output shown in Figure 3-6. Notice the binary output of this application. If you really want to understand how bits work, trying various numbers out with this program will help.

Looking at the Binary MyInteger: line in Figure 3-6, you can see that there are indeed four 1s in the binary version of the output. The highest 1 is in the 64 position and the lowest is in the 1 position. There are seven digits in the binary output, which means there are 25 leading 0s, just as the application says. There aren't any trailing 0s because the lowest position has a 1 in it.

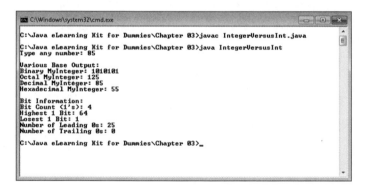

Figure 3-6

Perform Steps 5 and 6 again to rerun the application. This time, try a value of 170. The output changes to show how this number differs from 85. More importantly, this is an example of what happens when you reverse the values of the bottom eight bits (01010101 or 85 versus 10101010 or 170). Try other values to see what happens to the output.

Long versus long

The `Long` class provides all of the interesting features of the `Integer` class, but as an added bonus has the extended storage capacity of the `long` type. (A `long` can hold numbers from –9,223,372,036,854,775,808 to

9,223,372,036,854,775,807.) For example, you have access to the useful output methods such as `toBinary()`. The `Long` class also provides all of the bit manipulation features of the `Integer` class, so you can use it to create some really complex applications.

Scope is an important element of application development. The *scope* of a variable determines which parts of the application can see it. There are many ways in which Java uses scope to control variable visibility. One of those ways is to differentiate between global and local variables. A *global variable* is visible to every method within the class, while a *local variable* is visible only to the part of the application in which the variable is defined (such as a method).

It's time to see your first use of scope in action. In the following example, you use the `Long` class to learn how global and local scope works in a Java application.

Files needed: `LongVersusLong.java`

1. Open the editor or IDE that you've chosen to use for this book.

2. Type the following code into the editor screen.

```
// Import the required API classes.
import java.lang.Long;

public class LongVersusLong
{
   // Create a global variable.
   public static Long MyLong;

   public static void main(String[] args)
   {
      // Assign a value to the global variable
      // and display its value on screen.
      MyLong = Long.valueOf(500);
      System.out.println("MyLong = " + MyLong);

      // Call function1 to modify the value of
      // MyLong and display the result on screen.
      function1();
      System.out.println("MyLong in main() = "
        + MyLong);

      // Call function2 to modify the value of
      // MyLong and display the result on screen.
      function2();
      System.out.println("MyLong in main() = "
        + MyLong);
   }
```

```
public static void function1()
{
    // Assign a value to the global variable
    // and display its value on screen.
    MyLong = Long.valueOf(700);
    System.out.println("MyLong in function1() = "
      + MyLong);
}

public static void function2()
{
    // Create a local MyLong, assign it a value
    // and display its value on screen.
    Long MyLong;
    MyLong = Long.valueOf(900);
    System.out.println("MyLong in function2()= "
      + MyLong);
}
}
```

This application demonstrates two Java features you haven't yet had a chance to use in this book. First, it shows how to create and use methods other than main() in an application — in this particular case, two additional methods known as function1() and function2(). You'll see a lot more examples of how methods work throughout the book, but this is the simplest way to work with them. The main() method calls function1() and function2() as needed to perform tasks. Working with methods this way helps keep your code readable by preventing methods from getting too large.

The second feature is the use of a global variable. Notice that the declaration of MyLong appears outside of the methods. All of the methods can see the global version of MyLong so it has a global scope. The function2() method also has a variable named MyLong defined in it. This is a local variable. Only function2() can see this variable, so any changes you make to it only appear in function2(). When a method has a choice between a global variable and a local variable of the same name, it always uses the local variable by default.

3. **Save the code to disk using the filename LongVersusLong.java.**

4. **In your command prompt, type** javac LongVersusLong.java **and press Enter.**

The compiler compiles your application and creates a .class file from it.

5. **Type** java LongVersusLong **and press Enter.**

The application displays a sequence of outputs that demonstrate one way in which scope works in a Java application, as shown in Figure 3-7. Notice that function1() modifies the *global* variable, MyLong, so that main() also sees the change it makes. Meanwhile, function2()

modifies a *local* variable, `MyLong`, which means that `main()` *doesn't see* this change. The local copy of `MyLong` in `function2()` is invisible to `main()`.

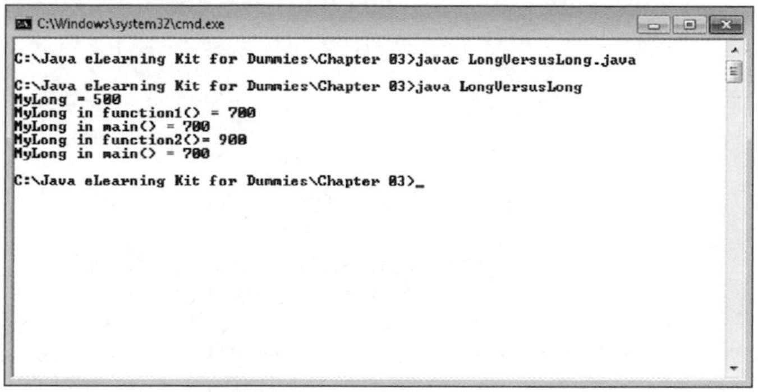

```
C:\Windows\system32\cmd.exe

C:\Java eLearning Kit for Dummies\Chapter 03>javac LongVersusLong.java

C:\Java eLearning Kit for Dummies\Chapter 03>java LongVersusLong
MyLong = 500
MyLong in function1() = 700
MyLong in main() = 700
MyLong in function2()= 900
MyLong in main() = 700

C:\Java eLearning Kit for Dummies\Chapter 03>_
```

Figure 3-7

PRACTICE

Create a `Long` version of the `IntegerVersusInt` example described in the "Integer versus int" section of the chapter and name it `LongVersusLong`. Everywhere you see the word Integer, replace it with the word Long. Now run the new application to see what happens. Most of the output is the same if you use the same input values. However, there is at least one important difference. (Hint: Look at the `Number of Leading 0s:` output.) Try typing a really large value that you can't use with the `IntegerVersusInt` program, such as 5,700,000,000 (without the commas). If you were to try a number this large with the `IntegerVersusInt` application, you'd see an error.

Float versus float

The `Float` class definitely makes working with `float` values easier, especially if the math you perform falls into the more esoteric range. For example, you can use the `Float` class to create a float value that contains either positive or negative infinity. There are concepts associated with `float` values that are well outside the scope of this book and if you're not working with that sort of math, you'll never need to worry about them. However, it's nice to know that the `Float` class makes it possible to do some amazing things with `float` values.

Floating point values approximate real numbers. In the following example, you see how the Float class can interact with floating point numbers and make them easier to work with.

Files needed: `FloatVersusFloat.java`

1. **Open the editor or IDE that you've chosen to use for this book.**

2. **Type the following code into the editor screen.**

```java
// Import the required API classes.
import java.lang.Float;

public class FloatVersusFloat
{
    public static void main(String[] args)
    {
        // Create some variables to work with.
        Float Value1 = Float.valueOf(11.55f);
        Float Value2 = Float.valueOf("11.55");
        Float Value3 = Float.parseFloat("0.1155e2");
        Float Value4 = Float.POSITIVE_INFINITY;

        // Show the actual values.
        System.out.println("Value1 = " + Value1);
        System.out.println("Value2 = " + Value2);
        System.out.println("Value3 = " + Value3);
        System.out.println("Value4 = " + Value4);

        // Determine some information about the values.
        System.out.println("\nValue1 Compared to Value2:
            " + Value1.compareTo(Value2));
        System.out.println("Value1 Compared to Value3: "
            + Value1.compareTo(Value3));
        System.out.println("Value1 Compared to Value4: "
            + Value1.compareTo(Value4));
        System.out.println("Value1 Infinite? "
            + Value1.isInfinite());
        System.out.println("Value4 Infinite? "
            + Value4.isInfinite());
        System.out.println("Value1 Integer Portion: "
            + Value1.intValue());
        System.out.println("Value3 as a String: "
            + Value3.toString());
        System.out.println("Value4 as a String: "
            + Value4.toString());
    }
}
```

The example begins by creating four `Float` objects, `Value1`, `Value2`, `Value3`, and `Value4`. When working with floating point values, you can assign a value using the `valueOf()` method, the `parseFloat()` method, or a constant, such as `Float.POSITIVE_INFINITY`. When you assign a numeric value, you either have to perform a cast, or you can simply add an f after the number to ensure Java knows that you mean to create a `float`, and not a `double`. The `parseFloat()` method is nice because you can use scientific notation with it. The value after the e is the exponent, so this method actually contains $0.1144 * 10^2$.

After creating the variables, the application begins working with them. When you want to compare two values, you must use the `compareTo()` method, just as you do with integer-based objects. Because floating point values can be infinite, the `Float` class provides the `isInfinite()` method. You can also work with just the integer portion of a floating point number, which means that you have full access to the features provided by integer-based values such as the `Integer` class. The example also shows what happens when you convert a floating point value to a string.

3. **Save the code to disk using the filename `FloatVersusFloat.java`.**

4. **In your command prompt, type** javac FloatVersusFloat.java **and press Enter.**

   The compiler compiles your application and creates a `.class` file from it.

5. **Type** java FloatVersusFloat **and press Enter.**

   The application outputs the results of the various floating point operations as shown in Figure 3-8.

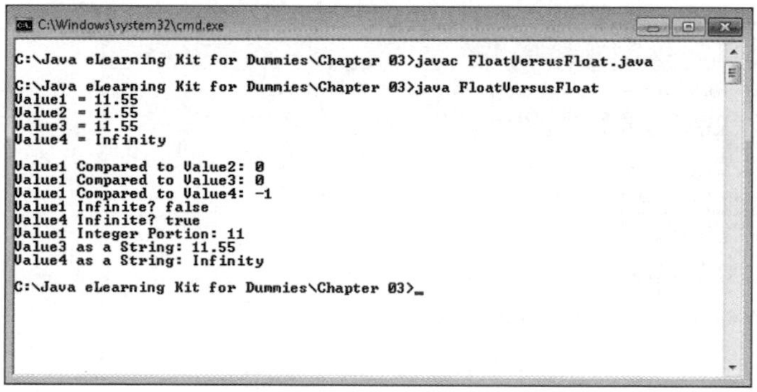

Figure 3-8

You should notice a few special things about the output in Figure 3-8. First of all, even if you provide input to the `Float` type in scientific notation, the number is stored as a standard float, so `"0.1155e2"` becomes 11.55. Second, any object that contains an infinite value outputs `Infinity` as its value. Third, you're seeing your first Java inconsistency. When you worked with the `Byte` version of `compareTo()`, it output the actual difference between the two numbers. The `Float` version of `compareTo()` outputs a 0 when the numbers are the same, a −1 when the first number is less than the second number (infinity is definitely greater than 11.55), and a 1 when the first number is more than the second number.

Most programming languages contain inconsistencies because the language develops over time and is the product of many developers' input. Always read the documentation to ensure you understand how a method works. In this case of `compareTo()`, the `Byte` and `Float` versions work differently, so you need to consider this difference when you write an application.

Double versus double

The `Double` type provides the same functionality as `Float`, except that it offers 64-bit precision. Consequently, you can perform the same sorts of tasks that you would with a `Float`. The differences between `Float` and `Double` are the same as those between `float` and `double`. A `Float` consumes less memory and could potentially offer slightly better speed, while a `Double` offers better precision (less error).

Create a `Double` version of the `FloatVersusFloat` example shown in the "Float versus float" section of the chapter. Replace every instance of the word `Float` with the word `Double`. If you run the application at this point, you'll run into something odd, as shown in Figure 3-9.

```
C:\Windows\system32\cmd.exe

C:\Java eLearning Kit for Dummies\Chapter 03>javac DoubleVersusDouble.java

C:\Java eLearning Kit for Dummies\Chapter 03>java DoubleVersusDouble
Value1 = 11.550000190734863
Value2 = 11.55
Value3 = 11.55
Value4 = Infinity

Value1 Compared to Value2: 1
Value1 Compared to Value3: 1
Value1 Compared to Value4: -1
Value1 Infinite? false
Value4 Infinite? true
Value1 Integer Portion: 11
Value3 as a String: 11.55
Value4 as a String: Infinity

C:\Java eLearning Kit for Dummies\Chapter 03>_
```

Figure 3-9

Notice that `Value1` doesn't contain the value you expected. That's because the code still assigns it the value of `11.55f` (for float). The example illustrates the inaccuracies that exist when using both `float` and `double`. To fix this problem, you must remove the `f` after `11.55` in your code so that Java uses a `double` to create `Value1`. The results will precisely match the `FloatVersusFloat` example at this point.

Boolean versus boolean

There really isn't much to say about the Boolean object type. It does offer some methods, such as valueOf(), but none of them are particularly compelling. You can't even offer an alternative output. About the only time where you might use the Boolean object type is when working with system information. The Boolean object type includes a getBoolean() method that lets you do things like access environment variables. This is one situation where you'll end up using the primitive type in your application in favor of the object type in most situations.

Character versus char

It may not seem as though you can do a lot with a single character, but the Character type really can do quite a lot. When you work with Character, you obtain a lot more than the value that char provides. For example, you can determine whether a character is of a particular type. This type also provides a number of ways to output the value.

Some of the Character methods and properties are beyond the scope of this book. For example, it's unlikely that you're going to want to modify individual bits within a Character, but the Character type provides the means for doing so.

In this exercise, you explore some of the more common ways to work with the Character type. Just be aware that you can do more.

Files needed: CharacterVersusChar.java

1. **Open the editor or IDE that you've chosen to use for this book.**

2. **Type the following code into the editor screen.**

```
// Import the required API classes.
import java.lang.Character;

public class CharacterVersusChar
{
    public static void main(String[] args)
    {
        // Create some Characters.

        Character Char1 = Character.valueOf('$');
        Character Char2 = Character.valueOf('a');
        Character Char3 = Character.valueOf('1');
```

```
// Determine some characteristics about the
// Characters.
boolean IsChar1Currency =
      (Character.getType(Char1) ==
       Character.CURRENCY_SYMBOL);

boolean IsChar2Lowercase =
      (Character.getType(Char2) ==
       Character.LOWERCASE_LETTER);

// Describe Char1.
System.out.println("It's " +
      IsChar1Currency
    + " that the " + Char1 +
    " is a currency symbol and its name is: "
  + Character.getName(Char1) + ".");

// Describe Char2.
System.out.println("It's " + IsChar2Lowercase +
      " that Char2 is lowercase and that " +
      Character.toUpperCase(Char2) +
      " is the uppercase version and " +
      Character.toTitleCase(Char2) +
      " is the title case version.");

// Describe Char3.
System.out.println("Char3 has a value of " +
      Character.getNumericValue(Char3) +
      ". It's " + Character.isDigit(Char3) +
      " that Char3 is a digit.");
   }
}
```

This example doesn't begin to show you everything the Character class can do with individual characters, but it does give you some ideas. To begin, there isn't anything fancy about creating a Character. The only option you have is the valueOf() method.

After you have a character to work with, you can start learning all sorts of things about it. For example, you can determine whether the character is a currency symbol or whether it's a lowercase letter. Whenever you want to learn about the kind of character you're working with, you call the getType() method and then compare the output against Character constants such as CURRENCY_SYMBOL.

Use the getName() method to obtain the official Unicode name for any character. Because these names are constant and unique, you can check the precise input the user has provided. Character also provides methods such as isDigit() that let you perform additional checks on the character value.

You have access to a number of output features. The `toUpperCase()`, `toLowerCase()`, and `toTitleCase()` methods are the ones that you'll use most often.

3. **Save the code to disk using the filename `CharacterVersusChar.java`.**

4. **In your command prompt, type** javac CharacterVersusChar.java **and press Enter.**

   The compiler compiles your application and creates a `.class` file from it.

5. **Type** java CharacterVersusChar **and press Enter.**

   Figure 3-10 shows the output of the `Character` class features used in this exercise.

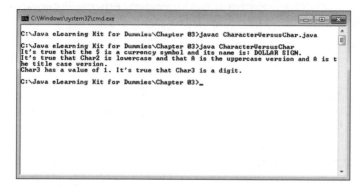

Figure 3-10

Using the New Date and Time API

In the past, Java lacked a good way to work with date and time values. Yes, there were two attempts to address the problem using the `Date` class first and then the `Calendar` class, but they proved clunky. Java 8 fixes this problem by creating an entire API devoted to date and time with special classes for each. The following sections describe the date and time API from an overview perspective.

Viewing the date and time API

Java developers have been asking for better date and time management functionality for a long time. Working with the older `Date` and `Calendar` classes was difficult, and you couldn't easily do things such as compare two time values. The new date and time API is immense, but it contains most of the features that developers have requested.

There are a lot of classes that you could use to interact with the date and time. However, you use the following classes most often:

- ✔ **Instant:** A specific point in time. The time value is defined as the number of nanoseconds that have passed since 1 January 1970.

- ✔ **LocalDate:** The date as it appears on the host system in a year, month, and day format. The output doesn't include the time zone or the time value.

- ✔ **LocalDateTime:** The date and time as it appears on the host system in a year, month, day, hours, minutes, and seconds format. The output doesn't include the time zone.

- ✔ **LocalTime:** The time as it appears on the host system in a format of hours, minutes, and seconds. The output doesn't include the time zone or date value.

- ✔ **MonthDay:** A month and day value without any corresponding year. You can use this value to represent recurring date values, such as anniversaries and birthdays.

- ✔ **OffsetDateTime:** The date and time as it appears on the host system in a year, month, day, hours, minutes, and seconds format. The output includes a time zone value.

- ✔ **OffsetTime:** The time as it appears on the host system in a format of hours, minutes, and seconds. The output includes a time zone value.

- ✔ **Year:** A year value without any other information. You could use this value for elements such as headings on a calendar.

- ✔ **YearMonth:** A year and month value without any corresponding day. You can use this value to represent recurring monthly events where the day of the event isn't important.

- ✔ **ZonedDateTime:** The date and time as it appears on the host system in a year, month, day, hours, minutes, and seconds format. The output includes an enumerated time zone value, such as America/Chicago. You can see a listing of the human-readable time zones at http://joda-time.sourceforge.net/timezones.html.

GO ONLINE

The Java 8 date and time API is so large that it would be impossible to cover in a single chapter, much less a section of a chapter. However, you can see the various classes used for the date and time API in detail at http://download.java.net/jdk8/docs/api/.

EXTRA INFO

A time zone shows the offset from Universal Time Coordinated (UTC). For example, Central Time in the United States has a UTC offset of −06:00, which means that it's six hours behind the International Atomic Time (TAI) that is maintained by the world time server. You can see the current world time server time at http://www.worldtimeserver.com/current_time_in_UTC.aspx.

Creating and using dates and times

The new date and time API provides considerable flexibility for working with both date and time values in your application. More important, you gain access to a number of new methods that make working with dates and times easier. The following example can't show everything that the date and time API is capable of doing, but it gives you a basic idea of what you can expect.

Files needed: `Java8DateTime.java`

1. Open the editor or IDE that you've chosen to use for this book.

2. Type the following code into the editor screen:

```java
// Import the required API classes.
import java.time.*;

public class Java8DateTime
{
    public static void main(String[] args)
    {
        // Display a time value.
        System.out.println("Local Values");
        System.out.println("Local Time: "
            + LocalTime.now().toString());

        // Display a date value.
        System.out.println("Local Date: "
            + LocalDate.now().toString());

        // Display both the time and the date.
        System.out.println("Local Date and Time: "
            + LocalDateTime.now().toString());

        // Display the date and time with time zone.
        System.out.println("\nTime Zone Values");
        System.out.println("Numeric Time Zone: "
            + OffsetDateTime.now().toString());
        System.out.println("Enumerated Time Zone: "
            + ZonedDateTime.now().toString());
    }
}
```

The classes you use most often when working with the date and time API are found in the `java.time` package. There are other packages that you may need from time to time, but when working with just date and time values, this is the only package you need.

This example shows how to obtain local time or date without regard to time zone and time or date with time zone included. You use time zone information when working with applications that could span a wide area. The time zone makes it possible to calculate the difference in time between New York and San Diego, as an example.

3. **Save the code to disk using the filename `Java8DateTime.java`.**

4. **In your command prompt, type** javac Java8DateTime.java **and press Enter.**

   The compiler compiles your application and creates a `.class` file from it.

5. **Type** java Java8DateTime **and press Enter.**

   Figure 3-11 shows the output of the various date and time classes used in this exercise. Notice that when you output either a date or a time alone, the value appears without special formatting. However, when you output date and time together, the output appears with a T between the date and the time to indicate the start of the time information.

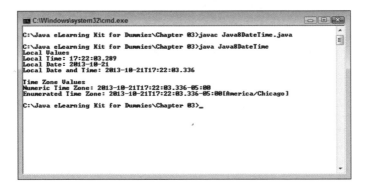

Figure 3-11

Working with Enumerations

In some cases, you want to create a list of specific values to use within an application. For example, you might want to create a list of month values from January to December so that it's not possible to select any other value. A list of values like this is called an *enumeration*.

Using this approach makes your application more reliable and reduces the chances of security risks because it isn't possible to supply a value that the developer didn't expect. People who want to break into your application (for any reason — not just as part of an intrusion) often look for ways to supply values that will cause the application to crash, which can cause data damage and potentially open the data to unauthorized viewing (among other issues). In addition, using enumerations can make your code easier to use. The following example demonstrates how to use a simple enumeration. You see a more complex example of enumerated values in Chapter 7.

Files needed: `Enumerations.java`

1. Open the editor or IDE that you've chosen to use for this book.

2. Type the following code into the editor screen:

```java
public class Enumerations
{
    // Create an enumeration.
    public enum Colors
    {
        Yellow,
        Blue,
        Red,
        Green,
        Purple
    }

    public static void main(String[] args)
    {
    }
}
```

This enumeration exists outside of the `main()` function within the class as a separate entity. You can also define enumerated values within separate files so that you can use them throughout one or more applications. All enumerations are `public` and use the `enum` keyword, followed by the name of the enumeration, which is `Colors` in this case. You then define a list of colors separated by commas.

3. Type the following code into the `main()` function:

```java
// Display an enumerated color by name.
System.out.println("The color is: " + Colors.Blue);

// Display an enumerated color by value.
System.out.println("The color is: " + Colors.values()[2]);
```

There are two common techniques for accessing enumerations. The first is directly by name, as shown in the first `System.out.println()` statement. This approach makes your code more readable and reduces any chance that someone will misinterpret the code.

The second technique is to access the enumeration by numeric value. Enumerated values begin at 0, so a value of 2 would point to the color `Red` in the list.

4. **Save the code to disk using the filename** `Enumerations.java`.

5. **In your command prompt, type** javac Enumerations.java **and press Enter.**

   The compiler compiles your application and creates a `.class` file from it.

6. **Type** java Enumerations **and press Enter.**

   Figure 3-12 shows the output of the enumeration you created.

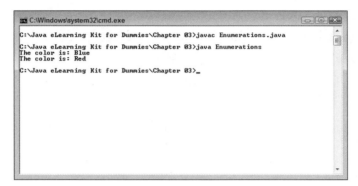

Figure 3-12

Summing Up

Here are the key points you learned about in this chapter:

- ✔ The `BigDecimal` data type helps you perform extremely accurate calculations using real numbers (those with both an integer and decimal portion).

- ✔ The `BigInteger` data type lets you perform huge calculations using integer numbers. It doesn't theoretically have a limit in size, other than the availability of memory in a system.

- ✔ Object versions of primitive types provide additional flexibility that makes it easy to manipulate the value the object contains.

- ✔ Application developers commonly use the binary (base 2), octal (base 8), decimal (base 10), and hexadecimal (base 16) numbering systems to create applications.

- ✔ The `Character` data type provides the means for detecting precisely what sort of character the variable contains.

> ✔ The new date and time API includes a number of date and time classes that you can use to work with date and time values.

> ✔ Enumerations provide a method for listing specific values that a user can't change.

Try-it-yourself lab

For more practice with the features covered in this chapter, try the following exercise on your own.

1. **Open the LongVersusLong application.**

2. **Add the code shown in bold to the** `function2()` **method.**

```
public static void function2()
{
    // Create a local MyLong, assign it a value
    // and display its value on screen.
    Long MyLong;
    MyLong = Long.valueOf(900);
    System.out.println("MyLong in function2()= " +
        MyLong);

    // Change the global MyLong, assign it a value,
    // and display its value on screen.
    LongVersusLong.MyLong = Long.valueOf(1000);
    System.out.println("Global MyLong in
        function2()= " +
        LongVersusLong.MyLong);
}
```

The new code lets `function2()` modify the global `MyLong` by providing a specific reference to it. Using `LongVersusLong.MyLong` forces `function2()` to ignore the default scope and use the global variable instead.

3. **Compile the application.**

4. **Run the application.**

The application provides output based on the new code you've added.

5. **Compare this output to the output you see in Figure 3-7.**

This version of the application demonstrates another feature of scoping rules in Java. It's possible to override the scoping rules in some cases, as long as the required variable isn't hidden from view (as in the case of the global `MyLong`).

Know this tech talk

boxing: The act of placing a value into an object for the purpose of manipulating the value with the help of the object's features.

casting: The act of converting one type into another type.

concatenation: The act of adding two strings together to create a single string. For example, if `String1` contains `Hello` (note the space after the word Hello) and `String2` contains `World`, concatenating the two strings would produce `Hello World`.

data: A series of 1s and 0s assigned to a specific location in memory.

escape character: A single special control character used to modify the output of an application. For example, the `/n` escape character adds an additional line between two lines of output.

escape sequence: Two or more escape characters used to modify the appearance of information on screen. For example, the `/t/t` escape sequence would add two tabs to the output, which would control the position of text on screen.

floating point number: An approximation of a real number, which is a number that has both an integer and a decimal portion, such as 5.1.

information: Data that has been assigned a type in order to give it meaning and make it possible to interpret what the data means.

object: A class used to hold a specific kind of data that has methods, properties, and events. An object can have special behaviors that let it interact with the data in unique ways.

overflow: An overflow occurs when an application attempts to create a value larger than the type is designed to hold. Java gets rid of the extra information and keeps just the bits that the type can successfully hold. Unfortunately, Java doesn't display an error message when this happens, so your application blissfully continues to run with the error in place. Use the `BigInteger` data type to prevent errors from occurring when performing integer math.

real number: A number that has both an integer and a decimal portion, such as 5.1. Some developers also call real numbers floating point numbers, but this isn't precisely true. A floating point number is merely an approximation of a real number.

scope: The visibility of a variable or method to other parts of an application.

unboxing: The act of removing a value from an object and placing it into the corresponding primitive type.

Chapter 4

Formatting Variable Content

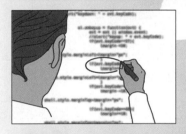

- ✔ Displaying output information in a particular way makes it *easier for the user to understand*.

- ✔ Creating a variable for percentages makes it *easier for the user to understand some fractional values*.

- ✔ Relying on escape sequences lets you *create specialized line formatting and use special characters*.

- ✔ Using date and time formatting helps you *display these values in the correct time zone and with the user's locale in mind*.

- ✔ Specifying currency values using the user's locale *ensures that the output reflects the proper currency symbols, thousands formatting, and decimal formatting*.

p until now, every application in this book has accepted the default methods of displaying output information. However, Java provides rich methods of formatting output so that it appears as you'd like it to appear, rather than as Java displays it by default. In fact, there are so many techniques that you'll find them listed throughout the book. The following sections tell you about some basic techniques that you'll find useful immediately.

Displaying Percentages

A percentage is normally going to appear in your application as a fractional amount in a `float` or `double`. Most developers want to display the percentage as a nicely formatted number (one that's understandable by humans) with a percent sign after it. In the following exercise, you create an application that formats a fractional number as a percentage.

Files needed: `DisplayPercent.java`

1. **Open the editor or IDE that you've chosen to use for this book.**

2. **Type the following code into the editor screen.**

```java
// Import the required API classes.
import java.text.NumberFormat;

public class DisplayPercent
{
    public static void main(String[] args)
    {
        // Set the interest rate.
        double Interest = .225;

        // Create a formatter to use.
        NumberFormat Percent =
            NumberFormat.getPercentInstance();
```

```
        // Set the maximum number of digits after the
        // decimal point.
        Percent.setMaximumFractionDigits(2);

        // Try displaying the interest.
        System.out.println("The interest is: "
            + Percent.format(Interest));
    }
}
```

The example doesn't do anything fancy. It begins by creating a `double` with the percentage rate.

To display a number as a percentage, you need to create a formatter. A formatter is a special class that does nothing but create nice-looking output. In this case, the application creates a `NumberFormat` object, `Percent`. Notice that you must call the `getPercentInstance()` constructor (the method used to construct the object from the class definition) in order to work with percentages.

Java assumes that you want to display percentages as whole numbers. However, you can change this behavior by calling the `setMaximumFractionDigits()` method. You can also set other values, such as the minimum number of digits used for both the integer and decimal portions of the output.

3. **Save the code to disk using the filename `DisplayPercent.java`.**

4. **In your command prompt, type** javac DisplayPercent.java **and press Enter.**

   The compiler compiles your application and creates a `.class` file from it.

5. **Type** java DisplayPercent **and press Enter.**

   Figure 4-1 shows the formatted percentage.

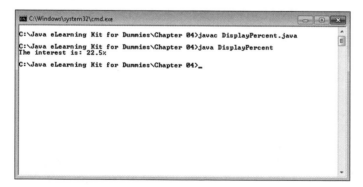

Figure 4-1

Using Escape Sequences

When you have some standard text, but you want to format it in a special way, you can use something called an escape character in order to tell Java to perform the formatting. (Here, an escape character means a character that "escapes" from the standard character presentation to do something special, such as move the cursor to the next line.) When you place a number of escape characters together, you get an escape sequence. Escape sequences aren't unique to Java — many other programming languages use them. In addition, escape sequences have been around for a long time. Even old mainframe systems use escape sequences. So, escape sequences are found on pretty much every platform and they're standardized across languages for the most part.

An escape character always begins with a backslash (\), followed by a special letter, such as n for creating a new line. Table 4-1 shows the escape characters that Java supports.

Table 4-1		Java Escape Characters
Character	*Purpose*	*Description*
\n	New line	Moves the cursor to the next line. Depending on the platform, it may not move the cursor to the beginning of the next line.
\t	Tab	Moves the cursor to the next tab position. Using tabs lets you precisely align output so that it appears as if you've used a table to hold the pieces of information.
\b	Backspace	Moves the character back one space without erasing the character on that space. When used correctly, and on the right platform, you can create overstrikes that combine two characters to produce special effects.
\f	Form feed	Ejects the current sheet of paper in a printer and starts fresh with the next sheet.
\"	Double quote	Produces a double quote without ending a quoted element in your code. This escape character is helpful when creating `String` objects that include a double quote.

continued

Table 4-1 *(continued)*

Character	Purpose	Description
\'	Single quote	Produces a single quote without ending a quoted element in your code. This escape character is helpful when creating a `char` that holds a single quote.
\\	Backslash	Because the backslash is used to create escape characters, you need a special method for including a backslash in your output.
\uDDDD	Unicode character	Produces the specified Unicode character when you provide an appropriate four-digit number. For example, a string that contains "\u00A9" will produce the copyright symbol.

It's time to see some of these escape sequences in action. In the following exercise, you create a series of string outputs that rely on escape sequences to produce the desired output. You'll see many of these escape sequences used in other parts of the book.

Files needed: `EscapeCharacters.java`

1. **Open the editor or IDE that you've chosen to use for this book.**

2. **Type the following code into the editor screen.**

```
public class EscapeCharacters
{
    public static void
        main(String[] args)
    {
        // Output various
        // strings using escape
        // sequences.
        System.out.println("Use
            the tab \\t character"
            + "\t to position
            things on screen.");
        System.out.println("Sometimes you want to move"
            + "\nto the next line");
```

GO ONLINE

It would be nice if everyone used the same character set, but it simply isn't the case. Consequently, a Unicode character of \u00BD normally produces an output of ½. However, the ASCII text provided at some versions of the Windows command line requires a value of /u00AB to produce the same result. Because different character sets work to different standards, you need to know which character set your application will use when you write it. You can find an incredibly extensive list of these character sets at http://www.i18nguy.com/unicode/codepages.html.

```
            // Replace \u00AB with \u00BD when working with an
            // application that actually follows the Unicode
            // standard.
            System.out.println("The carpenter removed a "
                    + "\u00BD\" from the piece of wood.");
        }
    }
```

The example uses the escape characters described in Table 4-1 to create sequences that produce a desired output. If you find that the /u00BD escape sequence doesn't produce the required ½ symbol, change it to /u00AB instead.

3. **Match each of the escape characters in the source code to the corresponding entry in Table 4-1 to determine what effect they'll produce.**

   It's essential to see how this code will work in your mind's eye if you can. After a while, you'll know from experience how things will look when viewing the escape characters, but it's helpful to try to figure them out from the outset.

4. **Save the code to disk using the filename `EscapeCharacters.java`.**

5. **In your command prompt, type** javac EscapeCharacters.java **and press Enter.**

   The compiler compiles your application and creates a `.class` file from it.

6. **Type** java EscapeCharacters **and press Enter.**

   Figure 4-2 shows the result of using the escape characters.

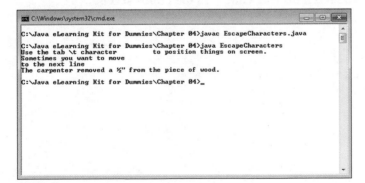

Figure 4-2

Displaying Date and Time

Java applications will use two distinct methods for working with date and time for the foreseeable future. The older method relies on the Calendar object. A newer method, introduced with Java 8, relies on the date and time API.

Each method has its own way of presenting information to the viewer. The older method is less flexible and requires more code, but it's the technique you see used in most Java applications today. The newer date and time API provides significant flexibility and offers a range of useful built-in formatting options that require little code. However, because Java 8 is so new, you won't see this technique used very often just yet. The following sections discuss formatting for both methods.

Using the Calendar object

Most people are quite picky when it comes time to display date and time because the world is a time-oriented place. It's important to see the date and time presented precisely as expected. The exercise in the "int" section of Chapter 2 exposed you to the `Calendar` object that provides access to the time and date on your computer. In the following exercise, you create output that matches specific criteria.

Files needed: `DisplayDateTime.java`

1. **Open the editor or IDE that you've chosen to use for this book.**

2. **Type the following code into the editor screen.**

```java
// Import the required API classes.
import java.util.Calendar;


public class DisplayDateTime
{
   public static void main(String[] args)
   {
      // Get the current date and time.
      Calendar MyCal = Calendar.getInstance();

      // Display the date and time on separate lines.
      System.out.format("%te %tB %tY",
            MyCal, MyCal, MyCal);
      System.out.format("\n%tl:%tM %tp",
            MyCal, MyCal, MyCal);
   }
}
```

The example begins by creating a Calendar object, MyCal. It then uses a new `System.out` method, `format()`, to produce formatted information. The `format()` method works by using special format codes as placeholders in the string. You then supply a variable to fill each of those placeholders. Table 4-2 describes each of these format codes.

Table 4-2	Example format() Method Formatting Codes
Code	**Description**
%tB	A locale-specific month name. The month will always appear as a complete name, such as January.
%tb	A locale-specific abbreviated month name, such as Jan for January.
%tm	A two-digit representation of the current month, where January is equal to 01.
%td	A two-digit day of the month without leading zeros. So, the first day of the month will appear as 1.
%te	A two-digit day of the month with leading zeros as needed. So, the first day of the month will appear as 01.
%ty	A two-digit year.
%tY	A four-digit year.
%tA	A locale-specific day of the week name. The day of the week will always appear as a complete name, such as Sunday.
%ta	A locale-specific abbreviated day of the week name, such as Sun for Sunday.
%tD	A shortcut method of outputting the date in %tm%td%ty form.
%tk	The hour using a 24-hour clock without leading zeros. So the first hour will appear as 1.
%tH	The hour using a 24-hour clock with leading zeros as needed. So the first hour will appear as 01.
%tl	The hour using a 12-hour clock without leading zeros. So the first hour will appear as 1.
%tI	The hour using a 12-hour clock with leading zeros as needed. So the first hour will appear as 01.
%tM	The minutes with leading zeros as needed. So the first minute of the hour will appear as 01.
%tS	The seconds with leading zeros as needed. So the first second of the minute will appear as 01.
%tL	The milliseconds with leading zeros as needed. So the first millisecond within the second will appear as 001.

continued

Table 4-2 *(continued)*

Code	Description
%tN	The nanoseconds with leading zeros as needed. So the first nanosecond within the second will appear as 000000001.
%tp	A locale-specific display of am or pm in lowercase.
%Tp	A locale-specific display of am or pm in uppercase.
%tz	The time zone offset from GMT, such as –0600 for United States Central time.
%tZ	The text time zone value, such as CST for Central Standard Time.

3. **Save the code to disk using the filename** DisplayDateTime.java.

4. **In your command prompt, type** javac DisplayDateTime.java **and press Enter.**

   The compiler compiles your application and creates a .class file from it.

5. **Type** java DisplayDateTime **and press Enter.**

   A Calendar object always contains the complete time, so MyCal has everything you need in it. The point is to get the date and time in the form you want them. As shown in Figure 4-3, this example outputs the date and time in a specific format.

LINGO

The term **locale** refers to someone's location when it comes to presentation of information. For example, if you live in Kansas, but type all of your documents in German, it's very likely that you'll use the German locale. Most people use the locale for the place in which they physically live, but as far as the computer is concerned, locale represents the country's rules that you use for formatting information such as date, time, numbers, and currency. The locale doesn't magically translate words into another language.

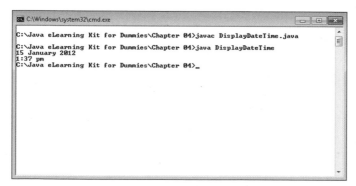

Figure 4-3

Modify the example as desired to output the time and date in other formats. Try various letter combinations from Table 4-2 to achieve the desired results. After each change to the code, perform steps 3 through 5 so you can see the result on screen.

Using the date and time API

The date and time API is designed to address the date and time handling limitations found in previous versions of Java. Part of the problem for many developers was a lack of formatting flexibility. Yes, you could usually get the output you wanted, but only after working with the code for a long time to get it. The following exercise demonstrates that Java 8 solves the problem of output by providing a number of easy-to-use options.

Files needed: `Java8DateTime.java`

GO ONLINE

Table 4-2 contains the most common formatting codes. You can create other codes as needed to obtain specific results. The article at `http://docs.oracle.com/javase/7/docs/api/java/util/Formatter.html` provides additional information about date and time formatting.

1. **Open the editor or IDE that you've chosen to use for this book.**

2. **Type the following code into the editor screen:**

```java
// Import the required API classes.
import java.time.*;
import java.time.format.*;

public class Java8DateTime
{
    public static void main(String[] args)
    {
        // Create a time and date object.
        ZonedDateTime theDateTime = ZonedDateTime.now();

        // Display some time values.
        System.out.println("Local Time: " +
            theDateTime.format(
                DateTimeFormatter.ISO_LOCAL_TIME));
        System.out.println("ISO Offset Time: " +
            theDateTime.format(
                DateTimeFormatter.ISO_OFFSET_TIME));
```

```
// Display a date/time value.
System.out.println("RFC 1123/RFC 822 Date/Time: " +
    theDateTime.format(
        DateTimeFormatter.RFC_1123_DATE_TIME));

// Display a custom date/time value.
System.out.println("Custom Date/Time: " +
    theDateTime.format(
        DateTimeFormatter.ofPattern(
            "dd MMM yyyy hh:mm:ss a zzzz")));
    }
}
```

The example begins by creating a `ZonedDateTime` object, `theDateTime`. A `ZonedDateTime` object can provide the date and time value using a numeric offset or a variety of named offsets, such as Central Daylight Time or CDT.

To output the date and time in a specific way, you need to use the `format()` method. You provide a formatter as input to this method. In most cases, all you really need is a `DateTimeFormatter` class object to perform the task. This class provides predefined formatters (such as `ISO_LOCAL_TIME`), or you can describe a format using a pattern. Table 4-3 describes each of these pattern codes.

GO ONLINE

The example doesn't even start to show everything that you can do with the `ZoneDateTime` object in the way of output. The description of the `DateTimeFormatter` class at `http://download.java.net/jdk8/docs/api/java/time/format/DateTimeFormatter.html` provides you with additional information.

Table 4-3	Example Patterns
Code	**Description**
'	Escape for text that would normally be considered a pattern character, such as a single letter *a*
' ' (two single quotes)	Single quote
[	Optional section start
]	Optional section end
a	AM or PM as needed to present the half of a 12-hour day
A	Number of milliseconds in the time value
D	Day of the year

Code	Description
d	Day of the month
E	Day of the week
e/c	Localized day of the week
F	Week of the month
G	Era (such as AD)
h	Hour of the day for a 12-hour clock (1 to 12)
H	Hour of the day for a 24-hour clock (0 to 23)
K	Hour of the day for a 12-hour clock (0 to 11)
k	Hour of the day for a 24-hour clock (1 to 24)
m	Minute of the hour
M/L	Month of the year
n	Nanoseconds of the second
N	Number of nanoseconds in the time value
O	Localized zone-offset
p	Add a padding character
Q/q	Quarter of the year
s	Second of the minute
S	Fraction of the second
u	Year
V	Time zone identifier such as America/Los_Angeles
w	The number of the week in the current year
W	The number of the week in the current month
X	Time zone offset (shows a *Z* for time zone 0)
x	Time zone offset
y	Year of the current era
Y	Year
z	Time zone name
Z	Time zone offset

3. Save the code to disk using the filename `Java8DateTime.java`.

4. **In your command prompt, type** javac Java8DateTime.java **and press Enter.**

The compiler compiles your application and creates a `.class` file from it.

5. **Type** java Java8DateTime **and press Enter.**

   This example shows just a few of the available formatting techniques. Figure 4-4 shows typical output. Notice that even though the `Zoned DateTime` object can provide a named zone output, it can also provide an offset output.

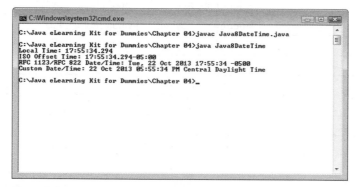

Figure 4-4

Displaying Currency Values

Displaying monetary amounts is particularly important because a decimal point in the wrong place can cause all kinds of trouble. It's also important to use the correct symbols. A monetary amount in pounds will definitely differ from one in dollars. In the following example you create locale-specific currency output for a numeric value.

Files needed: `DisplayCurrency.java`

1. **Open the editor or IDE that you've chosen to use for this book.**

2. **Type the following code into the editor screen.**

```java
// Import the required API classes.
import java.text.NumberFormat;
import java.util.Locale;
import java.math.BigDecimal;

public class DisplayCurrency
{
    public static void main(String[] args)
    {
        // Set the amount owed.
        BigDecimal MyMoney = new BigDecimal("19.95");
```

```
            // Create a formatter to use.
            NumberFormat Currency =
                    NumberFormat.getCurrencyInstance(Locale.US);

            // Try displaying the amount owed.
            System.out.println("The amount you owe is: "
                    + Currency.format(MyMoney));
        }
    }
```

The example begins by creating a monetary value using `BigDecimal`, which is the recommended way to work with monetary values. `MyMoney` contains the amount of money that's owed for this example. However, this value isn't formatted, so you don't know whether it's dollars, pounds, or yen.

The next step creates a `NumberFormat`, `Currency`, that's set up for currency values using `getCurrencyInstance()`. Notice the use of `Locale.US` to set the example to output dollars.

3. **Save the code to disk using the filename `DisplayCurrency.java`.**

4. **In your command prompt, type** javac DisplayCurrency.java **and press Enter.**

   The compiler compiles your application and creates a `.class` file from it.

5. **Type** java DisplayCurrency **and press Enter.**

   The example outputs the value in dollars. Figure 4-5 shows the formatted information.

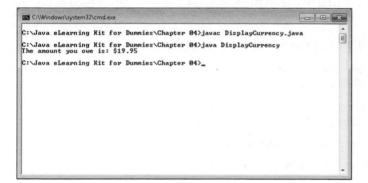

Figure 4-5

Try changing the code for this example to see the result of different locales. For example, try changing Locale.US to Local.UK to see the output in pounds. The monetary amount won't change, but the formatting will.

 # Summing Up

Here are the key points you learned about in this chapter:

- ✔ The NumberFormat object makes it possible to create properly formatted percent output.

- ✔ Escape characters make it possible to create nicely formatted output that works on just about every screen.

- ✔ Not all platforms use the same character set, so make sure you know which character set your platform uses before working with Unicode character output.

- ✔ Make certain that you use locale-specific date and time formatting when working with local times so that features such as month names appear the right way.

- ✔ The date and time API provides significantly greater flexibility than using the older Calendar object, but you must have Java 8 to use it.

- ✔ Java Currency features will only change the formatting of the output, not the actual value. In other words, Java won't take your dollar input and convert it to pounds.

Try-it-yourself lab

For more practice with the features covered in this chapter, try the following exercise on your own.

1. **Open the EscapeCharacters application.**

2. **Add code to the application that reproduces the first two columns of Table 4-1.**

   It helps to think of the positioning that you'll need to reproduce the table. Use tab and newline characters to carefully reconstruct the table.

3. **Compile the application.**

4. **Run the application.**

   Check the table you've produced for accuracy.

5. **Repeat Steps 2 through 4 until your table matches the first two columns of Table 4-1.**

6. **Repeat Steps 1 through 5 for Table 2-1 found in Chapter 2.**

   In this case, you need to add the other types of formatting described in this chapter.

Know this tech talk

constructor: A special method used to build an object from a class description. The constructor contains special code used to perform tasks such as initializing global variables. Every class has a default constructor, even if the code used to create the class doesn't contain one.

escape character: A single special control character used to modify the output of an application. For example, the /n escape character adds an additional line between two lines of output.

escape sequence: Two or more escape characters used to modify the appearance of information on screen. For example, the /t/t escape sequence would add two tabs to the output, which would control the position of text on screen.

formatter: A special type of class used exclusively for formatting output so it looks nice.

locale: The characteristics of application output that define a particular language. For example, some languages use a period for the decimal marker, while others use a comma. Formatting data with locale in mind makes it easier for people who speak other languages to use it.

Chapter 5

Working with Operators

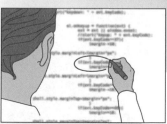

- ✔ Assigning data to a variable will *store the information while the application runs.*

- ✔ Use arithmetic operators to *modify the data value using various types of math.*

- ✔ Rely on unary operators to *perform self-contained data modification.*

- ✔ Employ relational operators to *check how data items compare.*

- ✔ Exercise operator precedence to *determine which operators have priority in your application.*

Operators are an essential part of Java application development. They do precisely as their name implies — they operate on the value contained within a primitive type or object in some way. Precisely how it operates on the value depends on the operator. In some cases, an operator will change the value in the variable, but in other cases, the operator simply uses the value to perform a specialized task, such as comparing two values. Java provides a wealth of operators that perform every task imaginable.

REMEMBER

The best way to understand how operators work and what they do is to group them into categories and then look at each category individually. That's precisely how this chapter approaches the topic. Each of the following sections describes a different operator category and shows how to use the operators within that category to your advantage. Here's a quick overview of the operators in this chapter:

✔ **Assignment operators** place the value you define into the variable. The basic assignment operator replaces the value in the variable. Combined assignment operators perform a math-related task and update the value in the variable. It's nearly impossible to write an application without making variable assignments of some sort.

✔ **Arithmetic operators** perform any math-related task, including addition, subtraction, multiplication, and division. Most applications need to perform math-related tasks, even if the user is unaware of the math functionality. You'll discover as the book progresses that math is an inescapable part of programming.

✔ **Unary operators** cause the variable to interact with its own content in some way, such as *incrementing* (adding to) or *decrementing* (subtracting from) the variable's value. In many respects, unary operators provide a shorthand that makes application code easier to understand and faster to write.

✔ **Relational and conditional operators** perform a comparison of some type and provide a result that reflects that comparison. These operators make it possible for applications to make decisions based on the content of variables.

If every operator had precisely the same precedence (priority), chaos would result because the computer wouldn't know which task to perform first. Because computers are logical and require well-ordered instructions, the developers of Java had to create an order in which operators are used when more than one of them appears in a single line of code. The order of precedence helps determine which task to do first, even if the order isn't clear from the way the code is written. You need to understand precedence in order to write good code. Otherwise, you may end up with code that assumes that the computer will be working with one operator first and only find out later that the computer really worked with another operator first.

LINGO

Precedence defines the order in which tasks are performed on a computer. Think priority when you see precedence. Just as you prioritize the work you need to do, the computer must also prioritize the work it must do. The order of precedence is essentially the same for all computer languages, and this order is borrowed from mathematicians. In short, the rules you learned for performing math tasks in school are the same rules that the computer uses to perform tasks. As a result, you'll likely find it easier to learn the order of precedence than you might initially think.

Storing Data Using Assignment Operators

You've already used assignment operators quite a bit in this book so far. In fact, almost every example has some type of assignment operator in it because it's nearly impossible to write an application without one.

Performing a simple assignment

The kind of assignment operator you'll use most often is a simple assignment. Simple assignments rely on the equal sign (=). In this exercise, you use a simple assignment to place a value in a primitive type and display it onscreen.

Files needed: `SimpleAssignment.java`

1. **Open the editor or IDE that you've chosen to use for this book.**

2. **Type the following code into the editor screen.**

```
public class SimpleAssignment
{
   public static void main(String[] args)
   {
      // Create a variable to hold the value.
      int MyInt;

      // Assign a value to the variable.
      MyInt = 2;

      // Display the content of the variable.
      System.out.println("MyInt = " + MyInt);
   }
}
```

In this example, the application begins by creating a storage container of type `int` with the name `MyInt`. At this point, `MyInt` doesn't contain anything — it's an empty storage container. In fact, if you were to try to do anything with `MyInt`, the Java compiler would report that you hadn't *initialized* the variable — you hadn't actually put anything in the storage container, in other words.

The next step places a value of 2 into `MyInt` using the assignment operator, `=`. This is a simple assignment. Nothing happens except that `MyInt` now contains a value. After `MyInt` contains something, you can display what it contains using the `System.out.println()` method.

3. **Save the code to disk using the filename `SimpleAssignment.java`.**

4. **In your command prompt, type** javac SimpleAssignment.java **and press Enter.**

The compiler compiles your application and creates a `.class` file from it.

5. **Type** java SimpleAssignment **and press Enter.**

You see the expected output of `MyInt = 2` as shown in Figure 5-1. The point here is that the application has made an assignment using the assignment operator.

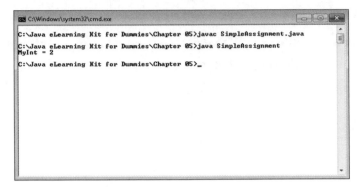

Figure 5-1

Performing a combined assignment

A *combined* assignment complicates the process by first performing a special operation on a value and only then performing a simple assignment. As a result, the content of the variable is updated in a specific way. The following list shows the common combined assignment operators.

- ✔ *=: Performs multiplication of the value within the variable by the number supplied to the right of the operator. The result is assigned to the variable.

- ✔ /=: Performs division of the value within the variable by the number supplied to the right of the operator. The result is assigned to the variable. When used with an integer type, the remainder is discarded.

- ✔ +=: Performs addition of the value within the variable with the number supplied to the right of the operator. The result is assigned to the variable.

- ✔ -=: Performs subtraction of the number supplied to the right of the operator from the number within the variable. The result is assigned to the variable.

- ✔ %=: Performs division of the value within the variable by the number supplied to the right of the operator. The remainder is assigned to the variable. This operator is used only with integer type variables.

Each of these operators performs a math operation followed by an assignment. In the following exercise, you use a simple assignment to place a value in a primitive type. The application then performs a number of combined assignments and places the result of each assignment onscreen.

LINGO

The % operator has a special name of **modulus**.

Files needed: `CombinedAssignment.java`

1. **Open the editor or IDE that you've chosen to use for this book.**

2. **Type the following code into the editor screen.**

```java
public class CombinedAssignment
{
    public static void main(String[] args)
    {
        // Create the initial variable and display
        // its value onscreen.
        int MyInt = 15;
        System.out.println("Initial value = " + MyInt);

        // Perform a multiply assignment.
        MyInt *= 3;
        System.out.println("Multiply assignment = " +
          MyInt);

        // Perform a divide assignment.
        MyInt /= 2;
        System.out.println("Divide assignment = " +
          MyInt);

        // Perform an addition assignment.
        MyInt += 6;
        System.out.println("Addition assignment = " +
          MyInt);

        // Perform a subtraction assignment.
        MyInt -= 12;
        System.out.println("Subtraction assignment = "
                + MyInt);

        // Perform a remainder assignment.
        MyInt %= 7;
        System.out.println("Remainder assignment = " +
          MyInt);
    }
}
```

The application begins by creating a variable and initializing it. If you try to use the variable without initializing it, the compiler will display an error message.

It's impossible to use a combined assignment operator without first initializing the variable. Doing so always results in an error because the combined assignment operator relies on the content of the variable as a starting point; therefore, the variable must contain something.

After the application creates the variable, it uses each of the common combined assignment operators to perform a task with the variable content. The application displays the result each time.

3. **View each step of the code carefully and write down the results that you think the application will display.**

   For example, the first call to `System.out.println()` displays a value of `15` because `MyInt` is assigned a value of `15`. This step asks you to determine what will happen after each of the remaining steps before you actually run the application.

4. **Save the code to disk using the filename `CombinedAssignment.java`.**

5. **In your command prompt, type** javac CombinedAssignment.java **and press Enter.**

   The compiler compiles your application and creates a `.class` file from it.

6. **Type** java CombinedAssignment **and press Enter.**

   You see the application outputs, as shown in Figure 5-2.

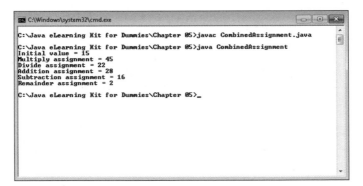

Figure 5-2

7. **Compare the results of your calculations against the actual application output.**

8. **If your results didn't match the output, view each step of the code again to determine where you derived an incorrect output.**

   This sort of exercise helps you understand the combined operators better. In addition, this is the sort of analysis that professional programmers use to learn new programming skills.

Change the numeric values used at each step of the applications, perform your analysis, and run the application again. Try various values to see how the application reacts. For example, try creating a value that will result in a negative output.

Performing Math Tasks with Arithmetic Operators

Most applications rely on math operations to perform part of their work, even when the user is unaware of such math. As this book progresses, you'll use math to perform tasks such as keeping track of the application status. Just how this happens is unimportant for now, but it is important to know that you use math relatively often when working with applications. Here's a rundown on the common math operators used in this book:

- ✔ *: Performs multiplication of the values within two variables.

- ✔ /: Divides the value within the variable on the right side of the operator by the value in the variable on the left side of the operator. The remainder is discarded when working with integer types.

- ✔ %: Divides the value within the variable on the right side of the operator by the value in the variable on the left side of the operator. However, in this case, the result is the remainder, rather than the quotient.

- ✔ +: Performs addition of the values within two variables.

- ✔ -: Subtracts the value of the variable on the right side of the operator from the value of the variable on the left side of the operator.

The following sections describe how to perform common math tasks by using the math operators. These sections are only an introduction to the topic. You'll see math operators used in the majority of the examples in this book.

Performing simple math tasks

You'll often need to perform simple multiplication, division, addition, or subtraction. The combined assignment operators described in the "Performing a combined assignment" section of the chapter provide the best way to perform single math tasks. In the following example, you see how Java performs math operations involving multiple operators or situations where the combined assignment operators don't work.

Files needed: `SimpleMath.java`

1. Open the editor or IDE that you've chosen to use for this book.

2. Type the following code into the editor screen.

```java
public class SimpleMath
{
    public static void main(String[] args)
    {
        // Create a series of variables to use.
        int X = 5;
        int Y = 10;
        int Z = 15;

        // Perform multiplication and display the
        // result.
        X = Y * Z;
        System.out.printf("%d * %d = %d%n", Y, Z, X);

        // Perform division and display the result.
        X = Z / Y;
        System.out.printf("%d / %d = %d%n", Z, Y, X);

        // Perform division using the modulus operator
        // and display the result.
        X = Z % Y;
        System.out.printf("%d %% %d = %d%n", Z, Y, X);

        // Perform addition and display the result.
        X = Y + Z;
        System.out.printf("%d + %d = %d%n", Y, Z, X);

        // Perform subtraction and display the result.
        X = Y - Z;
        System.out.printf("%d - %d = %d", Y, Z, X);
    }
}
```

The example begins by creating three `int` values, `X`, `Y`, and `Z`. There are many situations where you don't want to store the result of a calculation in the original variable so that you can reuse the original values in another calculation. In each case, the application performs a calculation and places the result in `X`. The code uses each of the values to display the calculation and its result.

This example is also the first one to use the `printf()` method. You use this method to create formatted output. Formatting works just as it does for the calendar example in the "Displaying Date and Time" section of Chapter 4. However, instead of using the date and time formatting strings described in Table 4-2 of Chapter 4, you use the formatting strings shown in Table 5-1 instead. Table 5-1 shows the most common formatting strings — Java does provide others that are used for special tasks.

Table 5-1		Common Java Formatting Strings
Code	*Specific Use*	*Description*
%b %B	General	Displays the Boolean value of the variable. When working with a Boolean variable (either primitive type or object), the result is the actual value of the variable. Other variables display `false` when the variable is null (hasn't been initialized) or `true` when the variable contains a value. The uppercase %B uses uppercase letters.
%s %S	General	Displays the string value of a variable — whatever the `toString()` method would normally display. The uppercase %S uses uppercase letters.
%c %C	Character	Displays the specified Unicode character using the rules of the `Character` data type. (See the "Character versus char" section of Chapter 3 for details.) The uppercase %C uses uppercase letters even if the character value would normally produce a lowercase output.
%d	Integral	Outputs an integer variable in decimal format.
%o	Integral	Outputs an integer variable in octal format.
%x %X	Integral	Outputs an integer variable in hexadecimal format. The uppercase %X uses uppercase letters.
%e %E	Floating point	Outputs a floating point variable using scientific notation. The uppercase %E uses uppercase letters.
%f	Floating point	Outputs a floating point variable using standard floating point (decimal) notation.
%g %G	Floating point	Outputs a floating point variable using either decimal or scientific notation depending on the precision of the variable. (The application uses the format that will provide the best output.) The uppercase %G uses uppercase letters.
%%	Percent sign	Outputs a percent sign. You can't use a single % sign because the % sign is used for other purposes when used alone.
%n	Newline character	Adds a newline character to the end of any output that you create. You can also use the \n escape character, but using %n is preferable in formatted output because it matches the remaining formatting strings.

3. **View each step of the code carefully and write down the results that you think the application will display.**

4. **Save the code to disk using the filename SimpleMath.java.**

5. **Type** javac SimpleMath.java **and press Enter.**

   The compiler compiles your application and creates a .class file from it.

6. **Type** java SimpleMath **and press Enter.**

The application outputs the formatted strings containing the values used for each math operation, as shown in Figure 5-3. If you change the values of X, Y, or Z, those changes will automatically appear in the output.

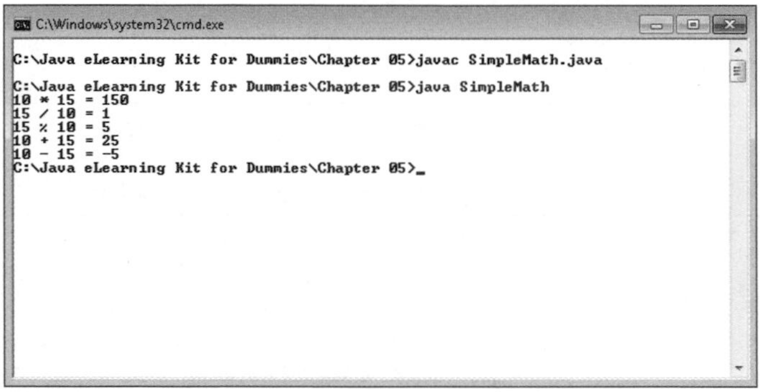

```
C:\Windows\system32\cmd.exe

C:\Java eLearning Kit for Dummies\Chapter 05>javac SimpleMath.java

C:\Java eLearning Kit for Dummies\Chapter 05>java SimpleMath
10 * 15 = 150
15 / 10 = 1
15 % 10 = 5
10 + 15 = 25
10 - 15 = -5
C:\Java eLearning Kit for Dummies\Chapter 05>_
```

Figure 5-3

7. **Compare the results of your calculations against the actual application output.**

8. **If your results didn't match the output, view each step of the code again to determine where you derived an incorrect output.**

PRACTICE

Try changing the values of X, Y, and Z in the example. Calculate the results of each of the changes before you run the application. Notice that the application automatically displays the appropriate values in the output for you.

Executing complex math tasks

Straightforward binary math operations are common enough, but many math tasks are more complex than that. As the math task becomes more complex, the requirement to understand how mathematicians perform their work becomes more important.

The same rules you learned in school for performing math apply to computers as well, so there's nothing new here. However,

LINGO

An **operator** is a symbol that defines a task to perform on an operand. An **operand** is either a variable or a constant. **Binary operators**, such as *, /, %, +, and -, require two operands — one on the left side of the operator and another on the right.

the computer doesn't just understand what you meant to say or write — the computer holds you to a strict interpretation of precisely what you write. The order and precedence of the math operations are important on the computer (as they would be to any moderately complex human communication).

> The basic rule to remember is that operations proceed from left to right, just as they do in school. Also, multiplication and division take precedence over addition and subtraction. The "Understanding Operator Precedence" section of this chapter provides you with a precise list of how each of the operators interact with each other.

This book can't describe everything there is to know about math — that's a topic for another book. However, you can discover some basic principles and use them to build your own examples. In the following exercise, you work through some complex math tasks to see how computers interpret the inclusion of multiple operators.

Files needed: `ComplexMath.java`

1. **Open the editor or IDE that you've chosen to use for this book.**

2. **Type the following code into the editor screen.**

```
public class ComplexMath
{
    public static void main(String[] args)
    {
        // Create a series of variables to use.
        int X = 5;
        int Y = 10;
        int Z = 15;
        int Result;

        // Addition and multiplication.
        Result = X + Y * Z;
        System.out.printf("%d + %d * %d = %d%n",
            X, Y, Z, Result);

        // Ordered addition and multiplication.
        Result = (X + Y) * Z;
        System.out.printf("(%d + %d) * %d = %d%n",
            X, Y, Z, Result);

        // Addition, subtraction, and multiplication.
        Result = X + Y - Y * Z;
        System.out.printf("%d + %d - %d * %d = %d%n",
            X, Y, Y, Z, Result);
```

```
// Ordered addition, subtraction, and multiplication
//  version one.
Result = X + (Y - Y) * Z;
System.out.printf("%d + (%d - %d) * %d = %d%n",
      X, Y, Y, Z, Result);

// Ordered addition, subtraction, and multiplication
//  version two.
Result = (X + (Y - Y)) * Z;
System.out.printf("(%d + (%d - %d)) * %d = %d%n",
      X, Y, Y, Z, Result);
   }
}
```

The example begins by creating three int values (X, Y, and Z) that act as inputs, as well as a single int (Result) that contains the result of any calculation. The example performs various math tasks with these inputs so that you can see how Java (and for that matter, most computer languages) will react. The screen output relies on the printf() method because it works so well for this type of display. To work through as many different results as needed, all you need to change are the three variable values at the beginning of the application.

In this case, the math operations are *mixed* — which means that they're a combination of addition and multiplication. However, the rules stated earlier are all in play. Remember from your math classes that parenthesis act to group operations that you want performed first — they have the highest priority in this example. The code could actually come from a textbook in this case — it doesn't truly feel as if you're writing a Java application so much as you're writing down an equation.

3. **View each step of the code carefully and write down the results that you think the application will display.**

4. **Save the code to disk using the filename ComplexMath.java.**

5. **In your command prompt, type** javac ComplexMath.java **and press Enter.**

   The compiler compiles your application and creates a .class file from it.

6. **Type** java ComplexMath **and press Enter.**

   The application outputs the formatted strings containing the values used for each math operation, as shown in Figure 5-4. If you change the values of X, Y, or Z, those changes will automatically appear in the output.

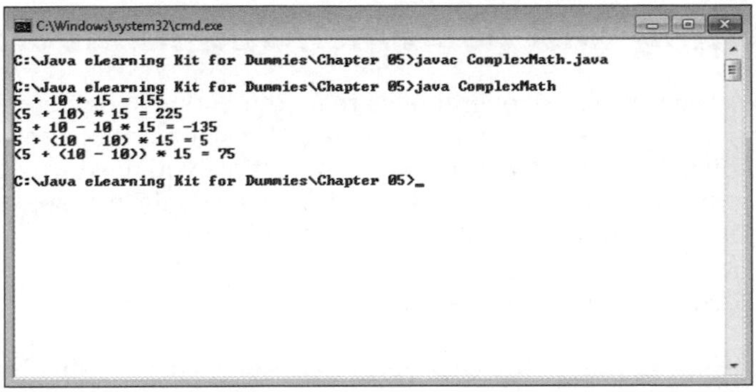
C:\Windows\system32\cmd.exe
C:\Java eLearning Kit for Dummies\Chapter 05>javac ComplexMath.java
C:\Java eLearning Kit for Dummies\Chapter 05>java ComplexMath
5 + 10 * 15 = 155
(5 + 10) * 15 = 225
5 + 10 - 10 * 15 = -135
5 + (10 - 10) * 15 = 5
(5 + (10 - 10)) * 15 = 75
C:\Java eLearning Kit for Dummies\Chapter 05>_

Figure 5-4

7. **Compare the results of your calculations against the actual application output.**
8. **If your results didn't match the output, view each step of the code again to determine where you derived an incorrect output.**

PRACTICE

Try creating other equations for the example. Remember to change both the equation in the code and your choice of string formatting you want used by the `printf()` method. (Refer to Table 5-1.)

Modifying Variable Content Using Unary Operators

Binary operators are those that require two operands (variables or constants) to work. A unary operator is one in which you need just the operator and its associated operand. The operators in the earlier "Performing Math Tasks with Arithmetic Operators" section are examples of binary operators. The following sections discuss unary operators, such as those used to increment or decrement the value in a variable.

LINGO

Unary operators perform an operation on a single operand, such as incrementing or decrementing the value within the operand. You must use a variable, and not a constant, when working with a unary operator in most cases.

Incrementing and decrementing numbers

The most common unary operations are incrementing and decrementing numbers. In most cases, an application uses these operations to keep count of something. However, you can use them anytime you need to increase or decrease the value of a variable by one. In this example, you see how the increment (++) and decrement (--) operators work.

Files needed: `IncrementDecrement.java`

1. **Open the editor or IDE that you've chosen to use for this book.**

2. **Type the following code into the editor screen.**

```java
public class IncrementDecrement
{
    public static void main(String[] args)
    {
        // Define a single variable.
        int X = 0;

        // Display the initial value.
        System.out.println("X = " + X);

        // Increment X and display the result.
        X++;
        System.out.println("X = " + X);

        // Decrement X and display the result.
        X--;
        System.out.println("X = " + X);
    }
}
```

The code in this example is straightforward. It begins by defining an `int` value, `X`. The code displays the initial value onscreen. It then increments X and displays the result. Notice that incrementing consists of adding ++ after the variable name. The same thing takes place when decrementing. You add a -- after the variable name.

3. **Save the code to disk using the filename `IncrementDecrement.java`.**

4. **Type** javac IncrementDecrement.java **and press Enter.**

   The compiler compiles your application and creates a `.class` file from it.

5. **Type** java IncrementDecrement **and press Enter.**

   The output shown in Figure 5-5 demonstrates how incrementing and decrementing works. As previously mentioned, this action works great for keeping count of things.

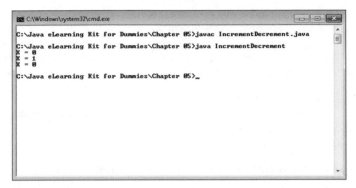

Figure 5-5

Understanding negation, bitwise Not, and Boolean Not

There are two types of unary operations that you should view together so that you don't misunderstand them later on. *Negation* is the act of setting a value to its negative version — the value of 2 becomes –2. Some math-related tasks require that you negate a value in order to use it. In some cases, people confuse negation with subtraction, but subtraction is a binary operation and negation is a unary operation.

Contrast negation with the bitwise *Not* operation, which you implement by using the ~ operator. The Not operation reverses each of the bits in a value. All of the 0s become 1s and vice versa. The Not operation is often used in Boolean-related tasks. It helps an application consider the logic of a task.

To make things even more confusing, there's a second Not operation called a *Boolean Not* operation that works on Boolean values. This operation relies on the ! operator. The bitwise operator (~) won't work on Boolean values and the logical operator (!) won't work on values other than Boolean.

LINGO

Negation is the act of setting a value to its negative equivalent. A value of 2 becomes –2.

LINGO

The term **bitwise** means to perform a task a single bit at a time, rather than using the entire value. So, a bitwise Not operation looks at each bit individually — any 1 becomes a 0, and vice versa. Consequently, when you have a value of 5, which in binary is 00000101, it becomes a negative six, which in binary is 11111010. Notice how the bits are precisely reversed in value.

It's time to compare and contrast how negation, bitwise Not, and Boolean Not work. In the following example, you see how an application can manipulate a number or Boolean value using each of these operators.

LINGO

Boolean values are either true or false. When you Not a Boolean value, you turn it from true to false, or from false to true.

Files needed: `NegationAndNot.java`

1. **Open the editor or IDE that you've chosen to use for this book.**

2. **Type the following code into the editor screen.**

```java
public class NegationAndNot
{
    public static void main(String[] args)
    {
        // Create the required variables.
        int X = 85;
        int Y = 0;
        boolean Z = true;

        // Display the current value.
        System.out.println("X = " + X);

        // Negate the value and display the result.
        X = -X;
        System.out.println("X = " + X);

        // Negate the value a second time and
        // display the result.
        X = -X;
        System.out.println("X = " + X);

        // Show the result of adding a value to its
        // Not value.
        Y = X + -X;
        System.out.printf(
                "Adding %d to %d = %d%n", X, -X, Y);

        // Set the value to its Not equivalent
        // and display the result.
        X = ~X;
        System.out.println("X = " + X);

        // Perform the Not operation again.
        X = ~X;
        System.out.println("X = " + X);
```

```
// Show the result of adding a value to its
// Not value.
Y = X + ~X;
System.out.printf(
        "Adding %d to %d = %d%n", X, ~X, Y);

// Show the Boolean Not operation.
System.out.println("Original Z = " + Z);
Z = !Z;
System.out.println("Z = " + Z);
Z = !Z;
System.out.println("Z = " + Z);
    }
}
```

This example begins by creating two variables. The first, an `int` named X, can use either negation or the bitwise Not operators. The second, a `boolean` named Y can use the Boolean Not operator. It's important to consider these operations as a sort of on/off switch. So, the application starts by showing the original value of each variable, and then the values change twice (on and then off).

3. **Save the code to disk using the filename `NegationAndNot.java`.**

4. **In your command prompt, type** javac NegationAndNot.java **and press Enter.**

   The compiler compiles your application and creates a `.class` file from it.

5. **Type** java NegationAndNot **and press Enter.**

   The code performs each of the tasks as described as shown in Figure 5-6. Notice that negation produces the precise negative of a number, while the bitwise Not produces the bitwise reversal of the variable's value. Likewise, a Boolean Not produces the reversal of the Boolean value.

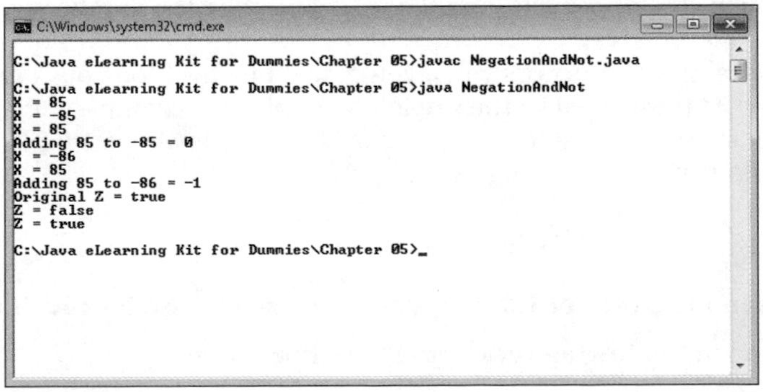

```
C:\Windows\system32\cmd.exe

C:\Java eLearning Kit for Dummies\Chapter 05>javac NegationAndNot.java

C:\Java eLearning Kit for Dummies\Chapter 05>java NegationAndNot
X = 85
X = -85
X = 85
Adding 85 to -85 = 0
X = -86
X = 85
Adding 85 to -86 = -1
Original Z = true
Z = false
Z = true

C:\Java eLearning Kit for Dummies\Chapter 05>_
```

Figure 5-6

Creating objects

Throughout this book, you create objects of various types. Java applications typically require one or more objects in order to work. In fact, the Java application itself is an object. Anytime you see the word class in a listing, you're talking about objects. Every application in this book is a class, which means that every application is an object.

It's important to realize just how objects work. When you create a class, what you're really creating is a blueprint. The blueprint describes how to create an object, but it isn't the object. To create an instance of a class (the object), you use the new operator. The new operator tells Java to create an instance of the requested object using the class you specify as a blueprint. An application can create as many instances of a class as required, provided there are enough system resources (such as memory) to do so.

Casting one type to another

The act of *casting* transforms one type of variable into another type. It's important to realize that casting isn't some sort of magic. As far as the computer is concerned, all of your data is 1s and 0s. The translation takes place, in part, in how your application views the data. When making a cast between disparate types, such as casting an integer type to a floating point type, the actual form of the data changes as well, but not in a way you need to worry about. (It all happens beneath the surface automatically.)

Casting can produce data loss. For example, if you cast a floating point type to an integer type, you'll lose the decimal portion of the floating point number. However, the integer portion will remain intact. When you cast a number held in a larger container, such as a long, to a smaller container, such as an int, you can lose the upper bits, and the actual value of the number can change.

In all cases, the cast occurs when you place the new type you want to use within parenthesis next to the original variable. For example, (float)MyInt would cast an int type to a float type. In the following example, you see how various kinds of casting work.

Files needed: TypeCasting.java

1. **Open the editor or IDE that you've chosen to use for this book.**
2. **Type the following code into the editor screen.**

```
public class TypeCasting
{
```

```java
public static void main(String[] args)
{
    // Define variables to use for the example.
    int MyInt = 65;
    long MyLong;
    float MyFloat;
    double MyDbl = 12345678901.123456;
    char MyChar = 'D';

    // Try casting an int to a long and display
    // the results.
    MyLong = (long)MyInt;
    System.out.printf("%d = %d%n", MyLong, MyInt);

    // Try casting an int to a float and display
    // the results.
    MyFloat = (float)MyInt;
    System.out.printf("%f = %d%n", MyFloat, MyInt);

    // Try casting a double to a float and display
    // the results.
    MyFloat = (float)MyDbl;
    System.out.printf("%f = %f%n", MyFloat, MyDbl);

    // Try casting a double to a long and display
    // the results.
    MyLong = (long)MyDbl;
    System.out.printf("%d = %f%n", MyLong, MyDbl);

    // Try casting a char to a long and display
    // the results.
    MyLong = (long)MyChar;
    System.out.printf("%d = %c%n", MyLong, MyChar);

    // Try casting an int to a char and display
    // the results.
    MyChar = (char)MyInt;
    System.out.printf("%c = %d%n", MyChar, MyInt);

    // Try casting a double to an int and display
    // the results.
    MyInt = (int)MyDbl;
    System.out.printf("%d = %f", MyInt, MyDbl);
}
}
```

The example begins by creating a number of variables of differing types. You've seen these types in action before and know from Chapter 2 that they have different presentations and different storage capacities. Simply casting one type to another may or may not work depending on the type and storage limitations.

3. **Examine the code before you compile it and determine which of the casts you think will fail.**

   You can create a list of the failures before you run the application. It's important to build knowledge of casts that will most definitely fail in real world applications.

4. **Save the code to disk using the filename `TypeCasting.java`.**

5. **In your command prompt, type** javac TypeCasting.java **and press Enter.**

   The compiler compiles your application and creates a `.class` file from it.

6. **Type** java TypeCasting **and press Enter.**

   You see the results of each of the casts, as shown in Figure 5-7. The left side always shows the cast value, and the right side always shows the original value. Notice in particular that the `double` type, `MyDbl`, is at the limit of the precision it can provide. The number displayed as output is a little less than expected in the last decimal position.

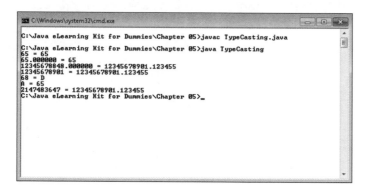

Figure 5-7

Notice that casting the `double` to a `float` compounds the error in the `double`. The small inaccuracy in the `double` is probably acceptable for many calculations, but the inaccuracy in the `float` is unusable. Because the values are somewhat close, this could actually end up as a subtle error in your code — one that could take a long time to find.

On the other hand, casting from a `double` to a `long` is probably acceptable as long as you can do without the decimal portion of the number. The integer portion of the output matches precisely.

It's interesting to note that casting between a `char` and a `long` and between an `int` and a `char` seems to work just fine. As previously noted, the computer sees a number, not a character.

A worst case cast occurs when the application tries to convert a `double` to an `int`. In this case, the output isn't even close. The numbers don't match at all. This is the sort of cast that can cause significant problems in an application.

Java allows even unusable casts when you specifically include one in your code. (The assumption here is that you know what you're doing.) Because the code doesn't provide any sort of an exception or compilation warning, this sort of error is extremely hard to find.

7. **Compare the results in your list to the actual results shown in Figure 5-7.**

   Creating a mental picture of how a cast can affect the output of your application is essential. Improper casts can cause all kinds of terrifying problems in applications. Many developers encounter this sort of error but don't recognize it until someone else points it out. Casts in code are always suspected points of failure, so always verify that a cast will actually produce the desired results.

Try changing the values of the variables in the example to see how a difference in value will affect the outcome of the casts. For example, it might be interesting to see what happens when you change the value of `MyInt` to 650.

Using Relational and Conditional Operators

Relational and conditional operators attempt to ascertain the *truth value* — whether something is true or not — of an expression. The operation results in a Boolean output that helps an application make a decision. The most common relations are comparisons between two operands using the following operators:

- ✔ `<`: Less than
- ✔ `<=`: Less than or equal to
- ✔ `==`: Equal

✔ >=: Greater than or equal to

✔ >: Greater than

✔ !=: Not equal

You'll use these operators quite a bit as the book progresses. However, you've probably already used them as part of a math class in determining the truth value of an expression, and you'll find that computers use them in the same way.

Computers also require some special operators for working with data in ways that humans understand intuitively. For example, a computer needs to know whether two variables are of the same type. These concepts are a little advanced, and you don't need to fully understand them now, but the following sections provide an overview of them as preparation for future chapters.

Finally, a special *conditional* operator set is available. Chapter 4 discusses conditional *statements,* but this is a conditional *operator,* so you see it demonstrated in this chapter. The conditional operator outputs one of two values depending on the truth value of the operand expression you provide. This is one of the few ternary operators that Java uses.

LINGO

Ternary operators require three operands to function properly. In the case of the conditional operator, it uses one operand to hold an expression that evaluates to true or false, a second operand that defines what to do when the expression is true, and a third operand that defines what to do when the expression is false.

Checking value equality

One of the more important truth tasks that applications perform is to check the equality of the values in two variables. This chapter presents some tricky situations in determining the truth behind equality in later chapters, but for now, it's important to concentrate on the operators themselves. The following exercise helps you understand how equality checks work.

Files needed: `DetermineEquality.java`

1. **Open the editor or IDE that you've chosen to use for this book.**

2. **Type the following code into the editor screen.**

```
// Import the required API classes.
import java.util.Scanner;
```

```java
public class DetermineEquality
{
    public static void main(String[] args)
    {
        // Create the scanner.
        Scanner GetInt = new Scanner(System.in);

        // Obtain the comparison values.
        System.out.print("Type the first number: ");
        int First = GetInt.nextInt();

        System.out.print("Type the second number: ");
        int Second = GetInt.nextInt();

        // Determine the equality of the two values.
        System.out.printf("It's %B that %d < %d%n",
            (First < Second), First, Second);
        System.out.printf("It's %B that %d <= %d%n",
            (First <= Second), First, Second);
        System.out.printf("It's %B that %d == %d%n",
            (First == Second), First, Second);
        System.out.printf("It's %B that %d >= %d%n",
            (First >= Second), First, Second);
        System.out.printf("It's %B that %d > %d%n",
            (First > Second), First, Second);
        System.out.printf("It's %B that %d != %d%n",
            (First != Second), First, Second);
    }
}
```

An important concept to grasp is that at least one of the checks performed by this example will be true. In fact, it's more likely that two or more checks will be true.

To make this example a little easier to use, it relies on a scanner that allows you to input two integer values. Any two integer values will do.

After the application reads the two values from the keyboard into `First` and `Second`, it performs a comparison of the two values. Notice how the code uses parentheses to change the order of precedence for the check so that the result is Boolean. Otherwise, these checks wouldn't work.

3. **Save the code to disk using the filename** `DetermineEquality.java`.

4. **In your command prompt, type** javac DetermineEquality.java **and press Enter.**

   The compiler compiles your application and creates a `.class` file from it.

5. **Type** java DetermineEquality **and press Enter.**

   The application asks you to input the first number.

6. Type 1 **and press Enter.**

The application asks you to input the second number.

7. Type 2 **and press Enter.**

The application outputs the results of the checks, as shown in Figure 5-8. Notice that multiple checks are true. For example, 1 is indeed less than 2 — 1 is also less than or equal to 2. These two values are also not equal to each other. The test you use depends on what sort of information you're trying to obtain.

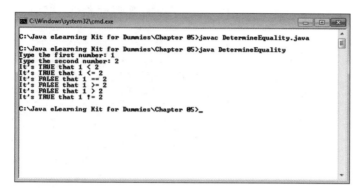

```
C:\Windows\system32\cmd.exe

C:\Java eLearning Kit for Dummies\Chapter 05>javac DetermineEquality.java

C:\Java eLearning Kit for Dummies\Chapter 05>java DetermineEquality
Type the first number: 1
Type the second number: 2
It's TRUE that 1 < 2
It's TRUE that 1 <= 2
It's FALSE that 1 == 2
It's FALSE that 1 >= 2
It's FALSE that 1 > 2
It's TRUE that 1 != 2

C:\Java eLearning Kit for Dummies\Chapter 05>_
```

Figure 5-8

8. Perform Steps 5 through 7 using values of 2 and 2.

Notice how the output changes to reflect the different values.

Try a range of values with the application to see how it reacts to different inputs. This application demonstrates how truth values work within the computer and will help you create better applications later in the book.

Performing a type comparison

The earlier "Casting one type to another" section of this chapter demonstrated how you can turn one type into another type. It also demonstrated that performing a cast can be a dangerous task at times because the cast may not produce the desired result. The following exercise demonstrates a technique you can use to determine the type of a variable. You can use this information to determine whether it's safe to perform a cast, among other tasks that you'll discover as the book progresses.

Files needed: `CompareType.java`

1. Open the editor or IDE that you've chosen to use for this book.

2. Type the following code into the editor screen.

```java
public class CompareType
{
    public static void main(String[] args)
    {
        // Define a variable that's an object.
        Integer MyInt = 22;

        // Display the type of MyInt.
        System.out.println(
            "MyInt is of type " + MyInt.getClass());

        // Check for the type of MyInt.
        System.out.printf(
            "It's %B that MyInt is of type Integer.%n",
            (MyInt instanceof Integer));
    }
}
```

Type is always associated with an object, so the example begins by creating a variable of type `Integer` named `MyInt`. The `getClass()` method always returns the class used to create the object. However, the easiest way to determine whether a variable is of a specific type is to use the `instanceof` operator. In this case, the application determines whether `MyInt` is of type `Integer`.

3. **Save the code to disk using the filename** `CompareType.java`.

4. **In your command prompt, type** javac CompareType.java **and press Enter.**

   The compiler compiles your application and creates a `.class` file from it.

5. **Type** java CompareType **and press Enter.**

   The example outputs the full name of the class used to create `MyInt`. It then shows the truth value of whether `MyInt` is an instance of type `Integer`, as shown in Figure 5-9.

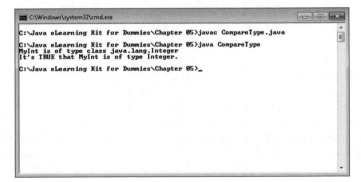

Figure 5-9

Performing a conditional evaluation

Java provides a special conditional evaluation operator that provides shorthand for the conditional statements that you'll discover in Chapter 6. The conditional evaluation operator (?:) requires three operands. The first is an expression that outputs a Boolean value. The second is an output that's invoked when the condition is true. The third is an output that's invoked when the condition is false. The following exercise demonstrates how this works.

Files needed: `ConditionalExpression.java`

1. **Open the editor or IDE that you've chosen to use for this book.**

2. **Type the following code into the editor screen.**

```java
// Import the required API classes.
import java.util.Scanner;

public class ConditionalExpression
{
    public static void main(String[] args)
    {
        // Create the scanner.
        Scanner GetAnswer = new Scanner(System.in);

        // Ask the user a question.
        System.out.print("Do you love the color blue?
          ");
        boolean Answer = GetAnswer.nextBoolean();

        // Determine which output to provide.
        String Result =
              Answer ? "You love blue!" : "You like
          orange.";

        // Display the result.
        System.out.println(Result);
    }
}
```

The example begins by asking the user a simple question, "Do you love the color blue?" The user needs to type **true** or **false**, depending on personal taste. The application assigns this answer to `Answer`. It then uses `Answer` as the first operand to the conditional evaluation operator. The second and third operands are strings in this case. Depending on the user's answer, the `String` variable, `Result`, can contain one of two values. The application ends by displaying `Result` onscreen.

3. **Save the code to disk using the filename** `ConditionalExpression.java`.

4. **In your command prompt, type** javac ConditionalExpression.java **and press Enter.**

   The compiler compiles your application and creates a `.class` file from it.

5. **Type** java ConditionalExpression **and press Enter.**

   The application asks the question.

6. **Type** true **and press Enter.**

   The application tells you that you love the color blue.

7. **Type** java ConditionalExpression **and press Enter.**

   The application asks the question.

8. **Type** false **and press Enter.**

   The application tells you that you like orange instead. Figure 5-10 shows how the conditional operator performs its work.

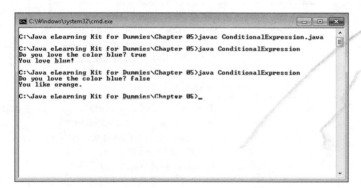

Figure 5-10

Understanding Operator Precedence

This chapter has discussed operator precedence quite a bit. It's essential to know how Java interprets the symbols you use to perform specific operations and in what order it interprets them. Otherwise, you could write an application with one result in mind and receive an entirely different result (as demonstrated by several of the examples in this chapter). Whenever you have a doubt as to how Java will interpret a symbol you use, you can rely on the information in Table 5-2 to help you.

Table 5-2		Java Operator Order of Precedence	
Priority	**Operators**	**Description**	**Associativity**
1	[]	Array index used to specify which array element to access.	Left
1	()	Method call or grouping. Grouping is especially important in that it changes the normal rules for interacting with operators, such as performing addition before multiplication.	Left
1	.	Member access used to interact with a member of an object.	Left
2	++	Prefix or postfix increment. Adds a value of 1 to the variable.	Right
2	--	Prefix or postfix decrement. Removes a value of 1 from the variable.	Right
2	+ -	Unary plus or minus. Sets the sign of the variable. The plus operator is never used because variables are positive by default. The minus operator negates the variable.	Right
2	~	Unary bitwise Not operator reverses the bits in a variable. In other words, it makes the variable the opposite of what it was. For example, a 5 (binary 00000101) becomes a −6 (binary 11111010).	Right
2	!	Unary Boolean Not operator is used in Boolean evaluations to turn `true` into `false` and `false` into `true`.	Right
2	(type)	Performs a cast to change the type of a variable into another type.	Right
2	new	Creates a new object based on the class provided.	Right
3	* / %	Performs the multiplication, division, and remainder math operations.	Left

Priority	Operators	Description	Associativity
4	+ -	Performs the addition and subtraction math operations.	Left
4	+	Concatenates two strings to produce a single string.	Left
5	<< >> >>>	Bitwise shift operators that are rarely used for application development. A discussion of these operators is beyond the scope of this book.	Left
6	< <=	Performs the logical comparison of two values for less than or less than and equal to.	Left
6	> >=	Performs the logical comparison of two values for greater than or greater than and equal to.	Left
6	`instanceof`	Tests whether an object is an instance of a particular class.	Left
7	==	Determines whether two values are precisely equal.	Left
7	!=	Determines whether two values are not equal.	Left
8	&	Bitwise AND operation that combines two values. A discussion of this operator is outside the scope of this book.	Left
8	&	Logical AND operation that combines the results of two logical evaluations. In many cases, both condition A and condition B must be `true` in order for an entire evaluation to be `true`.	Left
9	^	Bitwise exclusive or (XOR) operation that combines two values. A discussion of this operator is outside the scope of this book.	Left
9	^	Logical XOR operation that combines the result of two logical evaluations. In order to be true, either condition A or condition B must be `true`, but not both.	Left

continued

	Table 5-2 *(continued)*		
Priority	**Operators**	**Description**	**Associativity**
10	|	Bitwise OR operation that combines two values. A discussion of this operator is outside the scope of this book.	Left
10	|	Logical OR operation that combines the result of two logical evaluations. In order to be true, condition A or condition B, or both must be `true`.	Left
11	&&	Logical AND operation that's used as part of a logical expression to determine the truth value of both expressions. Both must be `true` for the entire expression to be `true`.	Left
12	||	Logical OR operation that's used as part of a logical expression to determine the truth value of both expressions. Either or both must be `true` for the entire expression to be `true`.	Left
13	? :	Performs a conditional assessment. See the "Using Relational and Conditional Operators" section of this chapter for details.	Right
14	=	Assigns the specified value to the variable.	Right
14	*= /= += -= %=	Combined operation and assignment. Java performs the requested operation, such as addition, and then assigns the result to the variable.	Right
	<<= >>= >>>= &= ^= |=	The combined assignment operators include a number of operators that perform bitwise operations. A discussion of these operators is outside the scope of this book.	

The Priority column of Table 5-2 is probably the most important because it defines the strict order in which Java interprets the symbols displayed in the Operators column. An operator higher in the table always takes precedence over an operator that's lower in the table.

The Associativity column is also important. In most cases, Java interprets symbols from left to right, which means that the symbols have a left *associativity*. However, in a few cases, the operator works from right to left. For example, when using the = operator, Java interprets the information to the right of the operator first, and it then assigns the result to the operand on the left of the operator. So the flow is from right to left, which makes the = operator right associative.

LINGO

Associativity is a math term that defines how elements in a binary operation interact. In most cases, Java uses left associativity. It begins from the left side of a group of operators and works toward the right side. For example, if you have 1 + 2 + 3 as an equation, Java adds 1 and 2 first, then adds 3 to the result of the first operation. You can control associativity by using parenthesis. The article at `http://math.about. com/od/prealgebra/a/ associative.htm` provides more information on this topic.

 Summing Up

Here are the key points you learned about in this chapter:

- ✔ Most applications use simple assignments to initialize variables.
- ✔ You must initialize a variable before you can modify it using a combined assignment operator.
- ✔ Combined assignment operators perform an operation on the variable by using a value to the right of the operator as input, and they then store the result in the variable.
- ✔ When performing math-related tasks, you must consider the order in which the values appear and the operations performed on them.
- ✔ Incrementing and decrementing are often used to keep track of the count of something.
- ✔ Negation produces the negative value of a number, while a bitwise Not produces the reversal of the bits within the number.
- ✔ A Boolean Not turns a `true` value into a `false` value, and vice versa.
- ✔ Use the `new` operator to create as many instances of an object as required by an application.

✔ Casting makes it possible to turn one variable type into another.

✔ Casting incorrectly can have serious side effects that could make the output of your application unusable.

✔ Relational and conditional evaluation operators make it possible to determine the truth value of an expression.

✔ It's possible that more than one relational operator will be true for a given expression.

✔ At least one relational operator will provide an output of true for a given expression.

✔ Determining the type of a variable can help you overcome issues with improper casting.

✔ The conditional evaluation operator is one of the few ternary operators provided by Java.

✔ Java always executes operations defined by operators with a higher precedence first.

✔ The associativity of an operator determines whether Java works with the right side or the left side first.

Try-it-yourself lab

For more practice with the features covered in this chapter, try the following exercise on your own:

1. **Open the ComplexMath application.**

2. **Change the application code to work with double values.**

   Use floating point values such as 2.3 or 3.5 to test the results.

3. **Go through the code you create to determine the expected output.**

   Track each line and provide a line-by-line summary of the results you expect to see.

4. **Compile the application.**

5. **Run the application.**

6. **View the results and match them to your expected results.**

7. **Perform Steps 2 through 7 for BigDecimal variables.**

   Each of the primitive or object types should react as expected to the math operations you create. Math is math. The kind of variable you use simply defines the storage container, not how the math will work.

Know this tech talk

- ✔ **associativity:** The order in which Java performs binary operations.

- ✔ **binary operator:** An operator that requires two operands to function. The addition operation, as specified by the + operator, is an example of a binary operator.

- ✔ **bitwise:** The act of modifying a value one bit at a time, rather than acting on the value as a whole.

- ✔ **class:** A blueprint written in code for creating objects. A class can include methods, properties, and events. The class defines specific ways to manipulate data in a safe manner.

- ✔ **grouping:** The act of using parentheses to show the preferred order of completing math tasks, rather than relying on the default order.

- ✔ **negation:** The act of setting a value to its negative equivalent. This means that a positive value becomes a negative value, and a negative value becomes positive. A value of 2 becomes –2, and a value of –2 becomes 2.

- ✔ **object:** An instance of a class created using the new operator.

- ✔ **operand:** The variable or constant used with an operator to produce a result from an operation. For example, when looking at A + B, A and B are both operands, + is the operator, and addition is the operation.

- ✔ **operator:** A special symbol or symbol set that performs a predefined task with a value within a variable — either a primitive type or an object. In some cases, operators change the value, but in others they simply perform a comparison and provide the result as output.

- ✔ **precedence:** The order in which Java interacts with operators when an equation or expression contains more than one operator. For example, Java always performs multiplication before it performs addition. Most of the rules of precedence are the same as those used by mathematicians.

- ✔ **ternary operator:** An operator that requires three operands to function. For example, the conditional operator requires three operands: the conditional expression, a true output, and a false output.

- ✔ **unary operator:** An operator that performs an operation on a single operand. For example, B++ is an example of a unary operator where B is the operand and ++ is the operator for an increment operation.

Chapter 6

Working with Conditional Statements

- Using a simple `if` statement allows your application to *decide whether to take a particular action.*

- Relying on the `if...else` statement lets your application *choose between two actions.*

- Placing one `if` statement within another helps your application *perform complex decision making.*

- Employing a `switch` statement lets the application *choose one action from multiple actions.*

- Defining a default option makes it possible for the application to *perform a specific task when no other tasks are selected.*

- Converting Boolean values to human-readable form *makes the application easier to use.*

"If you read this book from end to end, then you'll know quite a bit about Java when you're finished." This is a human form of a conditional statement. A conditional statement in an application begins with a condition and ends with a task. You use conditional statements every day. Another example of a conditional statement is, "Choose the item that most closely matches your age from this list for your prize." Programs can use that sort of conditional statement too! The main purpose of this chapter is to show you how to write conditional statements in a way that the computer understands; but from a logical perspective, you already know everything required to use conditional statements.

Using a Simple If Statement

The if statement is the easiest of the conditional statements to understand and you'll find that you use it often. An if statement consists of a condition that looks like this:

```
if (expression)
```

where expression is the condition that you want to check. The task associated with the if statement appears within curly braces like this:

```
{
    Tasks you want to perform ...
}
```

Every if statement follows the same pattern of condition followed by task. With this pattern in mind, in the following example you create an application that relies on an if statement to make a decision about a number that you type.

LINGO

Computers rely heavily on math used to express an idea to make certain decisions. Consequently, the condition part of a conditional statement is also called an **expression**. An expression always equates to a value of true or false, so it's a Boolean value. However, when you think about it, you use Boolean expressions in your daily conversation. For example, "If the item costs less than $5.00, then I'll buy it." The condition — item costs less than $5.00 — is a Boolean expression.

Files needed: `SimpleIf.java`

1. Open the editor or IDE that you've chosen to use for this book.

2. Type the following code into the Editor screen.

```java
// Import the required API classes.
import java.util.Scanner;

public class SimpleIf
{
    public static void main(String[] args)
    {
        // Create the scanner.
        Scanner GetInput = new Scanner(System.in);

        // Obtain a byte value.
        System.out.print("Type any number: ");
        int Input = GetInput.nextInt();

        // Determine whether Input is less than 5.
        if (Input < 5)
        {
            System.out.println("The input is < 5.");
        }

        // Determine whether Input is greater than or
        // equal to 5.
        if (Input >= 5)
        {
            System.out.println("The input is >= 5.");
        }
    }
}
```

This application obtains an integer value as input from the console. It then checks this value against the number 5 by using two `if` statements. The first statement determines whether `Input` is less than 5. If so, it outputs a message saying so. Likewise, the second statement determines whether `Input` is greater than or equal to 5 and outputs the appropriate message when true. The application will select one `if` statement or the other, but never both.

3. Save the code to disk using the filename `SimpleIf.java`.

4. In your command prompt, type javac SimpleIf.java **and press Enter.**

The compiler compiles your application and creates a `.class` file from it.

5. Type java SimpleIf **and press Enter.**

The application asks you to type a number. Make sure you type a whole number and not a floating point number or a character.

6. **Type** 4 **and press Enter.**

   The application outputs a message stating, `The input is < 5.`

7. **Repeat Steps 5 and 6, but substitute a value of 5 this time.**

   The application outputs a message stating, `The input is >= 5.`

8. **Repeat Steps 5 and 6, but substitute a value of 6 this time.**

   The application outputs a message stating, `The input is >= 5.`, as shown in Figure 6-1.

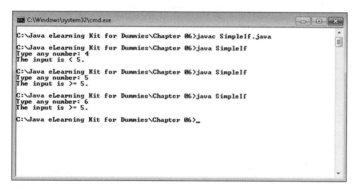

Figure 6-1

Performing One of Two Tasks with If. . .Else

The basic `if` statement could be used for every task. However, writing code using just the basic `if` statement can become boring and even introduce errors (bugs) into your application. Look again at the example in the "Using a Simple If Statement" section of the chapter, and you see that it has two `if` statements in it. The `if...else` statement makes it possible to perform precisely the same task using just one structure. The `if...else` statement says that if the condition is true, the application should perform one set of tasks, but if the condition is false, it should perform a completely different set of tasks.

LINGO

A **bug** is an error in the code that you write. Errors make your application behave in ways that you didn't anticipate. Anyone using your application will get results different from the results you wanted to provide them with. Bugs cause all sorts of problems. For example, a bug in the wrong place could cause your application to stop working or give a virus writer an opportunity to invade your application. Simplifying your code and using the appropriate statements is one way to decrease bugs.

The example in the "Using a Simple If Statement" section of the chapter is awkward and you can easily improve it. The following example shows how to use an `if...else` statement to make the code easier to read and understand. The change also reduces the risk of seeing a bug in the application.

Files needed: `UsingIfElse.java`

1. Open the editor or IDE that you've chosen to use for this book.

2. Type the following code into the editor screen.

```java
// Import the required API classes.
import java.util.Scanner;

public class UsingIfElse
{
   public static void main(String[] args)
   {
      // Create the scanner.
      Scanner GetInput = new Scanner(System.in);

      // Obtain a byte value.
      System.out.print("Type any number: ");
      int Input = GetInput.nextInt();

      // Determine whether Input is less than 5.
      if (Input < 5)
      {
         // Input is less than 5.
         System.out.println("The input is < 5.");
      }
      else
      {
         // Input is greater than or equal to 5.
         System.out.println("The input is >= 5.");
      }
   }
}
```

This application obtains an integer value as input from the console. It then checks this value against the number 5 by using an `if...else` statement. When Input is less than 5, the application performs the first task; but when it's greater than or equal to 5, the application performs the second task.

Interestingly enough, this version of the application is one line shorter than the previous version. When you use the various shortcuts shown in this chapter, you not only make your application less prone to errors, but you also save time typing code.

3. **Save the code to disk using the filename** `UsingIfElse.java`.

4. **In your command prompt, type** javac UsingIfElse.java **and press Enter.**

   The compiler compiles your application and creates a `.class` file from it.

5. **Type** java UsingIfElse **and press Enter.**

   The application asks you to type a number. Make sure you type a whole number and not a floating point number or a character.

6. **Type** 4 **and press Enter.**

   The application outputs a message stating, `The input is < 5.`

7. **Repeat Steps 5 and 6, but substitute a value of 5 this time.**

   The application outputs a message stating, `The input is >= 5.`

8. **Repeat Steps 5 and 6, but substitute a value of 6 this time.**

   The application outputs a message stating, `The input is >= 5.`, as shown in Figure 6-2.

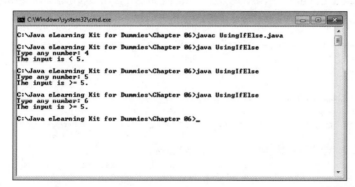

Figure 6-2

9. **Compare Figure 6-1 with Figure 6-2.**

   Notice that both versions of the application behave precisely the same.

Nesting If Statements

Sometimes a decision requires multiple levels. For example, if the ceiling is painted orange, then you may also need to decide whether the walls are painted yellow or red. Another form of multiple level decision-making is a menu. A user may have to decide between items A, B, or C, but isn't allowed to pick two at the same time (items A and B). Fortunately, you can create as many levels of `if` statements as required to handle this problem. Combining multiple levels of `if` statements to make complex decisions is called *nesting*.

Menus are one of the decision-making processes you'll encounter quite often in applications. Most real world decisions aren't just between *this* or *that*, but rather they involve shades of gray, as in "You must choose one item from a list of possible choices." The following example demonstrates how to use nesting to create a menu system.

LINGO

Nesting makes it possible to create multiple decision-making levels within an application. You can combine all sorts of statements into a cohesive unit in order to make a decision. Nesting lets you focus on a particular part of the decision-making process and perform the process one step at a time, rather than creating a horribly complex expression.

Files needed: `UseAMenu01.java`

1. **Open the editor or IDE that you've chosen to use for this book.**

2. **Type the following code into the editor screen.**

```
// Import the required API classes.
import java.util.Scanner;
import java.lang.Character;

public class UseAMenu01
{
   public static void main(String[] args)
   {
      // Create the scanner.
      Scanner GetChoice = new Scanner(System.in);

      // Obtain input from the user.
      System.out.println("Options\n");
      System.out.println("A. Yellow");
      System.out.println("B. Orange");
      System.out.println("C. Green\n");
      System.out.print("Choose your favorite color: ");
      char Choice = GetChoice.findInLine(".").charAt(0);

      // Convert the input to uppercase.
      Choice = Character.toUpperCase(Choice);

      // Determine if the input is an A.
      if (Choice == 'A')
         System.out.println("Your favorite color is
            Yellow!");
```

```
      // Determine if the input is a B.
      else if (Choice == 'B')
         System.out.println("Your favorite color is
            Orange!");

         // The input could be a C.
      else if (Choice == 'C')
         System.out.println("Your favorite color is
            Green!");
   }
}
```

The application begins by creating a `Scanner` (`GetChoice`) and using it to obtain `char` input (`Choice`) from the user. Because you can't be sure whether the user has entered an uppercase or lowercase letter, you need to convert the letter to uppercase. The code relies on the static method, `Character.toUpperCase()` to perform this task.

After the input is converted, the application uses it to make a choice. The user can input any of the three choices, but there's actually a hidden fourth choice. The user can also choose not to provide any of the specific input. For example, the user could type 3 instead of c or C. Consequently, the code must check the input up to three times in order to determine the user's choice.

3. **Save the code to disk using the filename UseAMenu01.java.**

4. **In your command prompt, type** javac UseAMenu01.java **and press Enter.**

   The compiler compiles your application and creates a `.class` file from it.

5. **Type** java UseAMenu01 **and press Enter.**

   The application asks you to choose a letter associated with a color.

6. **Type** A **and press Enter.**

   The application outputs the expected message.

7. **Repeat Steps 5 and 6, but substitute a value of b this time.**

   The application outputs the expected message again. Notice, however, that it doesn't matter whether the input is uppercase or lowercase, you still get the expected result.

8. Repeat Steps 5 and 6, but substitute a value of 3 this time.

The application doesn't output anything, as shown in Figure 6-3. Notice also in Figure 6-3 that the application provides a nice appearance for the menu system. For example, there is an extra line between Options and the list of options. That's the purpose of the \n escape code shown in the listing. Ending a string with a \n escape code will add an extra line and provide a pleasing appearance to the user.

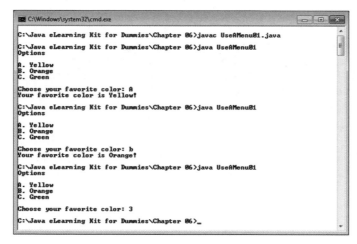

Figure 6-3

 Providing the right prompt can make a big difference in the usability of your application. For example, if you were to provide a list of valid options for the user of this application, such as Choose A, B, or C, you could make it less likely that the user will make an invalid choice. Even so, users do make invalid choices despite the best prompts, so your application code must also provide robust error handling.

Selecting from Multiple Conditions Using Switch

Just as there's a shortcut for using two `if` statements in the `if...else` statement, there's a shortcut for using multiple `if...else` statements to create a menu in the `switch` statement. The switch statement consists of a condition that looks like this:

```
switch (variable)
```

where `variable` contains a value you want to check against a number of constants. The constants appear as part of a `case` clause like this:

```
case value:
```

where `value` is a specific constant value you want to check. Finally, the task appears after the `case` clause and ends with a `break` clause like this:

```
task;
break;
```

You must include the `break` clause to tell the compiler when the task is finished.

The switch statement makes it possible to create a menu system in a way that's easy to read and a lot shorter to type. In the following example, you create an application that relies on the `switch` statement to allow the user to select from one of several options.

Files needed: UseAMenu02.java

1. **Open the editor or IDE that you've chosen to use for this book.**

2. **Type the following code into the editor screen.**

```java
// Import the required API classes.
import java.util.Scanner;
import java.lang.Character;

public class UseAMenu02
{
  public static void main(String[] args)
  {
    // Create the scanner.
    Scanner GetChoice = new Scanner(System.in);

    // Obtain input from the user.
    System.out.println("Options\n");
    System.out.println("A. Yellow");
    System.out.println("B. Orange");
    System.out.println("C. Green\n");
    System.out.print("Choose your favorite color: ");
    char Choice = GetChoice.findInLine(".").charAt(0);

    // Convert the input to uppercase.
    Choice = Character.toUpperCase(Choice);
```

```
// Choose the right color based on a switch
// statement.
switch (Choice)
{
   case 'A':
     System.out.println("Your favorite color is
       Yellow!");
     break;
   case 'B':
     System.out.println("Your favorite color is
       Orange!");
     break;
   case 'C':
     System.out.println("Your favorite color is
       Green!");
     break;
}
  }
}
```

This application begins precisely like the UseAMenu01 application does by displaying a menu of selections and asking the user to select one. In addition, it ensures that the input is converted to uppercase as needed. The switch statement compares Choice to three case clauses; A, B, and C. When Choice equals one of these constants, the application performs the task associated with that case statement and stops when it sees the break clause.

3. **Save the code to disk using the filename UseAMenu02.java.**

4. **In your command prompt, type** javac UseAMenu02.java **and press Enter.**

The compiler compiles your application and creates a .class file from it.

5. **Type** java UseAMenu02 **and press Enter.**

The application will ask you to choose a color.

6. **Type** A **and press Enter.**

The application outputs the expected message.

7. **Repeat Steps 5 and 6, but substitute a value of b this time.**

The application outputs the expected message again.

8. **Repeat Steps 5 and 6, but substitute a value of 3 this time.**

The application doesn't output anything, as shown in Figure 6-4.

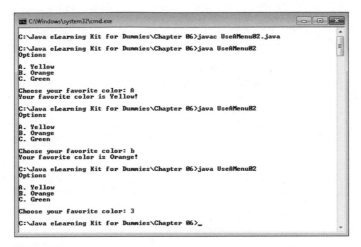

Figure 6-4

9. **Compare Figure 6-3 with Figure 6-4.**

Notice that both versions of the application behave precisely the same.

Executing a Default Task

The UseAMenu01 and UseAMenu02 applications suffer from a particular problem. When the user types an unexpected letter, number, or symbol, the application simply ends and doesn't display anything. This response is better than allowing the application to crash, but it hardly tells the user what went wrong. In this case, you need a default action to help the user understand what's wrong. Default tasks make it possible for the application to do *something,* even when the user doesn't provide the expected input. In the following exercise, you create a new version of UseAMenu02 and add a default task to it.

Files needed: UseAMenu03.java

1. **Open the editor or IDE that you've chosen to use for this book.**

2. **Type the following code into the editor screen.**

```
// Import the required API classes.
import java.util.Scanner;
import java.lang.Character;
```

```
public class UseAMenu03
{
  public static void main(String[] args)
  {
    // Create the scanner.
    Scanner GetChoice = new Scanner(System.in);

    // Obtain input from the user.
    System.out.println("Options\n");
    System.out.println("A. Yellow");
    System.out.println("B. Orange");
    System.out.println("C. Green\n");
    System.out.print("Choose your favorite color: ");
    char Choice = GetChoice.findInLine(".").charAt(0);

    // Convert the input to uppercase.
    Choice = Character.toUpperCase(Choice);

    // Choose the right color based on a switch
    // statement.
    switch (Choice)
    {
      case 'A':
        System.out.println("Your favorite color is
          Yellow!");
        break;
      case 'B':
        System.out.println("Your favorite color is
          Orange!");
        break;
      case 'C':
        System.out.println("Your favorite color is
          Green!");
        break;
      default:
        System.out.println(
            "Type A, B, or C to select a color.");
        break;
    }
  }
}
```

This application begins precisely like the UseAMenu02 application does by displaying a menu of selections and asking the user to select one. In addition, it ensures that the input is converted to uppercase as needed. The switch statement compares Choice with three case clauses: A, B, and C. When Choice equals one of these constants, the application performs the task associated with that case statement and stops when it sees the break clause.

Notice especially the default: clause of the switch statement. If the user doesn't make an appropriate choice, the code selects this option. In other words, the default: clause provides a form of error trapping. In this case, the application outputs a helpful message that reminds the user of the valid choices for the application.

3. **Save the code to disk using the filename** UseAMenu03.java.

4. **In your command prompt, type** javac UseAMenu03.java **and press Enter.**

The compiler compiles your application and creates a .class file from it.

5. **Type** java UseAMenu03 **and press Enter.**

The application asks you to choose a color.

6. **Type** A **and press Enter.**

The application outputs the expected message.

7. **Repeat Steps 5 and 6, but substitute a value of b this time.**

The application outputs the expected message again.

8. **Repeat Steps 5 and 6, but substitute a value of 3 this time.**

Notice that the application now outputs a helpful message to the user, as shown in Figure 6-5.

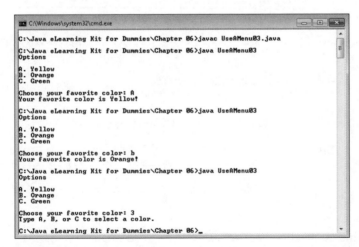

Figure 6-5

Displaying Boolean Values

This is the first chapter where you've really used Boolean values for their intended purpose — as decision making tools. However, you'll still find a need to display Boolean values from time to time. Most people understand `true` or `false`, but they don't find using `true` or `false` natural. Unfortunately, Java doesn't provide the means for displaying Boolean values in other ways, such as outputting yes or no, words the user will understand. In the following exercise, you construct a simple method for displaying Boolean values in human-readable terms, such as `yes` and `no`.

Files needed: `DisplayBoolean.java`

1. Open the editor or IDE that you've chosen to use for this book.

2. Type the following code into the editor screen.

```java
// Import the required API classes.
import java.lang.String;

public class DisplayBoolean
{
    public static void main(String[] args)
    {
        // Define a Boolean value.
        boolean BoolVar = true;

        // Change the Boolean value into a string.
        String BoolString = BoolAsString(BoolVar, "Yes",
            "No");

        // Display the result.
        System.out.println("The answer is " +
            BoolString + ".");
    }

    public static String BoolAsString(boolean BoolValue,
        String TrueString, String FalseString)
    {
        return BoolValue ? TrueString : FalseString;
    }
}
```

This application creates a simple `boolean` named `BoolVar` and sets it to `true`. It then creates a `String` value named `BoolString` that holds a human-readable version of the `BoolVar` value and displays this `String` on screen.

The secret to this example is the `BoolAsString()` method, which accepts three arguments as input and returns a `String` value.

- `BoolValue`: The Boolean value that you want to convert to a string.
- `TrueString`: The string you want output when `BoolValue` is true.
- `FalseString`: The string you want output when `BoolValue` is false.

The example returns the appropriate value based on a conditional statement. You initially saw conditional statements described in the "Performing a conditional evaluation" section of Chapter 5. This example presents a practical use for a conditional statement.

3. **Save the code to disk using the filename `DisplayBoolean.java`.**

4. **In your command prompt, type** javac DisplayBoolean.java **and press Enter.**

   The compiler compiles your application and creates a `.class` file from it.

5. **Type** java DisplayBoolean **and press Enter.**

   The application outputs a human readable string that matches the `BoolVar` value, as shown in Figure 6-6.

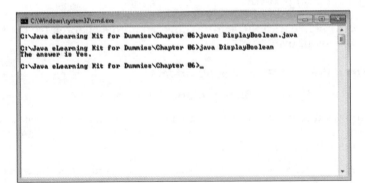

Figure 6-6

 Change the value of `BoolVar` to `false`. Compile and run the application. You should see the output change to match the new value of `BoolVar`. Try using other `TrueString` and `FalseString` values as well.

Summing Up

Here are the key points you learned about in this chapter:

- A conditional statement consists of a condition and a task. When the condition is `true`, the application performs the task.

- The condition portion of a conditional statement is also called an expression.

- Every conditional task could be performed by using a simple `if` statement, but using other conditional statement forms makes your application less prone to errors and also reduces the amount of typing you perform.

- The `if. . .else` statement lets your application choose between two courses of action depending on whether the expression you provide is `true` or `false`.

- Use the `switch` statement to allow the user to choose from a list of items.

- Rely on the `default` clause to provide a default action for your application when the user doesn't provide useful input.

Try-it-yourself lab

For more practice with the features covered in this chapter, try the following exercise on your own:

1. **Open the UseAMenu03 application.**

2. **Add a series of additional colors to the menu.**

   You want to change the menu to include additional `System.out.println("Letter. Color");` entries. Make sure each entry has a unique letter associated with it.

3. **Make the new menu entries functional by modifying the `switch` statement to accommodate them.**

   Each new color requires three lines of code similar to the code shown here:

   ```
   case 'A':
     System.out.println("Your favorite color is Yellow!");
     break;
   ```

4. **Change the default clause so that it provides the additional letters needed for the colors you added.**

5. **Compile the application.**

6. **Run the application.**

7. **Try each of the new menu entries.**

   Do the new menu entries work as you anticipated? If not, why not?

8. **Try typing letters, numbers, or other symbols that don't appear on the menu.**

   Does the default action still work as anticipated?

Know this tech talk

- ✔ **bug:** An error in the application code that causes your application to behave in a way that you didn't anticipate.

- ✔ **conditional statement:** A programming construct that consists of a condition (expression) and a task. When the condition is true, the application performs the task.

- ✔ **expression:** A mathematical description of the condition that you want the application to check. An expression normally includes a logical operator and always provides a Boolean output.

- ✔ **nesting:** The act of combining multiple levels of statement into a single super statement. The application executes upper levels of the statement first and then drills down into lower levels. Use nesting to make complex decisions where one decision affects several others.

Chapter 7

Repeating Tasks Using Loops

- ✔ Creating `for` loops allows an application to *perform a task a specific number of times.*

- ✔ Creating `while` loops allows an application to *perform a task until it has been completed.*

- ✔ Creating `for-each` loops allows an application to *perform tasks with collections of objects until every object in the collection has been used.*

Repeat after me, "Java is an amazing language!" Now say it again for good measure. There are many times in the real world when you repeat something. Likewise, applications have a need to repeat tasks. Doing them once isn't enough, in some cases. This chapter helps you understand how to perform the same task multiple times.

Performing Tasks a Set Number of Times

It's possible to perform every sort of repetitive loop using a `for` loop, but doing so would mean writing your code in odd ways. Even so, the `for` loop is the workhorse of the repetitive loop structures because it's easy to create, easy to debug, and easy to understand. The essence of a `for` loop is that the application performs a series of tasks a specific number of times.

Using the standard for loop

It's important to understand how a `for` loop is put together before you create your first one. The `for` loop begins with the word "for" followed by parentheses containing the following three items, separated by semicolons (;):

- ✔ A counter variable and the code used to initialize it, such as `int Current = 1`.
- ✔ A condition that will end the loop after a specific count, such as `Current <= 5`.
- ✔ A method for updating the counter variable so that the `for` loop can keep track of the current count, such as `Current++`.

The set of curly braces used to define the beginning and end of the `for` loop appears next. You place your code within the curly braces. In the following example, you create a `for` loop and then use it to see how `for` loops work.

Files needed: `StandardFor.java`

1. **Open the editor or IDE that you've chosen to use for this book.**

2. **Type the following code into the editor screen.**

```java
// Import the required API classes.
import java.util.Scanner;

public class StandardFor
{
    public static void main(String[] args)
    {
        // Create the scanner.
        Scanner GetChoice = new Scanner(System.in);

        // Ask the user how many times to say hello.
        System.out.print("Say \"Hello\" how many times?");
        int Count = GetChoice.nextInt();

        // Create a for loop.
        for (int Current = 1; Current <= Count; Current++)
        {
            // Perform the required task.
            System.out.println("Hello Number " + Current);
        }
    }
}
```

LINGO

A **counter variable** is a variable whose whole purpose is to track the current count of something. The variable doesn't actually add or subtract anything from the application data; rather, the purpose of the counter variable is to help the application perform the tasks you assign to it.

The application begins by asking the user how many times the application should say `Hello`. (Of course, a production application would ask other sorts of questions, but the principle is the same.) The answer the user provides is placed within `Count`.

The next step is to create a `for` loop where an `int` variable, `Current`, keeps track of the current count as the counter variable. The loop will continue to perform the tasks within the structure body until `Current` is greater than `Count`. Every time the loop starts, `Current` is incremented by one, so if `Count` is 5, the loop will execute five times.

Notice that this example uses an escape sequence \ " to display double quotes in the output. In many situations, you need to remember that escape sequences exist in order to achieve your goals.

3. **Save the code to disk using the filename** `StandardFor.java`.

4. **In your command prompt, type** javac StandardFor.java **and press Enter.**

    The compiler compiles your application and creates a `.class` file from it.

5. **Type** java StandardFor **and press Enter.**

    The application asks you how many times it should say `Hello`.

6. **Type** 5 **and press Enter.**

    The application outputs a series of `Hello` messages, as shown in Figure 7-1. Notice that the output includes the current value of `Current`. The value increases by 1 for each iteration of the loop, just as expected.

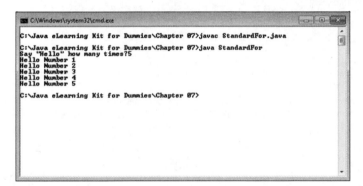

Figure 7-1

Using the break statement

There are times when you want to stop a `for` loop early. For example, you might detect a condition that would cause the loop to fail. Perhaps there aren't enough items to process, or your application detects some other issue. In this case, you can use the `break` statement to stop the `for` loop from doing any more work. In the following example, you add a `break` statement to the StandardFor application to stop it early.

Files needed: `UsingBreak.java`

1. **Open the editor or IDE that you've chosen to use for this book.**

2. **Type the following code into the editor screen.**

```java
// Import the required API classes.
import java.util.Scanner;

public class UsingBreak
{
    public static void main(String[] args)
    {
        // Create the scanner.
        Scanner GetChoice = new Scanner(System.in);

        // Ask the user how many times to say hello.
        System.out.print("Say \"Hello\" how many
          times? ");
        int Count = GetChoice.nextInt();

        // Create a for loop.
        for (int Current = 1; Current <= Count; Current++)
        {
            // Don't allow the application to say
            // hello more than three times.
            if (Current == 4)
                break;

            // Perform the required task.
            System.out.println("Hello Numnber " + Current);
        }
    }
}
```

This application looks much like the StandardFor application in the "Using the standard for loop" section of the chapter. However, it has the addition of an `if` statement that detects when `Current` is equal to four. When `Current` reaches this value, the application issues a `break` statement.

Notice that the `if` statement doesn't use curly braces in this example. A structure doesn't have to use curly braces if it only works with the next line of code. The `if` statement is associated only with the `break` statement in this case, so there's no need to use the curly braces.

3. **Save the code to disk using the filename `UsingBreak.java`.**

4. **In your command prompt, type** javac UsingBreak.java **and press Enter.**

The compiler compiles your application and creates a `.class` file from it.

5. **Type** java UsingBreak **and press Enter.**

   The application asks you how many times it should say `Hello`.

6. **Type** 2 **and press Enter.**

   The application outputs two `Hello` messages.

7. **Repeat Steps 5 and 6 using a value of 5 in place of 2.**

   You see only three `Hello` messages, as shown in Figure 7-2. The `break` statement doesn't hamper the application from outputting anything up to three `Hello` messages, but it doesn't allow anything over that number.

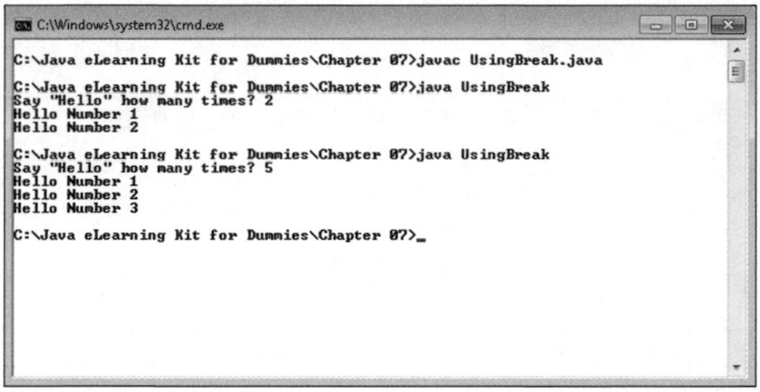
C:\Windows\system32\cmd.exe
C:\Java eLearning Kit for Dummies\Chapter 07>javac UsingBreak.java
C:\Java eLearning Kit for Dummies\Chapter 07>java UsingBreak
Say "Hello" how many times? 2
Hello Number 1
Hello Number 2
C:\Java eLearning Kit for Dummies\Chapter 07>java UsingBreak
Say "Hello" how many times? 5
Hello Number 1
Hello Number 2
Hello Number 3
C:\Java eLearning Kit for Dummies\Chapter 07>_

Figure 7-2

Using the continue statement

So far, you've seen a version of the `for` loop that performs a specific number of loops and another version that stops at a specific point using a `break` statement. A third version of the `for` loop performs a specific number of loops, but it skips some of the loops when conditions don't warrant performing the task. For example, the data that you need to process might not be of the right type or might be missing completely. This third form relies on the `continue` statement. The `continue` statement tells the `for` loop to go immediately to the next loop, rather than complete the current loop.

The best way to understand the difference between the `break` and `continue` statements is to contrast the output they provide. In the following exercise, you create an application that works almost precisely the same as the

EXTRA INFO

Just because the examples in this chapter look at the `break` and `continue` statements separately, that doesn't mean you can't combine them in a single `for` loop. The `break` and `continue` statements can appear wherever and whenever you need them. For example, you could choose to process part of a `for` loop and then continue on to the next loop if things aren't working out as expected. If an error occurs in the same `for` loop, you could choose to use a `break` statement to end it. A single `for` loop can also contain multiple instances of both the `break` and `continue` statements.

UsingBreak example in the "Using the break statement" section of the chapter and test it using the same approach. However, as you'll see, the resulting output differs because this example uses a continue statement instead of a break statement.

Files needed: UsingContinue.java

1. **Open the editor or IDE that you've chosen to use for this book.**

2. **Type the following code into the editor screen.**

```java
// Import the required API classes.
import java.util.Scanner;

public class UsingContinue
{
    public static void main(String[] args)
    {
        // Create the scanner.
        Scanner GetChoice = new Scanner(System.in);

        // Ask the user how many times to say hello.
        System.out.print("Say \"Hello\" how many
            times? ");
        int Count = GetChoice.nextInt();

        // Create a for loop.
        for (int Current = 1; Current <= Count; Current++)
        {
            // Don't allow the application to say
            // hello more than three times.
            if (Current == 4)
                continue;

            // Perform the required task.
            System.out.println("Hello Numnber " + Current);
        }
    }
}
```

The only difference between this application and the UsingBreak application is the continue statement that appears within the if structure. This difference may not seem like much, but it does control how the for structure works.

3. **Save the code to disk using the filename** UsingContinue.java.

4. **In your command prompt, type** javac UsingContinue.java **and press Enter.**

   The compiler compiles your application and creates a .class file from it.

5. **Type** java UsingContinue **and press Enter.**

   The application asks you how many times it should say Hello.

6. **Type** 2 **and press Enter.**

   The application outputs two Hello messages. In this case, output is precisely the same as the UsingBreak application because the condition provided by the if statement is never invoked.

7. **Repeat Steps 5 and 6 using a value of 5 in place of 2.**

   This time you see four Hello messages, as shown in Figure 7-3. Notice that the message when Current equals 4 is missing. However, because the continue statement lets the for structure process the next loop, you do see the output when Current equals 5.

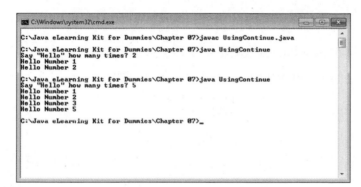

Figure 7-3

Modify the UsingContinue application so that it skips the number 3 and stops at the number 6. You'll need to use both a continue and a break statement to accomplish the task.

Nesting for loops

Sometimes you need to process something using multiple loops. For example, when working with tabular data, you might use one loop to process the rows and another loop to process the columns. There are multiple columns for each row, so the Columns loop appears within the Rows loop. Placing one repeating loop within another is called nesting the loops. Each iteration of the main loop executes the entire subordinate loop. So, when you start processing the first row, it executes all the column tasks for that row before moving to the next row.

The multiplication tables are one of the better ways to demonstrate nesting because you need to create a loop for rows and another for columns. In addition, you need to create the headings that show the numbers being multiplied, which means using an additional loop. In the following exercise, you create an application that demonstrates one method for creating the multiplication tables with code.

LINGO

Nesting is the process of enclosing one structure within another of the same type. Java uses nesting in a number of ways, so you'll see this term used quite often. When working with structures, one structure acts as a container to hold the other structure. The container structure is called the **main,** or **parent,** structure. The structure within the main structure is called the **subordinate,** or **child,** structure.

Files needed: `NestingLoops.java`

1. **Open the editor or IDE that you've chosen to use for this book.**

2. **Type the following code into the editor screen.**

```java
// Import the required API classes.
import java.util.Scanner;

public class NestingLoops
{
    public static void main(String[] args)
    {
        // Create the scanner.
        Scanner GetChoice = new Scanner(System.in);

        // Ask the user how many rows to provide.
        System.out.print("How many rows do you want? ");
        int Rows = GetChoice.nextInt();

        // Ask the user how many columns to provide.
        System.out.print("How many columns do you
          want? ");
        int Columns = GetChoice.nextInt();

        // Print out a column heading across the top.
        for (int ColNum = 1; ColNum <= Columns; ColNum++)
            System.out.print("\t" + ColNum);

        // End the column heading.
        System.out.println();
```

```
// Create a for loop for the rows.
for (int Row = 1; Row <= Rows; Row++)
{
    // Print out the current row number.
    System.out.print(Row + "\t");

    // Create a for loop for the columns.
    for (int Column = 1; Column <= Columns;
    Column++)
    {
        // Display a value for each column.
        System.out.print(Row * Column + "\t");
    }

    // Move to the next row.
    System.out.println();
}
    }
}
```

This application relies on multiple loops to perform its work. However, before it can do any work, the application must get some information from the user. It obtains the number of rows and columns that the user wants to see.

The first loop prints out the column numbers for the heading. Notice how this loop relies on an escape sequence (`"\t"`) to produce tabs between each column heading entry.

The second loop is nested. Because of the way your display works, the application always prints a row and all of the columns within that row, before moving on to the next row. The example prints out row heading elements at the beginning of each row.

3. **Save the code to disk using the filename `NestingLoops.java`.**

4. **In your command prompt, type** javac NestingLoops.java **and press Enter.**

   The compiler compiles your application and creates a `.class` file from it.

5. **Type** java NestingLoops **and press Enter.**

   The application asks you how many rows you want to see.

6. **Type 1 and press Enter.**

   The application now asks how many columns you want to see.

7. Type 5 **and press Enter.**

The application outputs a multiplication table containing headings, along with four rows and five columns of multiplication values, as shown in Figure 7-4.

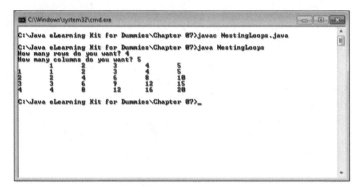

Figure 7-4

Modify the NestingLoops application so that it displays multiplication backward — showing the highest number first, and then proceeding to the lowest number. Being able to display output in any order you want is an important part of working with the for loop.

Executing Tasks Until Complete

You can create any looping situation you want by using a for loop. However, working with for loops isn't always convenient, and you'll find situations where checking for a condition, rather than taking a precise number of steps, works considerably easier. Java provides two methods for checking conditions. You can check the condition at the outset of the loop by using the while loop, or you can check the condition at the end of the loop by using a do . . . while loop. The following sections show how to use both loop types.

EXTRA INFO

As with a for loop, you can use the break and continue statements in either the while loop or do . . .while loop. The statements work precisely the same way. In addition, you can nest either loop to produce results similar to those shown for the for loop. The main difference in loops is how you define the beginning and end of the loop iterations.

Using the while loop

A while loop checks for a specific condition before it does any work. As long as the condition exists, the loop will continue performing the tasks you assign to it. Because it relies on a condition, the while loop has no specific ending count — you simply wait until a condition changes to end it. In this example, you compare the while loop against the for loop shown in the StandardFor application found in the "Using the standard for loop" section of the chapter.

Files needed: StandardWhile.java

1. **Open the editor or IDE that you've chosen to use for this book.**

2. **Type the following code into the editor screen.**

```java
// Import the required API classes.
import java.util.Scanner;

public class StandardWhile
{
    public static void main(String[] args)
    {
        // Create the scanner.
        Scanner GetChoice = new Scanner(System.in);

        // Ask the user how many times to say hello.
        System.out.print("Say \"Hello\" how many times?");
        int Count = GetChoice.nextInt();

        // Define a counter variable.
        int Current = 1;

        // Create a for loop.
        while (Current <= Count)
        {
            // Perform the required task.
            System.out.println("Hello Number " + Current);

            // Update the counter variable.
            Current++;
        }
    }
}
```

This application produces precisely the same output as the Standard For application when you provide the same input. However, the `while` loop requires that you do things a little differently. For example, notice that you must define a counter variable (`Current`) on a separate line of code — the `for` loop defines the counter variable as part of the `for` statement.

The condition part of the `while` statement is the same as the condition part (the second argument) of the `for` loop. However, to update the counter variable, `Current`, you must add another line of code within the `while` statement structure.

3. **Save the code to disk using the filename `StandardWhile.java`.**

4. **In your command prompt, type** javac StandardWhile.java **and press Enter.**

   The compiler compiles your application and creates a `.class` file from it.

5. **Type** java StandardWhile **and press Enter.**

   The application asks you how many times it should say `Hello`.

6. **Type** 5 **and press Enter.**

   The application outputs a series of `Hello` messages, as shown in Figure 7-5.

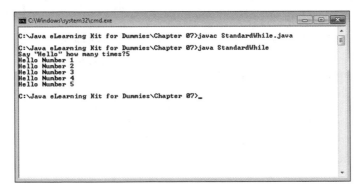

Figure 7-5

7. **Compare Figure 7-1 with Figure 7-5.**

   Notice that the output of the StandardFor application is precisely the same as the output of the StandardWhile application.

Now that you have a better idea of how the `while` statement works, use it to create versions of the UsingBreak, UsingContinue, and NestedLoops examples in this chapter. In each case, you need to make changes similar to the changes you've seen in this section. There's a special trick required to make the `continue` statement work in the `while` loop — remember that you must update the counter variable during each loop iteration. After you create each new application, ask yourself whether the `for` loop or the `while` loop is easiest to use in that particular situation.

Checking after the first execution with the do . . .while loop

A do . . . while loop works almost like a `while` loop. The difference shows up when the condition is checked. A do . . . while loop checks the condition at the end of the loop, which means that the loop will always run at least one time. In this example, you compare the do . . . while loop against the `for` loop shown in the StandardFor application. However, in this case, you'll also perform another test that shows the interesting difference in using a do . . . while loop.

Files needed: `StandardDoWhile.java`

1. **Open the editor or IDE that you've chosen to use for this book.**

2. **Type the following code into the editor screen.**

```java
// Import the required API classes.
import java.util.Scanner;

public class StandardDoWhile
{
    public static void main(String[] args)
    {
        // Create the scanner.
        Scanner GetChoice = new Scanner(System.in);

        // Ask the user how many times to say hello.
        System.out.print("Say \"Hello\" how many
            times? ");
        int Count = GetChoice.nextInt();

        // Define a counter variable.
        int Current = 1;
```

```
      // Create a for loop.
      do
      {
          // Perform the required task.
          System.out.println("Hello Number " + Current);

          // Update the counter variable.
          Current++;
      } while (Current <= Count);
    }
  }
```

The difference to note in this listing is that the condition isn't tested until *after* the loop has executed. Otherwise, everything else is the same as the StandardWhile loop example.

3. **Save the code to disk using the filename** `StandardDoWhile.java`.

4. **In your command prompt, type** javac StandardDoWhile.java **and press Enter.**

   The compiler compiles your application and creates a `.class` file from it.

5. **Type** java StandardDoWhile **and press Enter.**

   The application asks you how many times it should say `Hello`.

6. **Type** 5 **and press Enter.**

   The application outputs a series of `Hello` messages.

7. **Perform Steps 5 and 6 again, but substitute –1 for the input value.**

   The application still outputs a single `Hello`, as shown in Figure 7-6. In fact, you can type any negative number, 0, or 1 and still get a single `Hello` message from the application.

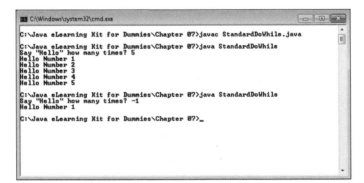

Figure 7-6

8. **Perform Steps 5 and 6 again using −1 with the StandardFor application.**

   The application exits without providing any output.

9. **Perform Steps 5 and 6 again using −1 with the StandardWhile application.**

   Again, the application exits without providing any output. Theoretically, you can provide this same behavior when working with a `for` loop, but it's complicated and using the `do . . . while` loop proves much easier to use.

> As with the `while` statement, it's important to see how the `do . . . while` statement compares with the `for` statement across a number of examples. Create versions of the UsingBreak, UsingContinue, and NestedLoops examples in this chapter using the `do . . . while` statement.

Interacting with Objects

The `for-each` loop is a special kind of loop in that you can use it with groups of things. It looks like a `for` loop in some respects because it doesn't actually use the keyword `for-each` — it uses the `for` keyword instead. However, the associated statement is different. The associated statement begins with a variable to hold one element of whatever sort of collection of elements you want to process like this:

```
for (char Letter
```

It then has a colon. This colon means "in." So, the statement now reads, for each `Letter` of type `char` in like this:

```
for (char Letter :
```

The last part is the collection of elements you want to process. Suppose you start with a `String` named `MyString`. You need to use the `toCharArray()` method to obtain a collection of `char` elements to process. So, the entire statement looks like this:

```
for (char Letter : MyString.toCharArray())
```

You read this statement as, "For each `Letter` of type `char` in the `MyString` `char` collection, do something." At this point, you can process each of the elements (`char` variables) in `MyString` as you normally would with any other structure.

For now, you really don't need to worry about what a collection of elements precisely means. You'll discover how these structures work in Chapter 10. The main focus of the sections that follow is to introduce you to the for-each loop, which you'll use quite often as the book progresses. So, for now, concentrate on the for-each loop as you work through the sections that follow.

Creating a basic for-each loop

A for-each loop can process any collection of objects that you want. In the example that follows, you create a collection of char variables from a String. A collection of this sort makes it easier to see how the for-each loop works and why it's such an important Java programming feature.

Files needed: StandardForEach.java

1. **Open the editor or IDE that you've chosen to use for this book.**

2. **Type the following code into the editor screen.**

```java
// Import the required API classes.
import java.lang.String;
import java.util.Scanner;

public class StandardForEach
{
    public static void main(String[] args)
    {
        // Create the scanner.
        Scanner GetString = new Scanner(System.in);

        // Obtain a string value.
        System.out.print("Type any string: ");
        String MyString = GetString.nextLine();

        // Process each character separately in a
        // for-each loop.
        for(char Letter : MyString.toCharArray())
            System.out.println(Letter);
    }
}
```

This example begins by obtaining a `String` from the user. The `String` can contain anything — numbers, letters, or special characters, as long as they aren't special characters, such as a tab.

The example then converts the `String` — `MyString`, in this example — to a collection of `char` variables by calling the `toCharArray()` method. It places each `char` in `Letter` and then displays `Letter` on screen. In short, the `for-each` loop is processing each letter in `MyString` separately.

3. **Save the code to disk using the filename `StandardForEach.java`.**

4. **In your command prompt, type** javac StandardForEach.java **and press Enter.**

   The compiler compiles your application and creates a `.class` file from it.

5. **Type** java StandardForEach **and press Enter.**

   The application asks you to type any string.

6. **Type** Hello **and press Enter.**

   The application outputs each letter that you've typed on a separate line of the output, as shown in Figure 7-7.

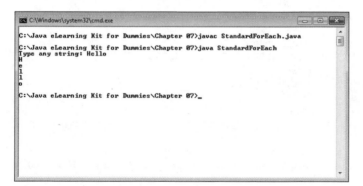

Figure 7-7

Using the for-each loop with enumerations

Chapter 3 introduces you to enumeration, a special kind of structure that makes it possible to create item lists. It's possible to use a `for-each` loop to list an enumeration. Instead of assuming that you know what a list contains (as the example in Lesson 3 does), you can use a for-each loop to ask what your options are. People commonly perform this task with real world lists, too, so it makes sense that Java supports this feature.

In this example, you create a Days of the Week enumeration and then use it to display the names to the user with a for-each loop. The user selects any of the entries by typing its associated number.

Files needed: UsingEnumerations.java

1. **Open the editor or IDE that you've chosen to use for this book.**

2. **Type the following code into the editor screen.**

```java
// Import the required API classes.
import java.util.Scanner;

public class UsingEnumerations
{
    // Create an enumeration to use in the
    // example.
    enum Days
    {
        Sunday,
        Monday,
        Tuesday,
        Wednesday,
        Thursday,
        Friday,
        Saturday
    }

    public static void main(String[] args)
    {
        // Create the scanner.
        Scanner GetDay = new Scanner(System.in);

        // Display the list of days on screen.
        for (Days ThisDay : Days.values())
            System.out.println(
                    ThisDay.ordinal() + "\t" + ThisDay);

        // Display a message asking the user to select
        // a day.
        System.out.print("Type the number of a day: ");

        // Get the number.
        int Selection = GetDay.nextInt();
```

```
        // Display the result.
        Days TheDay = Days.values()[Selection];
        System.out.println("You selected " + TheDay);
    }
}
```

Enumerations can appear just about anywhere in your code, but this example places the enumeration within the class structure, outside of `main()`. The enumeration is named `Days`, and it contains the days of the week.

Inside `main()`, the `for-each` loop lists each day of the week in turn. An enumerated entry has both a name and an ordinal value. The example shows you both of them.

After the application displays the days of the week for the user, it asks the user to select a particular day by typing its numeric value. The code uses this value to select a particular day from `Days` and place it in `TheDay`. The output from the example is the name of the day the user has selected.

3. **Save the code to disk using the filename `UsingEnumerations.java`.**

4. **In your command prompt, type** javac UsingEnumerations.java **and press Enter.**

   The compiler compiles your application and creates a `.class` file from it.

5. **Type** java UsingEnumerations **and press Enter.**

   The application displays the days of the week. It then asks the user to type a number corresponding to a particular day.

6. **Type** 1 **and press Enter.**

   The application outputs Monday as the day selected, as shown in Figure 7-8.

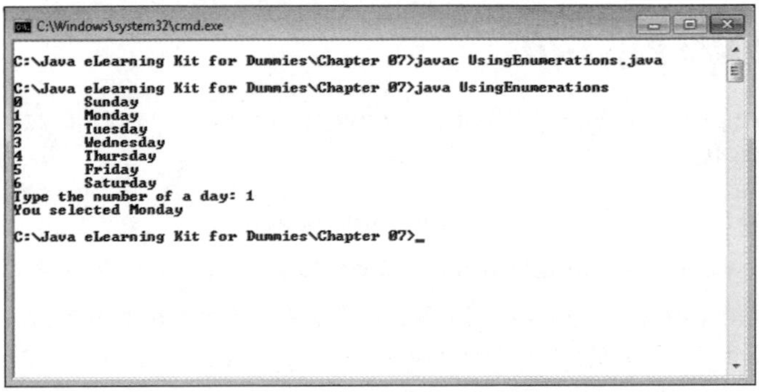

```
C:\Windows\system32\cmd.exe

C:\Java eLearning Kit for Dummies\Chapter 07>javac UsingEnumerations.java

C:\Java eLearning Kit for Dummies\Chapter 07>java UsingEnumerations
0       Sunday
1       Monday
2       Tuesday
3       Wednesday
4       Thursday
5       Friday
6       Saturday
Type the number of a day: 1
You selected Monday

C:\Java eLearning Kit for Dummies\Chapter 07>_
```

Figure 7-8

Summing Up

Here are the key points you learned about in this chapter:

- ✔ The for loop repeats a series of tasks a specific number of times.

- ✔ Use the break statement to stop a for loop from continuing to process tasks.

- ✔ Use the continue statement when you want to stop a single for loop from processing but want to continue with the remaining loops.

- ✔ Nest two or more sets of for loops when you need to process multiple dimensions or create a complex processing loop series.

- ✔ A while loop continues to repeat a series of tasks until a specific condition is met.

- ✔ The do . . . while statement acts much like the while statement, but it has the distinction of executing the tasks within its structure at least once, no matter what condition you might set for it.

- ✔ It's possible to repeat most forms of standard looping requirements by using the for, while, or do . . . while statements and your choice depends on convenience or personal taste.

- ✔ The for-next loop is special in that it works with each element in an enumeration, array, or collection. *NOT IN JAVA OR THIS BOOK.* ?

- ✔ The for-each loop relies on a special kind of for loop to do its work.

- ✔ You use the for-each loop to process individual elements of a collection of elements one element at a time.

- ✔ Using an enumeration can make it easier to work with your application.

Try-it-yourself lab

For more practice with the features covered in this chapter, try the following exercise on your own.

1. **Open the UsingEnumerations application.**

2. **Create a new enumeration that contains a list of colors.**

   Make sure you separate each color with a command and don't include any spaces in the color names.

3. **Rewrite the code to display the enumeration to the user with the for-each loop.**

4. **Change the code to ask the user to select a color and then display the color selection onscreen.**

5. **Compile the application.**

6. **Run the application.**

7. **Try each of the new color entries.**

   Do the new color entries work as you anticipated? If they don't, why not?

Know this tech talk

counter variable: A special sort of variable used to track the current count of something in the application. In most cases, a counter variable is a primitive integer type because counter variables only track whole numbers and don't require the extra features of an object variable type.

enumeration: A listing of like items that you can use to make your code easier to read. An enumeration makes it possible to refer to something using a human-readable term, even though the actual value is a number.

iteration: A single loop from a series of repetitive loops. A single iteration is one pass through the code in a repetitive loop structure.

nesting: Placing one structure within another structure of the same type. For example, nesting for loops places a subordinate `for` loop within a main `for` loop.

repetitive loop: A method of telling your application to perform a task more than once. The repetitive loop consists of a structure that defines where the loop begins and ends, some sort of condition used to determine how long to loop, and the series of tasks contained within the structure.

structure: A programming construct that begins with a statement that specifies the purpose of the structure. Normally curly braces ({ }) appear after the statement to define the statement body. One or more lines of code appear within the structure body to define the tasks performed by the structure.

Chapter 8
Handling Errors

- ✔ Defining error sources can help you *locate the errors with greater ease*.

- ✔ Catching errors, instead of letting them happen, lets you *control whether the application works as the user anticipates*.

- ✔ Throwing (deliberately causing) an error makes it possible for you to *tell the user something unexpected has happened*.

xcept for the simplest of applications, it's highly unlikely that you'll ever encounter an application that is error free. Errors in coding happen for a wide variety of reasons. It isn't enough to create an application that uses the correct code. The application must also have the right logic and use arguments in precisely the correct manner. In some cases, an error actually exists outside of the application, so the application doesn't even have control over whether the error occurs. The best the application can do is to handle the error so that the application doesn't crash and potentially damage the user's data.

There are situations where the code in a particular part of your application can't handle an error. Perhaps the code doesn't have enough information or it doesn't have the required rights to perform a task. In some cases, you need to interact with the user to allow the user to make the decision. These are just a few of the circumstances where your application actually has to signal an error. A Java application uses an exception to signal an error. You've seen exceptions in other chapters in this book. This is the first chapter where you'll discover how to throw an exception. *Throwing an exception* means to create one and send it to the caller.

LINGO

A **coding error** represents any action that the application takes that is outside of the anticipated behavior for that application. Errors can be dramatic, such as an application crash. However, errors are often more subtle, such as displaying incorrect output or producing an unexpected result. In some cases, errors aren't noticed by the user at all, but they do present opportunities for nefarious individuals to cause damage to the application, its data, or the system that supports it.

An **exception** is an alert of a sort. It describes an exceptional condition in your application and tells you that an error has occurred. Exceptions can happen for all sorts of reasons. The error might be in your code or in the application environment. For example, if your application tries to open a file that doesn't exist, the Java Runtime Environment (JRE) will generate an exception that tells your application about the error.

Throwing an exception means to create the exception object and then send it to the part of the application that called the current code. When your application throws an exception, it creates an object that tells others that it has encountered an error it can't fix. As the term suggests, throwing an exception is something your code does for exceptional conditions, when no other alternative is available.

Understanding Error Sources

There are many sources of error in an application. You may assume that the error is in the code, but often it isn't. The error could exist in a library or in some other code over which the application has no control. In some cases, the error has nothing to do with the code, but with the application environment. For example, the application may not have access to a resource that it requires to work. A file might be missing, or the network connection might be down. Users also cause errors by providing incorrect input.

For the most part, there aren't any errors that an application can't handle in some way when the application code is robust enough and has enough information to resolve it. However, before an application can do anything with an error, it must have the information required to resolve it. One of the best tools that a developer has to make an application robust enough to handle any errors is to classify the error and understand why it happens. That's the purpose of the following sections — to help you understand the nature of errors so that you can do a better job of fixing them.

Classifying when errors occur

Errors can occur at various times. However, you can broadly classify when an error will occur into two categories, at compile time and runtime, as described in the following sections.

Compile time

The compiler (javac for all the examples earlier in this book) converts your application code into Java byte code. During this process, it takes the human-readable code that you write and converts it into something that the Java Runtime Environment (JRE) understands. To perform this process, the compiler must *parse* the code, which means it reads the code in a manner that unambiguously determines precisely what you want the application to do, when you want it to do it, and how you want the task accomplished. If you break the rules for writing unambiguous code, the compiler displays an error message. This message is actually a kind of exception.

GO ONLINE

This single chapter can't hope to cover every possible source of errors or the resolution of those errors. Consider this chapter a good introduction to the most common problems. In fact, it may surprise you to learn that there are entire sites devoted to the topic of exceptions and exception handling! One of the better sources of information is the Introduction to Java Exception Handling tutorial at `http://tutorials.jenkov.com/java-exception-handling/index.html`. You can also find interesting articles on the topic, such as those found at `http://onjava.com/onjava/2003/11/19/exceptions.html` and `http://today.java.net/pub/a/today/2003/12/04/exceptions.html`.

Compile time errors are the easiest to handle because the compiler normally tells you precisely what's wrong and where the error has occurred. Even if the information isn't exact, the compiler will at least get you to the right area of the broken code so that you can look for the error it contains. The point is that you don't have to wait for the user to find this sort of error. To produce the compiled application, you must fix the error.

Runtime

The compiler can't find every error in your code. If the form of the code is correct (that is, you haven't made any mistakes in typing the elements that create the application), the compiler won't find the error. For example, if you initialize a numeric value to 5 instead of 4, the compiler can't find the error for you because the compiler has no idea that you really meant to type 4. These sorts of mistakes create *runtime errors* — those errors that happen at some point during the application execution.

LINGO

Parsing means to read the input you provide, such as code in human-readable form, and turn it into something else, such as Java byte code. An application can also parse user input. For example, a user could type a string that your application code turns into a number. So, parsing is the act of reading some type of input, interpreting that input in a specific way, and then producing output based on the interpreted input. A parser generates an error when the input isn't what it expects. For example, if the user inputs a string containing the letter C, and you expected a string containing a number, such as 123, the parser will generate an exception saying that the input is incorrect.

Runtime errors can occur at all sorts of times. Some errors are more likely to occur at specific times. The following list provides you with some ideas about when runtime errors are likely to occur:

- ✔ **Initialization:** When the application first starts — before it presents any sort of interface to the user or performs any useful work — it goes through an initialization phase. This is when setting a variable to the incorrect type or trying to use a variable before you initialize it will get noticed. Many resource-related errors also occur during initialization because most applications open required resources during this time.

- ✔ **Operating mode:** After an application initializes, it's in operating mode. If it has a user interface, it begins interacting with the user. This is the time when user input matters most. You'll also find incorrectly initialized variables at this time because the user (or the recipient of the application output, such as the system) will see that the output is incorrect. User requests for resources, such as a data file, also create errors during this time.

✔ **Background processing:** Most background processing errors result from the environment (such as the loss of a network connection), missing resources (such as a lost file), incorrectly initialized variables, or errors in how you told the application to perform a task. Some tasks are more commonly performed in the background than others are. For example, printing a document and downloading resources from the Internet are commonly performed in the background while the user continues to work with the application in the foreground.

✔ **Shutdown:** When the user (including the system accounts) tells the application it's no longer needed, the application goes through a shutdown phase. During this shutdown phase, the application closes files and performs other housekeeping chores that ensure the application doesn't leave a mess for the operating system. The most common errors that can occur during this phase are not releasing resources that your application has used and not saving data to disk. Of course, coding errors can occur at any time, and this phase of operation is no exception. You could tell the application to close five files when only four of them are actually open.

The JRE will present most runtime errors it detects to you as exceptions. However, the JRE won't catch every error in your application. You must also look at the output of your application to determine whether the output matches the expectations you have for a given input. Additionally, it's important to look at the state of any resources you use to ensure that they're not damaged in some way. For example, you need to ensure that any data you should save in a file actually ends up in the file when your application shuts down.

Distinguishing error types

Knowing when an error can occur is important. You need to understand when to look for a particular problem in your application. However, it's also important to understand *how* errors occur. The kind of error determines the strategy you use to find it and what you can do to fix it. Although some errors will require that you fix the code and update the application, some errors are fixed by retrying the operation or interacting with the user in some way. The following sections discuss the types of errors that you'll encounter most often.

Syntactical

A syntactical error is one in which the language you use to create your code is incorrect. For example, if you try to create an `if` statement that doesn't include the condition in parentheses, even when the condition is present on the same line as the `if` statement, that's a syntax error. The compiler will catch most of these errors for you. If the syntax of your code is incorrect, then in most cases the compiler can't use the code to create byte code for the JRE. Here's a list of the most common syntax errors:

- ✔ **Using incorrect capitalization:** One of the most common syntax errors that new developers make is to capitalize keywords, rather than use lowercase. Java is case sensitive, so using the proper case when you type your code is essential. This same error can occur with class names, variables, or any other code you type as part of your Java application. A variable named `MyVar` is always different from one named `myVar`.

- ✔ **Splitting a string over two lines:** In most cases, Java doesn't care if your code appears on one or more lines. However, if you split a string across lines so that the string contains a newline character, then the compiler will object. The answer is to end the string on the first line with a double quote, add a plus sign to tell the compiler you want to *concatenate* (add)

this string with another string and then continue the string on the
next line like this:

```
System.out.print("This is a really long " +
            "string that appears on two lines.");
```

✔ **Missing parentheses:** If you make a method call and don't include the
parentheses after the method name (even if you aren't sending any arguments to the method), the compiler registers an error. For example, this
code is incorrect because `print()` requires parentheses after it:

```
System.out.print;
```

✔ **Forgetting to import a class:** Whenever you want to use a particular
Java API feature, you must import the associated class into your application. For example, if your application contains `String userName;`,
then you must add `import java.lang.String;` to import the
`String` class.

✔ **Treating a static method as an instance method:** Static methods are
those that are associated with a specific class, while instance methods
are associated with an object created from the class. For example, when
you created the example in the section on nesting `if` statements in
Chapter 6, you used the `Character.toUpperCase()` static method.
If you'd tried to access the `toUpperCase()` method from a variable
instead, the application would generate an error.

✔ **Missing curly braces:** Anytime you want a Java feature to apply to multiple lines of code, you must enclose the entire block within curly braces
(`{}`). In most cases, the compiler will catch this error for you. For example, if you try to end a class without including the closing curly brace,
the compiler will generate an error. This is one error where the compiler
may not show you the precise location of the error because it can't
detect where the curly brace is missing — it simply knows that one is
missing. This sort of error can also create runtime errors. For example,
when an `if` statement is supposed to apply to multiple lines of code, but
you leave out the curly braces, the `if` statement affects only the next
line of code, and the application works incorrectly.

✔ **Forgetting the class or object name as part of a method call:** You always
include the class or object associated with a method before making the
method call. For example, `Character.toUpperCase()` and `System.
out.print()` are correct, but simply calling `toUpperCase()` or
`print()` is incorrect.

✔ **Omitting the `break` clause from `switch` statements:** It's easy to forget to
add the `break` clauses to a `switch` statement. In addition, the compiler
won't catch this error. As a consequence of leaving out the `break` clause,
your application will continue to execute the code in a `switch` statement
until it encounters a `break` clause or the `switch` statement is complete.

For example, the following comes from the section on executing a default task in Chapter 6, but the `break` clauses are commented out.

```java
// Import the required API classes.
import java.util.Scanner;
import java.lang.Character;

public class UseAMenu03
{
    public static void main(String[] args)
    {
        // Create the scanner.
        Scanner GetChoice = new Scanner(System.in);

        // Obtain input from the user.
        System.out.println("Options\n");
        System.out.println("A. Yellow");
        System.out.println("B. Orange");
        System.out.println("C. Green\n");
        System.out.print("Choose your favorite color: ");
        char Choice = GetChoice.findInLine(".").
            charAt(0);

        // Convert the input to uppercase.
        Choice = Character.toUpperCase(Choice);

        // Choose the right color based on a switch
        // statement.
        switch (Choice)
        {
            case 'A':
                System.out.println("Your favorite color is
                    Yellow!");
                //break;
            case 'B':
                System.out.println("Your favorite color is
                    Orange!");
                //break;
            case 'C':
                System.out.println("Your favorite color is
                    Green!");
                //break;
            default:
                System.out.println(
                        "Type A, B, or C to select a
                color.");
                //break;
        }
    }
}
```

When you execute this code and answer A, the application outputs all the possible responses, as shown in Figure 8-1. If you compare this output to the output shown in Figure 6-5, you'll see that the application isn't working correctly.

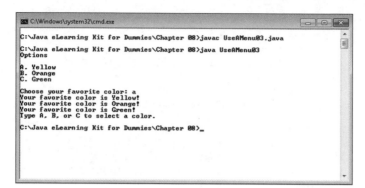

Figure 8-1

✔ **Omitting a `return` statement:** When you create a method that's supposed to return a value and then don't provide a `return` statement to return the value, the compiler will complain.

✔ **Mistyping the header for the `main()` method:** The compiler won't complain about this problem, but you'll see it immediately when you try to start the application. Java will complain that it can't find the `main()` method. Remember that a `main()` method must appear like this:

```
public static void main (String []args)
```

You can create many other syntax errors. As you've discovered by reading this list, the compiler will find some of them, the JRE will find others, but some, like omitting the `break` clause of a `switch` statement, are left for you to figure out. You'll discover more of these syntactical errors as the book progresses. Of the three main types of error, syntactical errors tend to be the easiest to find.

Semantic

Many people find the difference between semantic errors and syntactical (syntax) errors hard to understand, but they are different. You can see a semantic error when the syntax of your code is correct but the code usage isn't correct. The most common semantic error is one in which the code uses a variable that isn't initialized properly. Fortunately, the compiler finds this particular semantic error in most cases. Here's a list of other common semantic errors you need to know about.

✔ **Using an operator that doesn't apply:** In some situations, you might try to use an operator that doesn't apply to the variable or variables in question. For example, you can't use the increment operator (++) with a `boolean` variable. Newer versions of Java have become adept at finding this error, but you can still encounter difficulty figuring out precisely why an error occurs when you use the wrong operator in some cases. For example, `MyObj1 == MyObj2` won't compare the two objects — the equality operator works only with primitive types.

✔ **Using incompatible types:** This type of semantic error can be tricky because the compiler will flag some errors and not others. For example, if you try to assign a `float` to an `int` variable, the compiler displays an error message. On the other hand, if you assign an `int` to a `float` variable, the compiler performs an automatic type conversion to the `int` to make it a `float`. The problem with this second scenario is that it can silently introduce errors in your code, especially if you really did mean to use a `float`.

✔ **Losing precision during a conversion:** Sometimes you can apply casting incorrectly. For example, casting a `float` to an `int` works fine, but at the loss of the decimal portion of the number. This loss of precision can affect the output of your application in unexpected ways and cause the output to reflect a value other than the one you expected. The compiler never finds this sort of error because you have specifically applied a cast to the variable and the compiler expects that you know what you're doing.

✔ **Performing an impossible cast:** It's possible to convert between many different types in Java. However, no matter how much you'd like to convert a `boolean` value into an `int`, Java won't let you do it. The concept of performing the cast is syntactically correct, but you're applying it incorrectly, making this a semantic error that the compiler always catches.

✔ **Applying scoping incorrectly:** Any variable you declare inside a method has the same *scope* — visibility to other parts of the application, in other words — as the method. Consequently, you can't declare a `private static int` variable inside a method. Instead, you must define the variable globally like this:

```
public class PrivateVar
{
    // This declaration works.
    private static int PrivateInt = 3;

    public static void main(String[] args)
    {
        // This declaration doesn't work.
        private static int PrivateInt = 3;
    }
}
```

You'll encounter other types of semantic errors as the book progresses. For now, these are the most common problems you should look for in your code. Semantic errors tend to be harder to find than syntactical errors, but not nearly as hard as logical errors.

Logical

Logical errors can be extremely difficult to find because they don't reflect any sort of coding problem or an error in the use of Java language elements. The code runs perfectly as written — it just isn't performing the task that you expected it to perform. As a result, logical errors can be the hardest errors to find. You need to spend time going through your code looking for a precise reason for the error. Here's a list of common logical errors that Java developers encounter:

- ✔ **Using incorrect operator precedence:** The order in which Java interprets operators is important. Applications often produce the wrong result because the developer didn't include parentheses in the correct places. For example, the following example produces outputs of 11, 13, 9, and 8 from the four variables, all due to the location (or lack) of the parentheses.

```java
public class OperatorError
{
   public static void main(String[] args)
   {
      // Create some variables.
      int MyVar1 = 5 + 4 * 3 / 2;
      int MyVar2 = (5 + 4) * 3 / 2;
      int MyVar3 = (5 + 4) * (3 / 2);
      int MyVar4 = (5 + (4 * 3)) / 2;

      // Output the result.
      System.out.println(
            "MyVar1: " + MyVar1 +
            "\nMyVar2: " + MyVar2 +
            "\nMyVar3: " + MyVar3 +
            "\nMyVar4: " + MyVar4);
   }
}
```

- ✔ **Defining the wrong count:** Possibly the most common logical error is counting things incorrectly. People are used to starting counts with 1, and computers often start counts with 0. So, it's not uncommon to find that applications are precisely one off in performing a task, whether that task is running a loop or working with a collection of items.

- ✔ **Assuming a condition is true when it isn't:** Developers will often look at the statement used to define a condition and assume that the statement is true (or false) without verifying the logic of the statement. The use of an or statement when you really meant to use an and statement can also cause problems. The logic employed to make decisions causes many developers, even experienced developers, a lot of problems. Always verify your assumptions for conditional statements.

✔ **Relying on floating point numbers for precision work:** You can't assume that floating point numbers will deliver a specific number. This means you can't check a floating point number for equality to any specific value — you must instead use a range of values to perform the check. Floating point numbers are always an approximation in Java.

✔ **Relying on integer values to measure values:** Integers are great for counting items because they're precise. However, many integer math operations create imprecise results. This is especially true for division, because the remainder is always left off. (The number is rounded down.) Use floating point values or the BigDecimal object type when you need to measure something and precision is important.

✔ **Misplacing a semicolon:** It's possible to create Java code that compiles and runs perfectly well despite having a semicolon in the wrong place. Here's an example:

```java
public class ForLoopError
{
   public static void main(String[] args)
   {
      // Declare the variable.
      int Count;

      // Create the loop.
      for (Count=1; Count<=10; Count++) ;
      {
         // Output the result.
         System.out.println("Count is " + Count);
      }
   }
}
```

Notice that the semicolon appears immediately after the for statement, rather than after the code block as it should. Instead of printing individual values of Count, this example prints a single sentence that says Count is 11.

There are more ways to create logical errors than anyone can imagine. You'll see a number of additional examples as the book progresses.

Catching Errors

All the examples from this point on in the book will include *error trapping* in them. The examples won't bury you in error trapping, but they'll make good error trapping techniques part of the application code whenever possible (and the error trapping code doesn't completely hide the purpose of the example). With this in mind, the following sections provide an overview of the techniques used to catch errors. You'll see three different levels of error trapping commonly employed in Java applications.

Optional error handling

The phrase "optional error handling" is a bit of a misnomer. It's optional only because Java doesn't require you to perform it as part of using the various objects in your application. Every application you build should include some level of error handling, even if Java doesn't require you to add it. In fact, adding error handling to every application you create, even simple test applications, will help you become proficient in this aspect of Java programming and put you ahead of developers who don't follow this practice.

The example that follows builds on the ShowByte example found in the byte section of Chapter 2. That example causes quite a few problems because it doesn't include any error handling. A user can type values that don't work with the byte data type, resulting in an exception. This example corrects the flaws in that earlier example by providing error handling for those situations where the user types something unexpected.

Files needed: `ShowByte.java`

1. **Open the editor or IDE that you've chosen to use for this book.**

2. **Type the following code into the editor screen.**

```java
// Import the required API classes.
import java.util.Scanner;
import java.util.InputMismatchException;

public class ShowByte
{
    public static void main(String[] args)
    {
```

```
// Create the scanner.
Scanner GetByte = new Scanner(System.in);

// Ask the user for an input.
System.out.print("Type any number: ");

// Make sure that the value is acceptable.
try
{
   // Obtain a byte value.
   byte MyByte = GetByte.nextByte();

   // Display the value onscreen.
   System.out.println("The value of MyByte is: "
   + MyByte);
}
catch (InputMismatchException e)
{
   System.out.println("You must provide numeric
   input"
        " between -128 and 127!\n" +
   e.getMessage());
   return;
}
}
}
```

The basics of this example are precisely the same as the original ShowByte example. The application obtains input from the user and displays it onscreen.

The difference in this example is the try . . . catch statement. The try clause of the try . . . catch statement *traps* the error, which means that it detects that an exception has occurred. The catch clause of the try . . . catch statement takes over at this point and displays a helpful message to the user.

In the code example above, the catch clause handles a specific kind of error, the InputMismatchException object, e. Look again at Figure 2-4. The kind of error that you see for both of the incorrect inputs is an InputMismatchException. When you try an application and see information of this kind, you can use it to tailor the error handling that your application provides.

LINGO

Error handling is the act of resolving an exception that the application has trapped. In some cases, handling the error means displaying a message to the user and asking for a correction. However, error handling can take many forms, some of them completely automated and invisible to the user. This act is normally associated with the catch portion of a try . . . catch statement.

The e object also provides a number of interesting properties and methods. In this case, the example uses the getMessage() method to obtain any additional information that the exception can provide.

3. **Save the code to disk using the filename** ShowByte.java.

4. **In your command prompt, type** javac ShowByte.java **and press Enter.**

   The compiler compiles your application and creates a .class file from it.

5. **Type** java ShowByte **and press Enter.**

   The application asks you to type any number.

6. **Type** 3 **and press Enter.**

   The application outputs the expected value of 3.

7. **Type** java ShowByte **and press Enter. Then type** −15 **and press Enter.**

   The application outputs the expected value of −15.

8. **Type** java ShowByte **and press Enter. Then type** 128 **and press Enter.**

   The value you just typed is one larger than byte can support. However, instead of outputting the exception shown in Figure 2-3, the application now outputs the helpful message shown in Figure 8-2. Notice that this message tells the user what to do to correct the problem and also includes additional information provided by the exception itself.

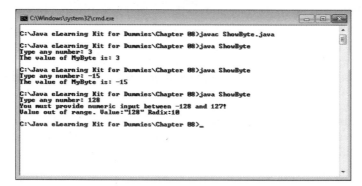

Figure 8-2

9. **Type** java ShowByte **and press Enter. Then type** C **and press Enter.**

   The application would normally output another exception, but in this case, it outputs a variant of the same helpful message, as shown in Figure 8-3. Using a helpful message of this sort makes it easier for the user to interact with the application, which also makes it more likely that the user will continue using it.

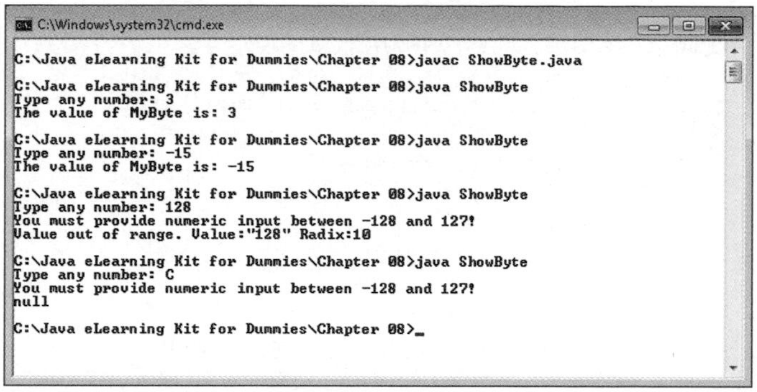

Figure 8-3

Notice that the output in Figure 8-3 shows `null` instead of additional information. Modify the `catch` clause of this example so that it outputs only the additional information when the `getMessage()` method has text to return to the user.

Handling more-specific to less-specific errors

Most applications can generate more than one exception. In addition, you may not be able to detect precisely which exceptions an application will generate. In this case, you need to provide multiple `catch` clauses for the `try . . . catch` statement. Each `catch` clause specializes in a particular kind of error. In addition, you can use generic exception handlers for those situations when your application encounters errors that aren't within the set that you originally anticipated.

In the following exercise, you create an application that can generate multiple kinds of errors. You then add error handling code to interact with each potential exception.

Files needed: MultipleException.java

1. **Open the editor or IDE that you've chosen to use for this book.**

2. **Type the following code into the editor screen.**

```java
// Import the required API classes.
import java.util.Scanner;
import java.util.InputMismatchException;
import java.lang.ArithmeticException;
import java.lang.Exception;
```

```java
public class MultipleException
{
    public static void main(String[] args)
    {
        // Create the scanner.
        Scanner GetInput = new Scanner(System.in);

        // Attempt to perform the task.
        try
        {
            // Ask the user for an input.
            System.out.print("Type the first number: ");
            int Value1 = GetInput.nextInt();

            // Ask the user for another input.
            System.out.print("Type the second number: ");
            int Value2 = GetInput.nextInt();

            // Create the output.
            int Result = Value1 / Value2;
            System.out.println("Value1 / Value2 = " +
            Result);
        }
        catch (InputMismatchException e)
        {
            // Determine whether there is error information
            // to display and output it.
            if (e.getMessage() != null)
                System.out.println("You must provide
                numeric input" +
                        " between -2,147,483,648 and
            2,147,483,647!\n"
                        + e.getMessage());
            else
                System.out.println("You must provide
                numeric input" +
                        " between -2,147,483,648 and
            2,147,483,647!");
            return;
        }
        catch (ArithmeticException e)
        {
            // Determine whether there is error information
            // to display and output it.
            if (e.getMessage() != null)
                System.out.println("You can't divide a
                value" +
```

```
                    " by zero!\n" + e.getMessage());
            else
                System.out.println("You can't divide a
                value" +
                    " by zero!");
            return;
        }
        catch (Exception e)
        {
            // Determine whether there is error information
            // to display and output it.
            if (e.getMessage() != null)
                System.out.println("The application is
                unable" +
                    " to determine precisely what went
            wrong.\n"
                    + e.getMessage());
            else
                System.out.println("The application is
                unable" +
                    " to determine precisely what went
            wrong.\n");
            return;
        }
    }
}
```

This example performs a simple task. It asks the user to provide two input values and then divides the first input value by the second. It doesn't seem as if too much could go wrong, but this code could generate at least two exceptions and potentially others.

As with the ShowByte example in the "Optional error handling" section of this chapter, the user could input a number that is either too large for the int type to handle or is simply an incorrect value, such as the letter C. Because the act of obtaining user input comes first, the example handles the InputMismatchException first. Notice that this version of the example also deals with the situation where e.getMessage() doesn't provide any information.

The user could also try to divide a number by 0, which generates the ArithmeticException. Because this exception can't occur when the user is inputting the numbers, it appears second in the list of catch clauses. Notice how the code simply piles one catch clause on top of another.

The two previous exceptions are specific. They occur for a specific reason and at a specific time. The application could potentially generate some other exception. There are many ways to handle this situation and the example shows just one of them. In this case, the application handles the general `Exception`. This overall class encompasses every other exception that the application could possibly generate. You must always include the generic `Exception` last or no other exception handling code will be called.

3. **Save the code to disk using the filename** `MultipleException.java`.

4. **In your command prompt, type** javac MultipleException.java **and press Enter.**

   The compiler compiles your application and creates a `.class` file from it.

5. **Type** java MultipleException **and press Enter.**

   The application asks you to type any number.

6. **Type the letter** C **and press Enter.**

   You see the expected error output shown in Figure 8-4.

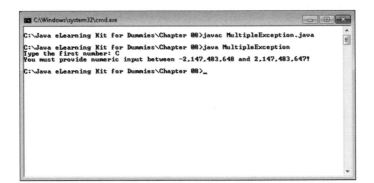

Figure 8-4

7. **Type** java MultipleException **and press Enter.**

   The application asks you to type any number.

8. **Type** 23 **and press Enter.**

   The application asks you to type another number.

9. **Type** 0 **and press Enter.**

   You see another exception message, but this time it tells you not to type 0 as the second number, as shown in Figure 8-5.

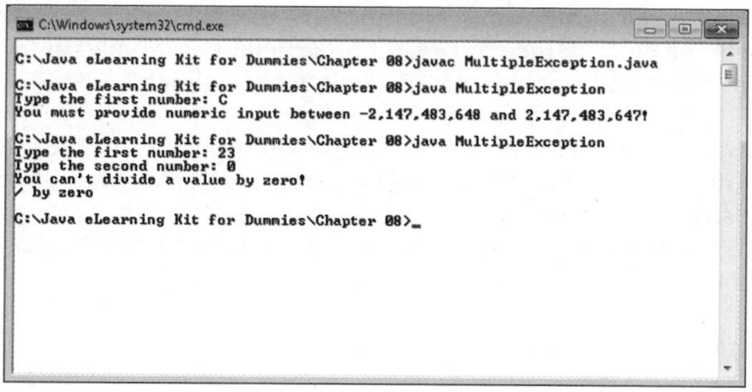

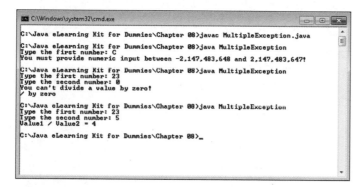

Figure 8-5

10. Repeat Steps 7 through 9, but this time type 5 **for the second number.**

You see the expected output shown in Figure 8-6.

Figure 8-6

Using Optional objects to avoid exceptions

Of all the exceptions you might see when working with Java, the NullPointer Exception (or NPE) is the most prevalent and sometimes the hardest to diagnose. A NullPointerException happens any time you pass a null value to a Java function that was expecting an actual value. The problem is that not every situation that creates an NPE is actually a problem.

Sometimes you expect to have a null value occur and need some method for dealing with it. For example, consider the situation where you want to find a specific value in a list of potential values. It's entirely possible that you won't find the value you want, resulting in a `null` value return. If you then try to process the `null` value, you get an NPE. Because you had expected `null` values to occur, finding the error can be horribly difficult.

Until now, it was hard for human developers to understand the black-and-white thinking of a computer. Java 8 now provides `Optional` objects to deal with the situation where a return value from a function is optional rather than required. The following exercise demonstrates how to use the `Optional` object to reduce the potential for unexpected NPEs.

Files needed: `OptionalObject.java`

1. **Open the editor or IDE that you've chosen to use for this book.**

2. **Type the following code into the editor screen:**

```java
// Import the required API classes.
import java.lang.String;

public class OptionalObject
{
    public static void main(String[] args)
    {
        // Create a test string and location.
        String MyString = "Hello World!";
        char Letter = 'a';

        // Obtain the character.
        String Chars = GetChar(MyString, Letter);

        // Print the result.
        System.out.println(
            "Found the letter: " + Letter +
            " " + Chars.length() + " times.");

        // Change the location.
        Letter = 'o';

        // Obtain the character.
        Chars = GetChar(MyString, Letter);

        // Print the result.
        System.out.println(
            "Found the letter: " + Letter +
            " " + Chars.length() + " times.");
    }

    public static String GetChar
        (String MyString, char SearchLetter)
    {
```

```
            // Create an output string.
            String OutString = "";

            // Check each character in the string.
            for (char ThisLetter : MyString.toCharArray())
               if (ThisLetter == SearchLetter)

                  // Add the character to the string.
                  OutString += new
                  Character(ThisLetter).toString();


            // Return the result.
            if (OutString.length() > 0)
               return OutString;
            else
               return null;
      }
   }
```

You wouldn't ever create code like this, but it provides a simple way to demonstrate how an NPE could occur. The code begins by creating a test string to use for locating specific letters. It also defines which letter to find — *a* in the first case, *o* in the second.

The call to `GetChar()` locates each instance of a character in the test string (or returns `null` when the character isn't found). When the character is found in the test string, `GetChar()` returns a string with each of these characters. Printing `Chars.length()` tells you how many times the character appeared.

Notice the technique that the example uses to convert a `char` to a `String`. In this case, the `char` is boxed into a `Character` object, and then the `toString()` method is used to create the required `String` output. The "Automatic boxing and unboxing" section of Chapter 3 gives you more details — this is an example of how you can use manual boxing to your advantage.

3. **Save the code to disk using the filename** `OptionalObject.java`.

4. **In your command prompt, type** javac OptionalObject.java **and press Enter.**

   The compiler compiles your application and creates a `.class` file from it.

5. Type java OptionalObject **and press Enter.**

You see the expected error output shown in Figure 8-7 because there is no letter "a" in the string "Hello World".

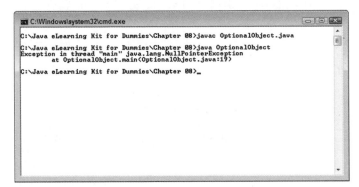

Figure 8-7

6. Change the code on the editor screen so it looks like this:

```java
// Import the required API classes.
import java.lang.String;
import java.util.Optional;

public class OptionalObject
{
    public static void main(String[] args)
    {
        // Create a test string and location.
        String MyString = "Hello World!";
        char Letter = 'a';

        // Obtain the character.
        Optional<String> Chars = GetChar(MyString,
            Letter);

        // Print the result.
        if (Chars.isPresent())
            System.out.println(
                "Found the letter: " + Letter +
                " " + Chars.get().length() + " times.");
        else
            System.out.println(Letter + " Not Found!");

        // Change the location.
        Letter = 'o';
```

```
      // Obtain the character.
      Chars = GetChar(MyString, Letter);

      // Print the result.
      if (Chars.isPresent())
         System.out.println(
               "Found the letter: " + Letter +
               " " + Chars.get().length() + " times.");
      else
         System.out.println(Letter + " Not Found!");
   }

   public static Optional<String> GetChar
      (String MyString, char SearchLetter)
   {
      // Create an output string.
      String OutString = "";

      // Check each character in the string.
      for (char ThisLetter : MyString.toCharArray())
         if (ThisLetter == SearchLetter)

            // Add the character to the string.
            OutString += new
            Character(ThisLetter).toString();


      // Return the result.
      if (OutString.length() > 0)
         return Optional.of(OutString);
      else
         return Optional.empty();
   }
}
```

To use the Optional object, you must import the required class into your application. The essential flow of the application is the same as before. However, now Chars is defined as an Optional<String>. This means that if the search letter isn't present in the search string, you can test for it using Chars.isPresent(). The result is that you don't need to worry about the NEP because it won't happen when the output String is null.

Notice the change in the GetChar() method as well. It has to return an Optional<String> now. In addition, you use the Optional.of() method to place the OutString value in the return value. When there are no letters to return, you use Optional.empty() instead.

7. **Save the code to disk by using the filename** `OptionalObject.java`.

8. **In your command prompt, type** javac OptionalObject.java **and press Enter.**

   The compiler compiles your application and creates a `.class` file from it.

9. **Type** java OptionalObject **and press Enter.**

   You see the expected error output shown in Figure 8-8 because the letter "a" doesn't appear in "Hello World", but the letter "o" does appear twice.

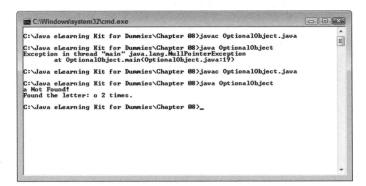

Figure 8-8

Throwing Errors

It's essential that your code makes every effort to fix a problem. However, there are times when your code simply doesn't have enough information, resources, rights, or some other requirement to fix a problem. When this happens, your code throws an error by using an exception object. The term *exception* is appropriate because it should be the exception to the rule, rather than the first act that the application performs. Even so, applications encounter errors that require exceptional measures, and the following sections describe how to deal with these sorts of situations.

Throwing errors during exceptional conditions

In the following exercise, you create an application that can generate multiple kinds of errors. Normally, you wouldn't throw an error if a value is in the wrong range — you'd display a message directly to the user instead. However, this example demonstrates how to throw and catch an error from within a method. As you might expect, this application includes error handling to catch a number of errors.

Files needed: ThrowException.java

1. **Open the editor or IDE that you've chosen to use for this book.**

2. **Type the following code into the editor screen.**

```java
// Import the required API classes.
import java.util.Scanner;
import java.util.InputMismatchException;
import java.lang.IllegalArgumentException;

public class ThrowException
{
    public static void main(String[] args)
    {
        // Create the scanner.
        Scanner GetInput = new Scanner(System.in);

        try
        {
            // Ask the user for an input.
            System.out.print("Type a number between 1 and
            10: ");
            int TheNumber = GetInput.nextInt();

            // Determine if the input is in the correct range.
            if ((TheNumber >= 1) && (TheNumber <= 10))
                // If so, display it.
                System.out.println("TheNumber = " +
                TheNumber);
            else
                // If not, throw an error.
                throw new IllegalArgumentException(
                        "The value of TheNumber is: " +
                TheNumber);
        }
        catch (InputMismatchException |
            IllegalArgumentException e)
        {
            // Determine whether there is error information
            // to display and output it.
            if (e.getMessage() != null)
                System.out.println("Please provide a
            value" +
                        " between 1 and 10!\n" +
            e.getMessage());
            else
                System.out.println("Please provide a
                value" +
                        " between 1 and 10!");
            return;
        }
    }
}
```

This example asks the user for an input between 1 and 10, and it then displays the number onscreen. Of course, the user could type something other than a number, which means that you must catch the InputMismatchException. The example provides the same sort of catch clause that you've seen in other examples in this chapter to handle this particular error.

In addition, the input number might not be between 1 and 10. Java can't detect this second error. The application detects the range of numbers by using an if statement. When the number is out of the specified range, the application throws an IllegalArgumentException, which is a specific kind of exception. The application could have used a simple Exception, but it's always better to throw a specific exception whenever possible to make the error easier to catch.

Notice that this example does something new: It uses a single catch clause to catch multiple exceptions. All you need to do to use this technique in your own applications is to separate the exceptions by using the or (|) operator.

3. **Save the code to disk using the filename ThrowException.java.**

4. **In your command prompt, type** javac ThrowException.java **and press Enter.**

   The compiler compiles your application and creates a .class file from it.

5. **Type** java ThrowException **and press Enter.**

   The application asks you to type a number between 1 and 10.

6. **Type the letter** C **and press Enter.**

   You see the expected error output shown in Figure 8-9.

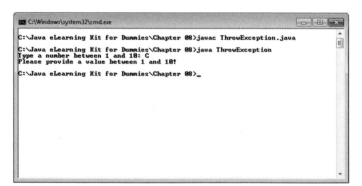

Figure 8-9

7. **Perform Steps 5 and 6 using the number 22 as the input.**

   You see the same error, but this time with additional information, as shown in Figure 8-10.

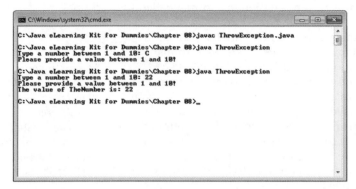

Figure 8-10

8. **Perform Steps 5 and 6 using the number 5 as the input.**

   This time the application displays the anticipated output, as shown in Figure 8-11.

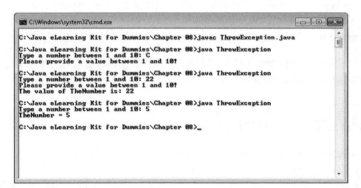

Figure 8-11

Passing errors to the caller

The examples in this book are just starting to get to the point where you're calling methods from `main()`. The `main()` method is always the top level of your application. As you call methods, the methods that you call form additional levels. For example, a method called from `main()` would be at the second level of your application. (See the example in the earlier "Using

Optional objects to avoid exceptions" exercise of this chapter.) If that method had to call another method, that method would be at the third level, and so on. Most applications are made up of many levels of calls. In fact, when you see an exception onscreen, it actually displays a list of the methods that called the current method in a format called the *call stack*.

Handling errors is an essential part of good programming practice. If you want robust applications that don't constantly crash, you need to provide good error handling. However, trying to handle an error when you don't have enough information to handle that error is also a problem. When your code attempts to fix an error at too low a level, it hides the error from a level that could possibly fix it. Yes, you want to fix an error at the lowest possible level, but not at the expense of providing a repair that could actually end up hiding something more serious.

LINGO

The **call stack** is a listing of methods and the order in which they are called by other methods. Knowing the call stack can help you locate the source of a potential error when it doesn't happen at the current level of the application.

When you find that a particular level of an application doesn't have the required resources, information, privileges, user access, or some other item needed to handle an error, then you issue a `throw` statement with the appropriate exception object. The previous level of the application will receive the exception and determine whether it can handle it. However, if the `main()` method receives the exception, then you must determine what to do with the error, or the application will crash. It's generally considered bad programming practice to simply let the application crash — you need to come up with some way to deal with errors that the application encounters.

Required error handling

Java provides two kinds of exceptions: checked (those monitored by the JRE) and unchecked (those that aren't monitored by the JRE). All the exceptions in the chapter so far are unchecked exceptions. You have the option of handling an unchecked exception. However, Java forces you to handle a checked exception. Your code won't even compile if you try to use a method that has a checked exception associated with it.

LINGO

A **checked exception** is one that the JRE is told by the class definition to monitor. The JRE forces the user of the class to provide handling for the exception to ensure that the class performs reliably.

All kinds of odd details are associated with checked and unchecked exceptions. An easy way to know whether an exception is checked is to know the parent class. All exceptions that are subclassed from the `Error` or `RuntimeException` classes are unchecked — every other exception is checked. The best practice is to handle every exception in your application, and you won't have to worry whether an exception is checked or unchecked. A great developer always handles potential errors — that's the bottom line.

In the following example, you create a class that relies on a checked exception. The class doesn't actually use this exception; this is simply a demonstration of how the Catch or Specify requirement works. After you create this class, you create an application that uses the class. When you initially create the application, you do so without exception handling so you can see how the compiler reacts to the lack of exception handling. The application then adds the required exception handling and you test it out.

Files needed: `RequiredException.java` *and* `UseRequiredException.java`

1. **Open the editor or IDE that you've chosen to use for this book.**

2. **Type the following code into the editor screen.**

```
// Import the required API classes.
import java.util.Scanner;
import java.util.
        InputMismatchException;
import java.io.IOException;

public class RequiredException
{
    public void DoDisplay()
        throws
        InputMismatchException,
        IOException
    {
        // Create the scanner.
        Scanner GetInput = new Scanner(System.in);

        // Ask the user for an input.
        System.out.print("Type a number between 1 and
            10: ");
        int TheNumber = GetInput.nextInt();
```

GO ONLINE

You really don't need to know too many details about the whole checked and unchecked requirement except that some exceptions are checked, and the compiler will tell you if you haven't handled them in your code. In this case, you simply add the required `catch` clause to your code. However, if you really do want to know how things work at a deeper level, you can read about this requirement at `http://docs.oracle.com/javase/tutorial/essential/exceptions/catchOrDeclare.html`. There's a lot of controversy about required error handling. You can read a simple statement of the controversy at `http://docs.oracle.com/javase/tutorial/essential/exceptions/runtime.html`. Unfortunately, this short article doesn't really discuss all the particulars of the controversy or provide you with examples. One of the best extended discussions of the topic (complete with examples) is at `http://tutorials.jenkov.com/java-exception-handling/checked-or-unchecked-exceptions.html`.

```
// Determine if the input is in the correct range.
if ((TheNumber >= 1) && (TheNumber <= 10))

   // If so, display it.
   System.out.println("TheNumber = " +
   TheNumber);
else

   // If not, throw an error.
   throw new IOException(
        "The value of TheNumber is: " +
   TheNumber);
   }
}
```

This example doesn't include a main() method, so you can't execute it as an application. This class simply contains a public method called DoDisplay() that you can access from other applications. When you call DoDisplay() from another application, it obtains input from the user, determines whether the input is in the desired range, and then outputs the number or raises an exception depending on whether the user has provided the correct information.

Notice that the method includes a new clause, throws. If you create a method that has the potential to throw an exception, you should always include the throws clause to tell other developers about the need to provide exception handling. This method can throw an InputMismatchException when the user types something other than a number. In addition, it can throw an IOException when the number is in the wrong range.

The code uses an IOException for demonstration purposes only. You really wouldn't use this kind of exception for the error that DoDisplay() could encounter. The IOException is a checked exception, so the example uses it to demonstrate how checked exceptions work.

3. **Save the code to disk using the filename RequiredException.java.**

4. **In your command prompt, type** javac RequiredException.java **and press Enter.**

The compiler compiles your application and creates a .class file from it.

5. **Create a new class named** UseRequiredException **by using the editor or IDE that you've chosen to use for this book.**

This new class must appear in the same folder as the RequiredException class that you created in Step 2.

6. **Type the following code into the editor screen.**

```
public class UseRequiredException
{
    public static void main(String[] args)
    {
        // Create the required object.
        RequiredException ThisTest = new
            RequiredException();

        // Use the DoDisplay() method to display a value.
        ThisTest.DoDisplay();
    }
}
```

This example simply creates an instance of the RequiredException class named ThisTest. It then uses ThisTest to access DoDisplay() to display a number onscreen.

Notice that you don't see any import statement in this part of the example. That's because the RequiredException class appears in the same folder as the UseRequiredException application. When two classes appear in the same folder, you don't have to import the first class to use it in the second class.

7. **Type** javac UseRequiredException.java **and press Enter.**

The compiler raises the error shown in Figure 8-12 to tell you that you must provide error handling for the DoDisplay() method.

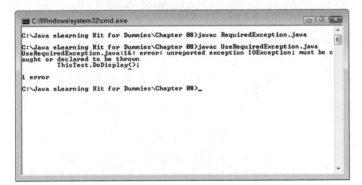

Figure 8-12

8. **Make the following changes (shown in bold) to the** UseRequired Exception **class.**

```
// Import the required API classes.
import java.io.IOException;
import java.util.InputMismatchException;

public class UseRequiredException
{
    public static void main(String[] args)
    {
        // Create the required object.
        RequiredException ThisTest = new
          RequiredException();

        // Attempt to perform the task.
        try
        {
            // Use the DoDisplay() method to display a
          value.
            ThisTest.DoDisplay();
        }
        catch (InputMismatchException | IOException e)
        {
            // Determine whether there is error information
            // to display and output it.
            if (e.getMessage() != null)
                System.out.println("Please provide a
                value" +
                        " between 1 and 10!\n" +
            e.getMessage());
            else
                System.out.println("Please provide a
                value" +
                        " between 1 and 10!");
            return;
        }
    }
}
```

The example now includes the required error handling. Because it's possible to handle both exceptions using a single message, the application places both in the same `catch` clause.

9. **Type** javac UseRequiredException.java **and press Enter.**

The compiler compiles your application and creates a `.class` file from it.

10. **Type** java UseRequiredException **and press Enter.**

    The application asks you to type any number.

11. **Type the letter** C **and press Enter.**

    You see the expected error output. (Refer to Figure 8-9.)

12. **Perform Steps 10 and 11 using the number 22 as the input.**

    You see the same error, but this time with some additional information. (Refer to Figure 8-10.)

13. **Perform Steps 10 and 11 using the number 5 as the input.**

    This time the application displays the anticipated output. (Refer to Figure 8-11.)

Modify the RequiredException class so that it relies on the Illegal ArgumentException. Make the required changes to the UseRequired Exception application as well. Even though the IllegalArgument Exception isn't a checked exception, you should still provide error handling for it.

Summing Up

Here are the key points you learned about in this chapter:

- ✔ Syntactical (syntax) errors normally result from writing Java code incorrectly.

- ✔ Semantic errors normally result when you write the Java code correctly but apply Java programming concepts incorrectly.

- ✔ Logical errors normally result when the Java code is both written and applied correctly, but the implementation of the task is incorrect.

- ✔ Syntactical errors are the easiest to fix, semantic errors come next, and logical errors are the hardest to fix.

- ✔ Trapping an error means detecting an exception object and doing something with it.

- ✔ Handling an error means resolving the exception by displaying a message to the user or relying on other means.

- ✔ All applications should include the appropriate error handling code.

- ✔ When providing complete error handling, always handle the most specific errors first, and then move on to less specific errors.

✔ Use `Optional` objects to help reduce the potential for errors in your application.

✔ Provide specific information whenever possible when throwing an error.

✔ Java makes it possible to catch multiple exceptions using a single `catch` clause.

✔ When the current level of the application can't handle an exception, make sure you pass it up to the next level.

✔ Checked exceptions ensure that anyone using the associated method provides the required error handling.

Try-it-yourself lab

For more practice with the features covered in this chapter, try the following exercise on your own:

1. **Open the UseAMenu03 application supplied with the source code for this book.**

2. **Fix the errors in this application.**

   This means removing the comments from in front of the `break` clauses.

3. **Compile the application.**

4. **Run the application.**

   Does the application run without error?

5. **Determine what sort of exception handling this application generates.**

   As a hint, try starting the application and simply pressing Enter at the prompt.

6. **Add the required error handling.**

   Make sure you add generic error handling for those situations where you can't anticipate what the user will do.

7. **Compile the application.**

8. **Run the application.**

   Does the error handling work as anticipated?

Know this tech talk

background processing: Tasks that an application performs behind the scenes. For example, when a user requests that an application print a document, the application performs this task in the background while the user continues to interact with the application in the foreground.

call stack: A listing of the methods that preceded the current method. Each method called the next in line in order to get to the current level of the call stack. Most applications have a large number of levels, so the call stack is an essential tool in fixing application errors.

checked exception: An exception that the JRE forces the user of a class to handle. The compiler actually checks to verify that you have provided handling for the exception and won't create a `.class` file for you if you don't provide the handling. The reason to use checked exceptions is to ensure that a class and the objects created from it perform reliably.

error: Any unexpected or unanticipated application behavior, including actions or results that fall outside the realm of expected application output.

error handling: The act of resolving an exception that the application has trapped by displaying a message to the user or taking other action.

error trapping: The act of detecting an exception and passing this information to a `catch` statement that resolves the correct exception object.

exception: A special object that defines an error condition within an application. The exception tells where the error has happened and what sort of error has happened. In some cases, the exception may provide additional bits of information that the recipient can use to resolve the error.

foreground processing: Priority tasks that an application performs as part of interacting with the user (including the system). For example, the user interface for any application is a foreground processing task. In most cases, foreground processing occurs at a higher priority than background processing to ensure that the application can meet user demands in a timely manner.

parse: The act of interpreting input and producing an output based on that input. For example, when a programmer provides code to a Java compiler, the compiler produces Java byte code as output. Likewise, when a user provides a numeric string as input, a parser can produce a numeric value as output.

throw: The act of creating an exception object and passing it to the caller of the current code. Throwing an exception means that the current code can't resolve the error and requires help to fix it. The exception object will help the caller understand what has happened and enable the caller to fix the problem in many situations.

Chapter 9
Creating and Using Classes

- Develop an understanding of class structure that *helps you create better classes.*

- Understand how variable scope *affects how and when you use variables in your application.*

- Begin writing classes that *demonstrate the full capabilities of class construction.*

- Design a test application that fully *demonstrates how to use a complete class definition.*

- Use anonymous classes to *perform ad hoc tasks that don't require the use of formal classes.*

- Use lambda expressions to *perform tasks using significantly less code* than more traditional techniques.

1. How does class inheritance affect the way I write my classes?

Inheriting from another class can greatly reduce the amount of work you need to do, as described on page

2. When I create new classes and use them in my application, is it possible to access methods, properties, and other features of the superclass?

Java makes it possible for your class to see the features of the superclass, as described on page

3. What precisely is a default scope?

The default scope is the visibility of a class feature within a given circumstance without using any special modifiers, as summarized on page

4. Why would I ever want to modify the default scope?

Modifying the default scope makes it possible to hide features from prying eyes and makes it possible to create classes that are less likely to fail due to security and reliability concerns, as shown on page

5. When would I need to create more than one *constructor* — the element that allows for use of special variables or performs other setups — for my class?

Using multiple constructors makes it possible to create versions of a class with extended functionality or reduced coding requirements, as defined on page

6. Is it possible to get the functionality of a class without going through the trouble of creating one?

Anonymous classes make it possible to create ad hoc classes that you use for a single purpose without defining the class formally, as shown on page

7. How can I create a concise anonymous class that has just one method?

Lambda expressions provide the means to define a special kind of anonymous class that has only one functional interface and one method, as described on page

You probably realize by now that you've been creating classes in every chapter of this book. It's impossible to create a Java application without creating a class. In fact, you created an example in the "Required error handling" section of Chapter 8, where you accessed the features of a simple class from another Java class. However, the ways in which you've used classes so far have been relatively simplistic — Java is capable of considerably more complexity, which is the point of this chapter.

Classes have a specific structure. Just as the blueprints used to create buildings have certain features and follow predefined formats, so do the classes you create. Otherwise, the JRE could never interpret your design and use the class to construct objects within an application.

As part of designing a class, you must also understand how to show and hide data and code elements in your class, which means that this chapter must provide some additional information about scope. Using scope correctly makes your class more secure because you can hide data from prying eyes. A properly scoped variable also makes the class more reliable by making it less likely that someone will be able to fill the variable with incorrect data. Another good reason to employ scope is to make your class easier to use by hiding details that other developers don't need to see in order to use the class.

Java has had *anonymous inner classes* (usually shortened to *anonymous classes*) to create ad hoc classes where a formal class description is unnecessary or overkill. For example, you might use an anonymous class to change the standard behavior of a formal class in just one instance. Using an anonymous class makes your code cleaner, shorter, and easier to understand. It also helps optimize the code in many cases so it conceivably runs faster. Java 8 also includes a new feature called *lambda expressions* that make the code even shorter. A lambda expression is a special kind of anonymous class that contains just one functional interface and one method, so you can describe what to do with a bare minimum of code. The result is that anyone viewing your code will be able to focus on what the code does rather than the structure around the code.

Understanding the Structure of Classes

A building contractor can understand a blueprint designed by an architect because both of them use the same set of rules and conventions. When you create a class, you're the architect. The blueprint you create must communicate your ideas to the computer, which plays the role of the builder. For this communication to work, you must both use the same rules and conventions. The following sections describe the rules and conventions for creating classes in Java by dividing the task into functional areas, such as writing a method.

Calling methods

You've worked with a number of method types in the book. However, you really haven't seen how methods are put together until now. A *method* describes an action that the object can perform. Even though most of the class examples to this point have had just one method, a class can have any number of methods that it requires.

In looking at methods, note that every method can have the following parts:

✔ **Modifiers (optional):** The modifiers change the way the class behaves. For example, if you make a class `private`, the method is visible only to other methods within the class. When you create an object from the class, the object's user can't access the private method.

A method can have more than one modifier attached to it. For example, you can use `public` and `static` together to make the method visible outside of the class as part of the class itself, rather than as part of an object created from the class. The `main()` method found in most of the examples so far in the book is both `public` and `static`.

LINGO

A **convention** is an agreement or a contract between you and the JRE. In fact, when you read other documentation, it may actually use the term *contract* to express the idea of a convention. No matter what term you use, the convention expresses the responsibilities of each party in defining the class and building it as an object. In some respects, you can also view a convention as a custom — the set of practices that Java developers have created for developing classes. There isn't a right or wrong about the conventions that Java uses; this set of practices is simply what Java developers have created over time as the most efficient way of defining a class.

EXTRA INFO

You can't call a non-static method from a static method. The non-static method is associated with an *object* — an instance of the class — while the static method is associated with the class itself. To access the non-static method, you must create an object. You can, however, access a static method from a non-static method. The static method always exists, even before the object is created. Therefore, the static method is always accessible.

✔ **Return type (required):** Every method has a return type. The return type defines the information that the method returns to the caller after it has completed its work. When you don't have anything to return to the caller, you set the return type as `void`. For example, the `main()` method has a return type of `void` because it doesn't return anything to the caller.

A method can have only one return type, even if that return type is a complex type that can contain multiple values.

✔ **Method name (required):** Every method must have a name. Otherwise, you couldn't call the method. Here are some additional considerations for the method name:

- The method name must begin with a letter — any letter will do.

- You can't begin a method name with a number or special character.

- Numbers can appear anywhere else in the method name.

- The only special character you can use is the underline (_). For example, a method name can't include an ampersand (&).

✔ **Argument list (optional):** If the method requires information from the caller to perform a task, you can supply one or more arguments (or *parameters* as some people call them) in a list contained within parentheses. Here are some additional considerations for arguments:

- The argument includes the argument type followed by the argument name. For example, if you want to supply an `int` value called `MyInt`, type **int MyInt.**

- Argument names and types follow the same constraints as any other variable.

- You must separate multiple arguments with commas. For example, if the `MyMethod()` method requires an `int` called `MyInt` and a `float` called `MyFloat`, the argument list would be `MyMethod(int MyInt, float MyFloat)`.

- If there are no arguments, the method name must be followed by a pair of empty parentheses.

EXTRA INFO

Using camelcase is the standard convention for creating methods and variable names, but the Java compiler doesn't enforce this convention. *Camelcase* is where you begin each word in a method or variable name with a capital letter, except for the first word. The first word is always lowercase. For example, if you create a method named `checkForDoubles()`, the convention is to start the first word, `check`, as lowercase, but to show `For` and `Doubles` with initial capitalization. Some developers, including myself, prefer *pascalcase*, where every word of a method or variable name is capitalized. In this case, `CheckForDoubles()` would have every word capitalized. Using pascalcase for the methods and variables you create helps differentiate them from methods and variables that are part of the Java Application Programming Interface (API). No matter which casing you use, you must apply it consistently. Remember that Java treats `checkForDoubles()` as a different method from `CheckForDoubles()`.

✔ **Exception list (optional):** The exception list defines which exceptions a method is likely to encounter and throw. The exception list begins with the keyword `throws`, followed by a list of exception classes. You've already seen an example of how this feature works in the "Required error handling" section in Chapter 8.

✔ **Method body (required):** A method isn't much use without code that tells what tasks to perform. The method body always appears within curly braces (`{ }`).

Using the preceding rules, the shortest method declaration you can create is one that uses the default scope, is accessible as part of an object, accepts no parameters, returns no values, and contains no code. Even though the following method is completely useless, it will compile, and you can call it in your code:

```
void MyMethod()
{
}
```

The sections that follow demonstrate more practical methods than `MyMethod()`, but it's important to know the absolute minimum amount of code needed to create a method. The main reason to use methods is to group lines of code together in such a manner that they perform a single defined task. In addition, you should make a method small enough so that the code it contains is easily understood by you and everyone who follows you.

Allocating properties

One of the issues that tends to confuse many new Java developers (and some experienced Java developers as well), is the concept of properties in Java. Some languages have a formal mechanism for working with properties, but Java doesn't provide this mechanism. In addition, there's some level of confusion about the terminology that Java uses for specific program elements that are related to properties. This section uses a specific set of terms that reflect the terminology used by the majority of Java developers, but you should expect to see other usages as you look around online.

A *property* is a value that you can access as part of the class or the object created from the class. You use properties to provide access to a global variable, which is also called a *field*. The "Long versus long" section in Chapter 3 contains the first example of a global variable in the book. The best practice is to always make fields `private` and then rely on special getter and setter methods to access them. The combination of field, getter, and setter is a property in Java. Here's a typical example that uses an `int` named `MyInt`.

```
// Create the MyInt field.
private int MyInt = 0;

// Obtain the current value of MyInt.
public int getMyInt()
{
    return MyInt;
}

// Set a new value for MyInt.
public void setMyInt(int MyInt)
{
    this.MyInt = MyInt;
}
```

In this example, the code declares a private variable, MyInt, and assigns it a value of 0. The getter, getMyInt(), provides the current value of MyInt to the caller, while the setter, setMyInt(), lets the caller change the value of MyInt. The reason you want to use properties is so that you have better control over how a caller interacts with MyInt. By using setters and getters, you make it possible to do tasks such as verify the range of values that a caller provides and then throw an exception when the input is incorrect in some way.

To protect a field from damage, such as receiving incorrect data values, you must declare it as private and rely on getters and setters to access it. The getters and setters must provide any checks required to ensure the caller interacts with the private field correctly.

LINGO

A **field** is a kind of global variable that holds data that the class or object manages. Some developers extend the term *field* to include all sorts of other meanings, but this book uses *field* to specifically mean a globally accessible variable.

LINGO

Getters and **setters** are special methods that provide access to fields. Using getters and setters helps you control field access and reduces the chance that the field will be used incorrectly.

Considering inheritance

Just as you inherited specific features from your parents, every class you create inherits certain features from a parent or superclass. When you don't define a specific inheritance for a class, it uses the Object class as its superclass.

Inheritance is important because it helps define the characteristics of any class you create, and using the right class as a parent can save considerable time when you're creating a new class. In addition, you can access features of the parent class by using the super keyword. The best way to see how inheritance works is to play with it in an example.

In the following example, you create a class that tells you about its class name and the name of its superclass. The purpose of this example is to help you understand how inheritance works by using a simple set of classes.

Files needed: ParentClass.java, SimpleClass.java, *and* UseSimple Class.java

LINGO

A **superclass** is the parent class of the current class. Every class you create has a superclass (parent class). The default superclass is Object, but you can inherit from many other classes in the Java API to produce some amazing results.

1. **Open the editor or IDE that you've chosen to use for this book.**

2. **Type the following code into the editor screen.**

```
// Import the required API classes.
import java.lang.String;

public class ParentClass
{
    // Create a method that returns a special string.
    public String GetClassName()
    {
        return "This is the ParentClass";
    }
}
```

The example begins with the parent class, the one that the SimpleClass that you'll define next inherits from. Notice that ParentClass has just one method, GetClassName(), that returns a String to the caller. As with most of the classes in the book so far, ParentClass inherits from Object, which is the default inherited class.

3. **Using the standard commands of your editor or IDE, save this file as ParentClass.java.**

4. **In your command prompt, type** javac ParentClass.java **and press Enter.**

The compiler compiles your application and creates a .class file from it.

5. **Create a new class named SimpleClass by using the editor or IDE that you've chosen to use for this book.**

This new class must appear in the same folder as the ParentClass class that you created in Step 2.

6. **Type the following code into the editor screen.**

```
// Import the required API classes.
import java.lang.String;

public class SimpleClass extends ParentClass
{
    // Override the same method in the parent class and
    // output a special string.
    public String GetClassName()
    {
        return "This is the SimpleClass";
    }

    // Provide the means for getting the string from
    // the parent class.
    public String GetSuperClass()
    {
        return super.GetClassName();
    }
}
```

This class inherits all the functionality of ParentClass. Notice the use of the extends keyword in this class declaration. A Java class can inherit from only one parent.

The next thing you should notice is that this class also has a GetClassName() method that returns a String to the caller. The String is different, but otherwise, the method is completely the same. This technique is called *overriding the method*. You override a method when you want to provide a different behavior for the method in the child class.

LINGO

Overriding a method means to supply a different version of a method in a class that inherits from a parent class. In many cases, the parent class has only a simple method that doesn't specifically address the needs of the child class.

Now that SimpleClass has an implementation of GetClassName(), you may think it's impossible to access this method in ParentClass. Fortunately, Java has a way to get around this problem. Look at GetSuperClass() and you see the super keyword used as a means of accessing GetClassName() in ParentClass from SimpleClass.

7. **Using the standard commands of your editor or IDE, save this file as SimpleClass.java.**

8. **In your command prompt, type** javac SimpleClass.java **and press Enter.**

The compiler compiles your application and creates a .class file from it.

9. **Create a new class named `UseSimpleClass` using the editor or IDE that you've chosen to use for this book.**

   This new class must appear in the same folder as the `SimpleClass` class that you created in Step 6.

10. **Type the following code into the editor screen.**

```
// Import the required API classes.
import java.lang.String;

public class UseSimpleClass
{
    public static void main(String[] args)
    {
        // Create an instance of the simple class.
        SimpleClass Test = new SimpleClass();

        // Display the SimpleClass string.
        System.out.println(Test.GetClassName());

        // Display the string from the parent class.
        System.out.println(Test.GetSuperClass());
    }
}
```

   This example simply creates an instance of the `SimpleClass` class named `Test`. It then uses `Test` to access the `GetClassName()` and `GetSuperClass()` methods to display the class names from `SimpleClass` and `ParentClass`.

By following this example carefully, you see how inheritance works at a simple level in Java. The remainder of the book will provide additional examples of inheritance because it's an important and somewhat complex topic (too complex to discuss in just one example).

11. **Save the file, then type** javac UseSimpleClass.java **in your command prompt and press Enter.**

   The compiler compiles your application and creates a `.class` file from it.

12. **Type** java UseSimpleClass **and press Enter.**

   You see the output shown in Figure 9-1. The application is able to display both the `SimpleClass` and `ParentClass` strings by relying on the inheritance features that Java provides.

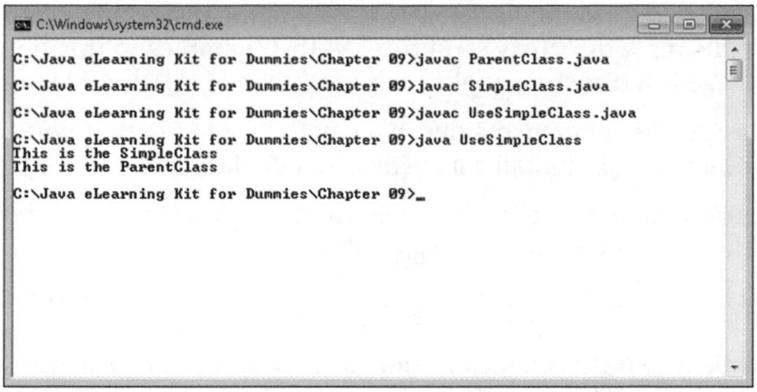

Figure 9-1

Defining Variable Scope

As your applications become more complex, the need to consider scope becomes ever more important. The main reason is that you can inadvertently introduce a bug into your application by not observing scoping rules. This can result from a field or other member being used incorrectly by the application (such as adding an incorrect data value or accessing a method at the wrong time or with incorrect data). In addition, incorrect scoping can leave the door open for outsiders to interact with your application in unforeseen ways (such as a virus). The following sections assume that you've already read the scoping information in the "Long versus long" section in Chapter 3.

Considering default scope

The default scope occurs when you don't specifically assign a scope to a class element. Because many Java developers have no idea what the default scope is for some elements (and using a default scope means that your code isn't documented), it isn't used very often. Even so, you need to know what the default scope is for various elements because some Java developers do rely on it. However, before you can understand the default scope, you need to consider *visibility* — the measure of which application elements can see a member. Java provides the following levels of visibility (in general order of encapsulation):

✔ **Package:** The container used to hold a number of classes. When working with a simple directory structure, as the examples in this book do, the package is a directory that holds a number of .class files.

✔ **Class:** A class usually resides in a single .java file that you compile into a .class file. It contains a single class declaration.

✔ **Method:** An element can reside in the class or as part of a method. The method acts as a container to hold the element.

✔ **Block:** An element can reside within a code block, such as a for loop.

Scope partially depends on the location used to declare an element. For example, a variable that's defined within a block (such as a for loop) is visible only within that block. When you try to use the variable outside of the block, Java displays an exception. Taking visibility into account, Table 9-1 describes the various levels of scope within the Java environment.

Table 9-1	Java Scoping Rules			
Visibility	*private*	*(default)*	*protected*	*public*
Accessible from the class	X	X	X	X
Accessible from the package		X	X	X
Accessible from any child class			X	X
Accessible anywhere				X

Table 9-1 shows how the default scope fits into the scheme of things. For example, if you declare a method by using the default scope, any method can use it as long as it resides in the same package. In addition, if you create a class that inherits from the class containing the method, the subclass can use the method as long as it resides in the same package. However, if the subclass exists outside the current package, it can't use the method. In short, the default scope is a little more restrictive than the protected scope but less restrictive than the private scope.

In the following example, you create a parent class that has methods that have a private, default, protected, and public scope. In the same folder, you create a child class that attempts to access these methods. In a different folder, you create another child class that attempts to access these methods as well (so you can see the difference between default and private scoping). Finally, you add an application to test everything.

Files needed: ScopeParent.java, ScopeChild1.java, ScopeChild2. java, *and* TestScope.java

1. **Open the editor or IDE that you've chosen to use for this book.**

2. **Create a subdirectory in your project folder named** inside.

3. **Create a** .java **file in the** inside **subdirectory named** ScopeParent.java.

4. **Type the following code into the editor screen.**

```java
// Define the package for this class.
package inside;

public class ScopeParent
{
    // Create a private method.
    private void PrivateMethod()
    {
        System.out.println("The parent's private
            method.");
    }

    // Create a default method.
    void DefaultMethod()
    {
        System.out.println("The parent's default
            method.");
    }

    // Create a protected method.
    protected void ProtectedMethod()
    {
        System.out.println("The parent's protected
            method.");
    }

    // Create a public method.
    public void PublicMethod()
    {
        System.out.println("The parent's public
            method.");
    }
}
```

This is the first time you've seen the `package` keyword used. In this case, the `package` keyword tells you that this file exists in the `inside` subdirectory. As you begin writing more complex Java, you'll find that you use the `package` keyword for nearly every class you create to ensure the class resides in a specific package.

The `ScopeParent` class is defined as `public`, but you could also define it as a default scope class. Inside this class, you find various methods, each of which relies on a different scope.

Notice that the default scope method, `DefaultMethod()`, is the only one that doesn't include a scope keyword. Leaving out the scope keyword always defines an element that uses the default scope.

5. **Save this file as `ScopeParent.java` in the `inside` directory.**

6. **In your command prompt, type** javac inside/ScopeParent.java **and press Enter.**

   The compiler compiles your application and creates a .class file from it.

7. **Create a .java file in the `inside` subdirectory named `ScopeChild1`. java by using the editor or IDE that you've chosen to use for this book.**

8. **Type the following code into the editor screen.**

```java
// Define the package for this class.
package inside;

public class ScopeChild1 extends ScopeParent
{
    // Access the private method.
    public void UsePrivate1()
    {
        super.PrivateMethod();
    }

    // Access the default method.
    public void UseDefault1()
    {
        super.DefaultMethod();
    }

    // Access the protected method.
    public void UseProtected1()
    {
        super.ProtectedMethod();
    }
```

```
    // Access the public method.
    public void UsePublic1()
    {
        super.PublicMethod();
    }
}
```

As with the `ScopeParent.java` file, this class defines itself as belonging to the inside package. The class tries to use each of the methods in the parent class by accessing them with the `super` keyword.

9. **Using the standard commands of your editor or IDE, save this file as `ScopeChild1.java` in the `inside` directory.**

10. **In your command prompt, type** javac inside/ScopeChild1.java **and press Enter.**

    At this point, you see an error message telling you that you can't access the private member, `PrivateMethod()`, of the `ScopeParent` class, as shown in Figure 9-2. Java never allows you to access the private members of a superclass from the subclass.

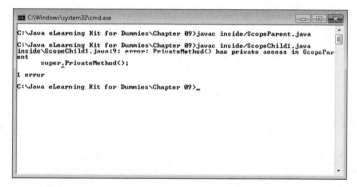

Figure 9-2

11. **Edit the `ScopeChild1` class to remove the `UsePrivate1()` method (delete all of the code shown below).**

    ```
    // Access the private method.
    public void UsePrivate1()
    {
        super.PrivateMethod();
    }
    ```

12. **Save the file, then type** javac inside/ScopeChild1.java **in your command prompt and press Enter.**

    The compiler compiles your application and creates a `.class` file from it.

13. **Create a subdirectory in your project folder named `outside`.**

14. **Create a `.java` file in the `outside` subdirectory named `ScopeChild2.java` by using the editor or IDE that you've chosen to use for this book.**

15. **Type the following code into the editor screen.**

```
// Define the package for this class.
package outside;

//Import the required application classes.
import inside.ScopeParent;

public class ScopeChild2 extends ScopeParent
{
    // Access the default method.
    public void UseDefault2()
    {
        super.DefaultMethod();
    }

    // Access the protected method.
    public void UseProtected2()
    {
        super.ProtectedMethod();
    }

    // Access the public method.
    public void UsePublic2()
    {
        super.PublicMethod();
    }
}
```

`ScopeChild1` and `ScopeChild2` have some interesting differences. First, notice that the `package` declaration defines this particular package as `outside`, not `inside`. Second, because this is part of the `outside` package, you must import `ScopeParent` before you can use it. `ScopeChild2` can't see `ScopeParent` until you import it because the two `.class` files aren't in the same directory.

The example is essentially the same as `ScopeChild1` except that it doesn't attempt to access the `PrivateMethod()` of the `ScopeParent` class. You already know that it isn't possible to access this method because it isn't accessible in `ScopeChild1`.

16. **Using the standard commands of your editor or IDE, save this file as `ScopeChild2.java`.**

17. **In your command prompt, type** javac outside/ScopeChild2.java **and press Enter.**

You see an error message telling you that you can't access `DefaultMethod()` from `ScopeChild2`, as shown in Figure 9-3. Now you're seeing the true meaning of the scoping rules in Table 9-1. Even though `ScopeClass1` can access `DefaultMethod()` without problem, this same method is inaccessible outside of the package.

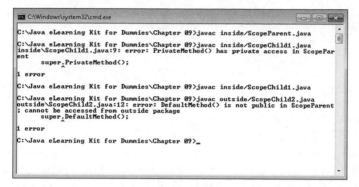

Figure 9-3

18. Edit the `ScopeChild2` class to remove the `UseDefault2()` method (delete all of the code shown below).

```
// Access the default method.
public void UseDefault2()
{
    super.DefaultMethod();
}
```

19. **Save the file and then type** javac outside/ScopeChild2.java **in your command prompt and press Enter.**

    The compiler compiles your application and creates a `.class` file from it.

20. **Create a new class named `TestScope` by using the editor or IDE that you've chosen to use for this book.**

    This new class must appear in the main folder of your application, not in either the `inside` or `outside` subdirectories.

21. **Type the following code into the editor screen.**

```
// Import the required application classes.
import inside.*;
import outside.ScopeChild2;

public class TestScope
{
    public static void main(String[] args)
    {
        // Create the required objects.
        ScopeChild1 Child1 = new ScopeChild1();
        ScopeChild2 Child2 = new ScopeChild2();

        // Use each of the accessible methods in Child1.
        Child1.UseDefault1();
        Child1.UseProtected1();
        Child1.UsePublic1();
```

```
        // Use each of the accessible methods in Child2.
        Child2.UseProtected2();
        Child2.UsePublic2();
    }
}
```

All the classes that this example uses reside in other directories as part of other packages. The application imports all the classes in the inside package by using the asterisk (*) wildcard character. The application specifically imports `outside.ScopeChild2`.

The example instantiates objects from both `ScopeChild1` (`Child1`) and `ScopeChild2` (`Child2`). The application then calls each of the accessible methods in these two objects.

22. Save the file, then type javac TestScope.java **in your command prompt and press Enter.**

The compiler compiles your application and creates a `.class` file from it.

23. Type java TestScope **and press Enter.**

Figure 9-4 shows the output. As you can see, the scoping rules work as expected to hide some items and make other items accessible. The same principles hold true when you're working with fields, getters, setters, and other class elements.

```
C:\Windows\system32\cmd.exe                                           — □ ▒

C:\Java eLearning Kit for Dummies\Chapter 09>javac inside/ScopeParent.java

C:\Java eLearning Kit for Dummies\Chapter 09>javac inside/ScopeChild1.java
inside\ScopeChild1.java:9: error: PrivateMethod() has private access in ScopePar
ent
        super.PrivateMethod();
             ^
1 error

C:\Java eLearning Kit for Dummies\Chapter 09>javac inside/ScopeChild1.java

C:\Java eLearning Kit for Dummies\Chapter 09>javac outside/ScopeChild2.java
outside\ScopeChild2.java:12: error: DefaultMethod() is not public in ScopeParent
; cannot be accessed from outside package
        super.DefaultMethod();
             ^
1 error

C:\Java eLearning Kit for Dummies\Chapter 09>javac TestScope.java

C:\Java eLearning Kit for Dummies\Chapter 09>java TestScope
The parent's default method.
The parent's protected method.
The parent's public method.
The parent's protected method.
The parent's public method.

C:\Java eLearning Kit for Dummies\Chapter 09>_
```

Figure 9-4

Set the `ScopeParent` class to use the default scope by removing the `public` keyword at the beginning of the class declaration. What happens to the application now that the entire `ScopeParent` class scope has changed? Feel free to continue experimenting with the three classes in this example to see what happens when you change the scoping rules for each of the classes.

Observing scope within a block

Developers often experience problems figuring out why an application is misbehaving when encountering a block access problem. The basic guideline is that any variable you create within a block is defined only within that block. For example, when you look at the following code, you see a typical block access scenario.

```
// Create a variable inside a block.
for (int i = 0; i < 10; i++)

   // Display the value of that variable.
   System.out.println("The value of i is: " + i);

// Access outside the block doesn't work.
System.out.println("The value of i is: " + i);
```

The example displays the value of i within the for loop (a type of block) without problem. However, trying to access i outside the block isn't acceptable because the variable isn't defined. The compiler will catch this error.

Another potential problem occurs when a variable is defined in the application and also within a block. Because this situation is likely to create problems, newer versions of Java won't allow the sort of code shown here:

```
public static void main(String[] args)
{
   // Define a variable.
   int i = 0;

   // Create a variable inside a block.
   for (int i = 0; i < 10; i++)

      // Display the value of that variable.
      System.out.println("The value of i is: " + i);

   // Access outside the block doesn't work.
   System.out.println("The value of i is: " + i);
}
```

The compiler won't always prevent you from shooting yourself in the foot. In many situations, the developer does something with the variable and doesn't understand the consequences. For example, the following code is perfectly legal in Java:

```
public static void main(String[] args)
{
   // Define a variable.
   int i = 0;
```

```
// Create a variable inside a block.
for (i = 0; i < 10; i++)

    // Display the value of that variable.
    System.out.println("The value of i is: " + i);

    // Access outside the block doesn't work.
    System.out.println("The value of i is: " + i);
}
```

The `for` loop displays the values 0 through 9 because of the condition within the `for` loop declaration. The final call to `System.out.println()` displays a value of 10, not 0 or 9 as some developers might expect. The `i++` part of the declaration occurs, and then the condition is evaluated, so the final value of `i` is 10, not 9 because it has to be 10 in order for the condition to become `false`. The point of this section is that you must consider how a block works with a variable in order to determine whether you can access the variable and what the value will contain on exit from the block.

Defining a Class with Event Support

You've seen a number of classes and class components in the chapter. For example, you've already seen how to create methods and properties. The previous sections have also demonstrated the importance of scope to your classes. However, so far you haven't seen any information about working with events and you really haven't seen a class of any complexity. The following sections introduce you to a class that uses events and because it uses events, requires a little more complex construction method.

Defining an event

An *event* is anything that happens within the class that the class must convey to the outside world. For example, when a user clicks a button, the button must tell the outside world that it has been clicked. Knowing that the button has been clicked allows other code to react to that event. The method that performs this task is known as an *event handler*.

LINGO

An **event** is an occurrence of a predefined action within a class, such as a button click, that the class must tell outsiders about.

In the following example, you create a class that defines an event. The event isn't useful by itself — it simply describes an action that can occur within a

class. The action need not even be specific —
you can create a generic event, as is the case in
this example that can define any action.

Files needed: MyEvent.java

1. **Open the editor or IDE that you've chosen**
   to use for this book.

2. **Type the following code into the editor screen.**

```
// Import the required API classes.
import java.util.EventObject;

// An event object contains the information required
// to describe the event.
public class MyEvent extends EventObject
{
    // The event object must include this special
    // constructor that accepts an object with
    // the event information in it.
    public MyEvent(Object EventArgs)
    {
        // Your code doesn't actually have to do
        // anything with the event; the superclass does.
        super(EventArgs);
    }
}
```

Any event definition you create must inherit from EventObject or
similar event-based class. Consequently, this class begins by importing
java.util.EventObject and then inheriting from it.

A *constructor* is a special method that
defines how a class should create an
object. The default constructor doesn't do
anything other than create the object, and it
takes no input arguments. A generic constructor does more than simply create the
object (for example, it can initialize variables), but it doesn't require any input
argument either. An event can't rely on
either a default or a generic constructor.
This is one case where you must create a special constructor that
accepts some sort of input. The example shows the simplest possible
implementation — it accepts an Object, EventArgs. Notice that the
constructor is the only method that doesn't require that you provide a
return value and it also has precisely the same name as the class.

LINGO

An **event handler** is a special
method that performs tasks based
on the occurrence of an event.

LINGO

A **constructor** is a special method
that doesn't have a return value. It
describes how to create an object
from the class. Constructors
always have the same name as
the class.

If you plan for your event to perform some special processing, you'd include it in the constructor or as part of other methods within the class. However, your class need not implement any special behavior to work. The example simply calls the parent class' constructor with `EventArgs` to accomplish the work it needs to do.

Unless you want to perform a lot of extra coding, your event class must call the parent class' constructor (as shown in this example) at some point. Otherwise, you need to implement all of the event behaviors in your code (a potentially messy and error-prone process).

3. **Using the standard commands of your editor or IDE, save this file as** MyEvent.java.

4. **In your command prompt, type** javac MyEvent.java **and press Enter.**

   The compiler compiles your application and creates a `.class` file from it.

Creating an event listener interface

When a class generates an event, there must be something to listen and react to the event. Otherwise, when the event is fired, nothing will happen. An event listener waits for an event to happen and then passes this information out to other classes by calling methods that have registered themselves with the event listener.

Unfortunately, you don't know precisely how everything is going to work until someone actually creates a class definition that uses the event. Your event requires a listener, but you don't know how to put it together. In short, you realize that there has to be an interface between the event and an event listener, but you don't know how to implement that interface. A special sort of class, called an *interface,* lets you tell Java that something is needed, but you don't know precisely what.

LINGO

An **event listener** waits for events to happen. When it detects an event, it tells any class that has registered itself with the event listener about the event. In short, an event listener is a manager that makes it possible to react to events within a class.

In the following example, you create an interface that describes the interaction required between a class that defines an event and one that uses the event. The interface doesn't provide an implementation; it merely describes what must happen.

Files needed: `MyEventListener.java`

1. **Open the editor or IDE that you've chosen to use for this book.**

2. **Type the following code into the editor screen.**

   ```
   // Import the required API classes.
   import java.util.EventListener;

   // An event listener listens for an event to occur.
   public interface MyEventListener extends EventListener
   {
       // When the event happens, the event listener tells
       // everyone about it.
       public void EventHappened(MyEvent Event);
   }
   ```

   Describing what an event listener interface does takes considerably longer than writing the event listener interface code. In this case, `MyEventListener` inherits from `EventListener`. It defines a single method, `EventHappened()`, that specifies a single method used to tell classes that an event has happened.

3. **Using the standard commands of your editor or IDE, save this file as `MyEventListener.java`.**

4. **In your command prompt, type** javac MyEventListener.java **and press Enter.**

   The compiler compiles your application and creates a `.class` file from it.

LINGO

An **interface** is a class that describes a relationship between a class and the outside world, without providing an implementation (functional code) of that relationship. Without any functional code, an interface can only tell how the relationship should look, not how it actually works.

Implementing the event as part of a class definition

At this point, you have an event and an event listener description. So, you have the resources for telling everyone that an event has occurred, but you have no mechanism to deliver or manage the event. An event class uses the event and the event interface, along with some management code, to make it possible to *fire* events (make them happen) and to manage a list of *event handlers* (classes that want to hear about the event and are listening for it).

In the following example, you create an interface that describes the interaction required between a class that defines an event and one that uses the event. The interface doesn't provide an implementation; it merely describes what must happen.

Files needed: `SampleEventClass.java`

1. Open the editor or IDE that you've chosen to use for this book.

2. Type the following code into the editor screen.

```
// Import the required API classes.
import javax.swing.event.EventListenerList;

// An event class manages the event. It provides the
// means for adding and removing listeners and also
// firing the event when it happens.
public class SampleEventClass
{
    // Create a variable to hold a list of listeners,
    // which are applications that want to know
    // about the event.
    protected EventListenerList ListenerList =
        new EventListenerList();

    // Add an event listener to the list.
    public void AddEventListener(MyEventListener
        Listener)
    {
        ListenerList.add(MyEventListener.class,
        Listener);
    }

    // Remove an event listener from the list.
    public void RemoveEventListener(MyEventListener
        Listener)
    {
        ListenerList.remove(MyEventListener.class,
        Listener);
    }

    // Fire the event, tell everyone that something has
    // happened.
    public void FireEvent(MyEvent Event)
```

```
{
    // The event manager must tell each of the
    // listeners in turn, so you need a list of
    // listeners.
    Object[] Listeners = ListenerList.
      getListenerList();

    // Process each of the event listeners in turn.
    for (int i = 0; i < Listeners.length; i+=2)
    {
        // An event list could contain any number of
        // events,so you need to ensure you
        // process only the listeners that want to
        // hear about this particular event.
        if (Listeners[i] == MyEventListener.class)
        {
          // Fire the EventHappened method using the
          // event argument supplied by the caller.
          ((MyEventListener)Listeners[i+1]).
        EventHappened(Event);
        }
    }
  }
}
```

More than one method can listen for events generated by your event class. As a result, you need some means of managing a list of these classes. You have a lot of options for performing this task at your disposal, but using `javax.swing.event.EventListenerList` is the easiest method available.

The example begins by creating an `EventListenerList`, `ListenerList`. It then provides methods for adding methods to (`AddEventListener()`) and removing methods from (`RemoveEventListener()`) the list. These methods rely on functionality provided as part of the `EventListenerList` class — you don't implement the functionality yourself.

The `FireEvent()` method is the centerpiece of this class. When this method is called, the caller is saying that an event has happened and that the object created from this call should tell everyone about it. The method takes one input, a `MyEvent` object, `Event`. This input argument says that a specific kind of event has happened.

To tell everyone who's said they want to know about the event, the `FireEvent()` method begins by obtaining the list of methods that appear in `ListenerList`. An odd aspect of `ListenerList` is that the entries appear in every other element. You don't need to worry about why this is the case — you simply have to know that it is. Consequently, the code creates a `for` loop that looks at every other element.

The list you create could contain any number of event listeners, each of which is waiting for a different event. The example ensures that the class of the event listener entry is precisely the same as the `MyEventListener.class`, so that you know it's the right kind of event listener. When this is the case, the code calls the `EventHappened()` method within that class to tell it that the event has happened.

3. **Using the standard commands of your editor or IDE, save this file as `SampleEventClass.java`.**

4. **In your command prompt, type** javac SampleEventClass.java **and press Enter.**

   The compiler compiles your application and creates a `.class` file from it.

Demonstrating use of the event in a class

You now have a means of using an event within a class. The example class isn't very complex. However, it does incorporate everything you've learned to date about creating classes, plus it adds the information you need to know in order to add events to a class. The following example shows a simple class that lets you create an event implementation and then interact with it in a meaningful way.

Files needed: `DemoClass.java`

1. **Open the editor or IDE that you've chosen to use for this book.**

2. **Type the following code into the editor screen.**

```
public class DemoClass
{
    // The event manager class isn't the same as an
    // event manager. DoEvents is the object that
    // actually manages the event for this class.
    private SampleEventClass DoEvents = new
        SampleEventClass();

    public DemoClass()
    {
        // You must add each object created from this class
        // to the event listener list. Each object will
        // receive a separate notification.
```

```
        DoEvents.AddEventListener(new MyEventListener()
        {
            public void EventHappened(MyEvent Event)
            {
               if ((int)Event.getSource() >= 4)
                   System.out.println("Number is too
        high!");

                if ((int)Event.getSource() <= 0)
                    System.out.println("Number is too
        low!");
            }
        });
    }

    // Create a field to manipulate for this class. The
    // field could represent any data.
    private int Value = 0;

    // Obtain the current value of the field.
    public int getValue()
    {
        return Value;
    }

    // Set the value of the field directly.
    public void setValue(int Value)
    {
        // Create an event object that contains
        // the value that the caller attempted to
        // use.
        MyEvent Event = new MyEvent(Value);

        // When the caller tries to set the value too
        // high or too low, the class must fire the
        // event. Otherwise, it can change the contents
        // of Value.
        if ((Value <= 3) & (Value > 0))
           this.Value = Value;
        else
           DoEvents.FireEvent(Event);
    }

    public void AddOne()
    {
        // Create an event object containing the
        // current contents of Value.
        MyEvent Event = new MyEvent(Value);

        // Make sure that Value isn't getting too
```

```
            // high.  If so, fire an event.
            if (Value <= 3)
                Value++;
            else
                DoEvents.FireEvent(Event);
        }

        public void SubtractOne()
        {
            // Create an event object containing the
            // current contents of Value.
            MyEvent Event = new MyEvent(Value);

            // Make sure that Value isn't getting too
            // low.  If so, fire an event.
            if (Value > 0)
                Value--;
            else
                DoEvents.FireEvent(Event);
        }
    }
```

The big thing is not to get overwhelmed by this class; take it one element at a time. The code begins by creating a `SampleEventClass` object, `DoEvents`, to manage the event that this class generates. You use `DoEvents` to interact with the events that this class generates in a meaningful way — a way that you'll discover later on.

The constructor comes next. Notice that this is a generic constructor — one that doesn't require any input arguments. However, it adds the instance of this class — the object created from `DemoClass` — to the event listener list by calling `DoEvents.AddEventListener()`. To make things easy for this example, the event handler appears directly as part of the method call. It's a call to `EventHappened()`, which takes an argument of the `MyEvent` type, `Event`. When the information contained within the event (obtained by calling `getSource()`) is greater than or equal to 4, the application displays a message that the number is too high. Likewise, an event value less than or equal to 0 generates a message saying that the number is too low.

This is an actual class that does something other than work with events. The next step is to create an `int` named `Value` with an initial value of `0`. The class manipulates the data in `Value` and generates events based on that content. The `getValue()` and `setValue()` methods are the getter and setter for `Value`. Notice that `setValue()` provides the special feature of checking the input value. When the input value is in the desired range, `setValue()` lets it pass. However, when the input value is outside of the desired range, rather than set the value, `setValue()` generates an event by calling `DoEvents.FireEvent()`. To make this call, setValue() must create a new MyEvent object, Event, that contains the incorrect value, Value. The event handler, EventHappened(), receives this information and displays the appropriate message.

The AddOne() method increments Value, while SubtractOne() decrements Value. Both of these methods also check Value for incorrect information and act accordingly.

3. **Using the standard commands of your editor or IDE, save this file as DemoClass.java.**

4. **In your command prompt, type** javac DemoClass.java **and press Enter.**

The compiler compiles your application and creates a .class file from it.

Using the Class with Events

At this point, you have a class to use. All you need to do is create an application to use it. In the following example, you create an application that exercises DemoClass.

Files needed: UseEvent.java

1. **Open the editor or IDE that you've chosen to use for this book.**

2. **Type the following code into the editor screen.**

```
public class UseEvent
{
    public static void main(String[] args)
    {
        // Create a copy of the demonstration class.
        DemoClass TestClass = new DemoClass();

        // Value will start at 0, so keep adding 1
        // until Value should equal 5.
        TestClass.AddOne();
        System.out.println(TestClass.getValue());
        TestClass.AddOne();
        System.out.println(TestClass.getValue());
        TestClass.AddOne();
        System.out.println(TestClass.getValue());
        TestClass.AddOne();
        System.out.println(TestClass.getValue());
        TestClass.AddOne();
        System.out.println(TestClass.getValue());
```

```
            // Now that Value is at 4 (we couldn't make it
            // equal 5), keep subtracting 1 until Value
            // should equal -1.
            TestClass.SubtractOne();
            System.out.println(TestClass.getValue());
            TestClass.SubtractOne();
            System.out.println(TestClass.getValue());
            TestClass.SubtractOne();
            System.out.println(TestClass.getValue());
            TestClass.SubtractOne();
            System.out.println(TestClass.getValue());
            TestClass.SubtractOne();
            System.out.println(TestClass.getValue());

            // Try setting the value directly.
            TestClass.setValue(3);
            System.out.println(TestClass.getValue());
            TestClass.setValue(5);
            System.out.println(TestClass.getValue());
            TestClass.setValue(-5);
            System.out.println(TestClass.getValue());
        }
    }
```

The application begins by creating a DemoClass object, TestClass. It then exercises the resulting object by testing all of its methods, properties, and events. The application begins by incrementing the value in TestClass until it exceeds the recommended value. Now that TestClass is at its limit, the application decrements the value it contains until it's too low. Finally, the application tries setting the value in TestClass directly. In short, TestClass demonstrates the implementation of a range check. You can't take it beyond the anticipated boundaries.

3. **Using the standard commands of your editor or IDE, save this file as UseEvent.java.**

4. **In your command prompt, type** javac UseEvent.java **and press Enter.**

   The compiler compiles your application and creates a .class file from it.

5. **Type** java UseEvent **and press Enter.**

   You see the output shown in Figure 9-5. Notice that the event handler generates a message every time the application tries to exceed the predefined range. In addition, the value remains at the last known good value.

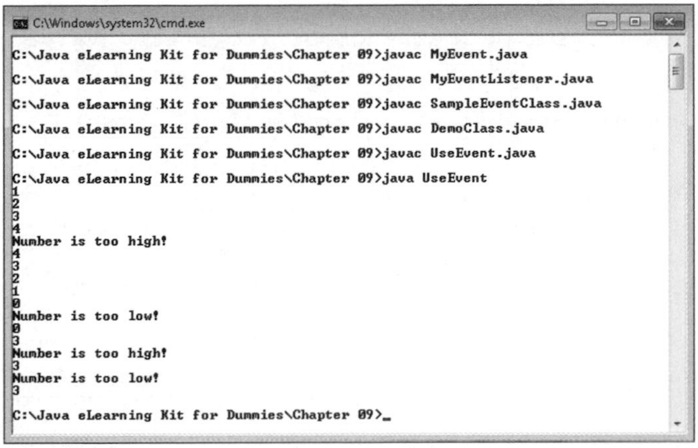

Figure 9-5

Working with Anonymous Inner Classes

Sometimes you don't really need to create a formal class definition in order to make your application work correctly. For example, it's possible to add event-handling support to an application without going through all the work you saw earlier in this chapter. An anonymous class can make your code easier to understand and more elegant. The example that follows shows a basic use of an anonymous class when working with an interface.

> **LINGO**
>
> An **anonymous inner class**, also known simply as an **anonymous class**, provides a shortcut method for creating classes that have limited functionality when a formal class declaration is unneeded or unwanted. For example, if you normally use the functionality of another class without modification but need to modify that functionality for just one purpose, then an anonymous class can be really helpful.

Files needed: `AnonymousClass.java`

1. **Open the editor or IDE that you've chosen to use for this book.**
2. **Type the following code into the editor screen:**

```
public class AnonymousClass
{
   // Create an interface that describes
   // something to do.
   interface DoSomething
   {
      // Specify a method for doing something.
      void SaySomething();
```

```
    // Specify a second method.
    void SaySomethingSpecific(String Value);
}

public static void main(String[] args)
{
    // Create an instance of the interface using an
    // anonymous class.
    DoSomething DoIt = new DoSomething()
    {
        // Define the functionality of the methods
        // within the interface.
        public void SaySomething()
        {
            System.out.println("I'm saying something!");
        }

        public void SaySomethingSpecific(String Value)
        {
            System.out.println(Value);
        }
    };

    // Actually use the anonymous class.
    DoIt.SaySomething();
    DoIt.SaySomethingSpecific("I'm saying something
        specific");
}
}
```

In this case, the example begins with an interface named DoSomething
that contains two methods: SaySomething() and SaySomething
Specific(). An interface doesn't provide any sort of implementation —
it simply states what needs to be done.

The main() method begins by creating an instance of DoSomething
that defines the implementation as an anonymous class. Notice that
you must define both methods contained in DoSomething, even if you
plan to use only one method in your application. The point is that there
is a class definition here, but it doesn't have a name. Notice that the
anonymous class declaration ends with a semicolon.

To use the anonymous class functionality, you call one of the methods
contained within the DoIt object as shown later in the code. If the
example didn't include the anonymous class, the code wouldn't compile
because you'd only have an interface and it isn't possible to instantiate
an interface.

3. **Using the standard commands of your editor or IDE, save this file as** `AnonymousClass.java`.

4. **In your command prompt, type** javac AnonymousClass.java **and press Enter.**

   The compiler compiles your application and creates a `.class` file from it.

5. **Type** java AnonymousClass **and press Enter.**

   You see the output shown in Figure 9-6. As you can see, the code calls each of the anonymous class methods in turn.

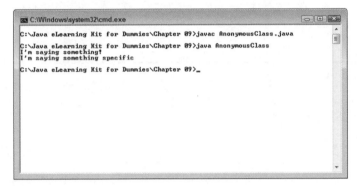

Figure 9-6

Working with Lambda Expressions

Many things could be said about lambda expressions — all of them are confusing. The easiest way to think about lambda expressions is as a concise form of anonymous class. You use lambda expressions when an anonymous class would have a single functional interface that has only one method.

Lambda expressions rely on a shorthand method for defining what task they perform that lends elegance to your application code. You use the arrow operator (->) to define the two parts of a lambda expression. The left side defines any arguments input to the one method in the interface, while the right side contains the interface implementation as defined by that one method. The following example makes things a lot clearer for you as you work through your first lambda expression.

Files needed: `LambdaExpression.java`

1. **Open the editor or IDE that you've chosen to use for this book.**

2. **Type the following code into the editor screen:**

```
public class LambdaExpression
{
   // Create an interface that describes
   // something to do.
   interface DoSomething
   {
      // Specify a method for doing something.
      void SaySomethingSpecific(String Value);
   }

   public static void main(String[] args)
   {
      // Create an instance of the interface using a
      // lambda expression.
      DoSomething
         DoIt = (Value) -> { System.out.
         println(Value); };

      // Actually use the lambda expression.
      DoIt.SaySomethingSpecific("Saying something
         specific!");
   }
}
```

The example begins by creating an interface, just as you would when working with an anonymous class. However, notice that this version of `DoSomething` contains only one method. If your interface requires two methods, you must use an anonymous class implementation instead.

Creating the lambda expression requires you to complete these four tasks:

- Define the type of the lambda expression (`DoSomething` in this case), which is the name of the interface you want to use.

- Define the name of the object that will hold the lambda expression (`DoIt` in this case).

- Specify any input arguments based on the interface definition (`Value` in this case). Notice that you don't define the variable type — Java infers the variable type for you.

- Create an expression that implements the interface. Notice that the expression appears on the right side of the arrow operator.

Using the resulting lambda expression is much the same as using an anonymous class. You simply specify the name of the object, the method it contains, and any arguments required for that method.

3. **Using the standard commands of your editor or IDE, save this file as** `LambdaExpression.java`.

4. **In your command prompt, type** javac LambdaExpression.java **and press Enter.**

The compiler compiles your application and creates a `.class` file from it.

5. **Type** java LambdaExpression **and press Enter.**

You see the output shown in Figure 9-7.

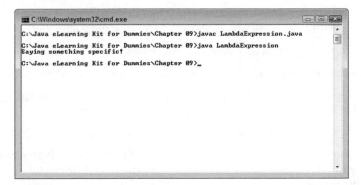

Figure 9-7

Summing Up

Here are the key points you learned about in this chapter:

- ✔ Methods provide the means of telling a class or object to perform a specific task.

- ✔ A method declaration includes the method scope, whether it's static or non-static, the return type, method name, argument list, and method body.

- ✔ Properties provide the means of interacting with data inside of a class or object.

✔ A property declaration includes the property scope, whether it's static or non-static, type, variable name, and initial value.

✔ Using getters and setters helps protect the data managed by your class from improper use by the caller.

✔ Every class you create in Java inherits from a parent class of some sort.

✔ A class that you create inherits from the `Object` class.

✔ Use the private scope to completely hide class elements.

✔ Use the default scope to hide class elements from access outside the current package.

✔ Use the protected scope to hide class elements from access outside of subclasses.

✔ Use public scope to allow access of class elements by anyone.

✔ A class that relies on events uses an event class to define that event.

✔ Event listeners wait for events to happen and then react to them.

✔ An implementation of an event as part of a class requires that you provide a means to register and unregister event handlers.

✔ You must provide a means of firing the event.

✔ Anonymous classes make it possible to express tasks by using significantly less code than would otherwise be needed when using more traditional techniques.

✔ Lambda expressions provide a shortcut method for creating specialized versions of anonymous classes that have just one functional interface and one method.

Try-it-yourself lab

For more practice with the features covered in this chapter, try the following exercise on your own:

1. **Open the `ParentClass.java` file supplied with the source code for this book.**

2. **Add a new method named `AnotherString()` and have it return "This is another string" to the caller.**

   Use the `GetClassName()` method as an example of how you should create the new method.

3. **Open the UseSimpleClass application.**

4. **Add a call to** `System.out.println(Test.AnotherString());` **at the end of the** `main()` **method.**

   Adding this call will test the new `AnotherString()` method.

5. **Compile the application.**

6. **Run the application.**

   What happens when you run the application? What does this result tell you about inheritance?

Know this tech talk

anonymous inner class: A special kind of unnamed class that contains one or more interfaces and one or more methods. You use an anonymous class when a formal class declaration is unneeded or unwanted. Because an anonymous class has no name, you can't reference it outside the class in which it exists.

constructor: A special type of method used to create an object from a class. Every class comes with at least one constructor, the default constructor.

event: A special occurrence within a class that the class makes outsiders aware of.

event handler: A special method that's designed to react to events generated by another class.

event listener: A special class that's designed to listen for events that occur within another class.

field: A variable that's defined as part of a class or an object.

interface: A class that defines unimplemented methods. Any class inheriting from an interface must provide implementations of the described methods.

getter: A special method used to obtain the value of a field and make it accessible outside the class or object.

lambda expression: An anonymous class that contains just one functional interface and one method. Normally, a lambda expression is designed to perform a task by using the shortest possible code.

method: The means of telling a class or object to perform a specific task.

override: To replace the implementation of a method in a parent class with a new implementation in a child class. Often, the parent class supplies a simple method that doesn't address the requirements of the child class.

package: A container used to hold multiple classes together. The simplest package relies on a subdirectory of a directory structure. A package is always defined using the package keyword in the .java file.

property: The means of accessing a value stored by a class or object.

setter: A special method used to change the value of a field from outside of the class or object.

superclass: The parent class of the current class. You access the superclass by using the super keyword.

Chapter 10

Accessing Data Sets Using Arrays and Collections

✔ Using arrays makes it possible to *create lists of items that you want to process.*

✔ Most developers *view two-dimensional arrays as a sort of data table.*

✔ Java allows you to create arrays with any number of dimensions so that you can *express that data in a natural (intuitive or real world) way.*

✔ Sometimes an array isn't the right answer, so Java also *provides array-like structures that have other qualities that make them perfect for storing data in specific ways.*

✔ Even though arrays and collections store lists of data, you *use collections to manipulate data in the same way that a database does.*

✔ When creating collections and other complex types, you can *use annotations to make the purpose of the collection or type clearer* without affecting application execution.

*J*ust about everyone makes lists. You create a grocery list before going

to the store and create lists of tasks you must perform at work. Lists

are a natural way of keeping track of data of various sorts. Java

provides lists in the form of arrays. The easiest way to think of arrays is as

electronic lists that help you manage the data in your application.

Not every list you create has just one dimension. For example, you might end up creating a table that not only tells what to do, but when and where to do it. Tables are two-dimensional lists — they're composed of rows and columns. People naturally create tables when they need to track data that's too complex for a simple list. Likewise, Java provides you with access to two-dimensional arrays that work much like tables do.

Sometimes you need even more than two dimensions. For example, when you try to decide how to manage stock in a warehouse, you use a three-dimensional list to do it — height, width, and depth. Woodworkers commonly use three-dimensional lists, too. In fact, humans use multi-dimensional lists all the time without really thinking about it. Java can meet your needs in this regard as well.

Arrays could meet every listing need. However, some forms of specialty lists are so common that Java provides special objects for them. For example, when you're making pancakes, you often create a stack of them. When you finish the stack, you take the last item you put on it first and then move down toward the first item. Likewise, we're all familiar with lines called *queues* at the bank and shopping center, where the first person in line is also the first person to leave it. Java provides an assortment of special list types that are really offshoots of the array but provide special logic for managing the list with greater ease: stack, queue, and deque (double-ended queue).

LINGO

An **array** is a kind of electronic list. It's a grouping of individual data values — normally of the same type — that you treat as a single entity. You use an array as a sort of container for managing a list of data.

LINGO

A **stack** is a special type of array that forces you to remove the last item you added to the list first. This is a Last In, First Out (LIFO) structure that acts much like a stack of pancakes, where you take the topmost pancake from the stack first when you're having breakfast.

LINGO

A **queue** is a special type of array that forces you to remove the first item you added to the list first. This is a First In, First Out (FIFO) structure that acts much like a line at the bank. The first person in line is the first person served.

Finally, this chapter discusses a truly specialized form of array with intelligence called a *map*. Most people think about this sort of object as a collection. When you have a DVD collection, you think about more than a simple stack of disks. The content of each DVD takes on special importance, and you often categorize DVDs by type and list them in order of title. It's the use of these database-like qualities that changes an array from a simple list to a type of collection called a map. The following sections describe all these forms of Java lists. In addition, you discover a new method of documentation for complex types called *annotations* that you'll find very helpful as your applications become more complex.

Performing Basic Array Tasks

An array is simply a list. It can be a list of anything — any primitive or object type. In most cases, an array is a list of like items. For example, if you create an `int` array, then all the items in that list are `int` values. The following sections describe how to create, initialize, *iterate* (examine each value), and otherwise manipulate arrays.

Defining an array

Always think of an array as a list of items. With this in mind, when you want to define an array, you begin with the type of the item you want to create. For example, if you want to create an array of integer values, you start with the `int` primitive type in most cases. The type is followed by a pair of square brackets (`[]`), which is then followed by the array name. You've seen an array defined for every application in the book. The `main()` method declaration always includes one, as shown here:

```
public static void main
        (String[] args)
```

LINGO

A **deque** is a special kind of array that lets you add or remove items from either end of the list. However, you can't access items in the middle of the list. A deque can act as either a stack or a queue depending on the need at the time. It lets a developer create a list where items that a program can't act on now are put back into the list for later processing.

LINGO

A **collection** is a list of complex items that you manage in the same way that you would a database. Java provides the `Map` object for this purpose. The list isn't structured in a concrete fashion — you can reorder it as needed and process it in a more comprehensive way than other Java types.

GO ONLINE

This chapter goes through a lot of information very quickly. Fortunately, you can find a number of sources of additional help online. For example, you can find an excellent tutorial about arrays at `http://docs.oracle.com/ javase/tutorial/java/ nutsandbolts/arrays. html`. Another interesting tutorial appears at `http://www. learn-java-tutorial. com/Java-Arrays.cfm`. Make use of as many resources as you can while you begin your Java journey to ensure you get up to speed as quickly as possible.

In this case, `args` is an array of type `String`. It contains the list of string values provided at the command line. You'll see additional array examples as the chapter progresses.

Initializing an array

Before you can use an array, you must initialize it. Initializing an array is a two-step process:

1. Instantiate the array so that you have an array object to work with.

2. Provide a value for each element in the array.

The elements in an array are accessed using a unique number. The numbers begin at 0 and continue through one less than the total number of elements. For example, if you have an array with ten elements, they're numbered from 0 through 9. To access a particular element, you use the array's name, followed by the number enclosed in square brackets. The following code shows a typical array definition and initialization:

LINGO

An **array element** is an individually accessible item in the list. Every element is a single item of the same type as the array. For example, when you define an `int []` array, each element within the array is of type `int`.

```
// Define an array of integer values.
int[] MyArray;

// Instantiate MyArray.
MyArray = new int[5];

// Define the individual array values.
MyArray[0] = 0;
MyArray[1] = 1;
MyArray[2] = 2;
MyArray[3] = 3;
MyArray[4] = 4;
```

This code creates an `int []` array named `MyArray`. It instantiates this array to hold five entries by calling `new int[5]`. The code then initializes each of the individual array values by accessing the individual elements, 0 through 4.

Using the for-each loop with arrays

Defining an array and filling it with data are two essential parts of working with arrays — the parts that you perform every time you use an array. However, when you have an array filled with data, you normally want to *do* something with that data. In the following exercise, you define an array, fill it with data, and then use a `for-each` loop to display the values in each array element.

Files needed: `SimpleArray.java`

1. **Open the editor or IDE that you've chosen to use for this book.**

2. **Type the following code into the editor screen.**

```java
public class SimpleArray
{
    public static void main(String[] args)
    {
        // Define an array of integer values.
        int[] MyArray;

        // Instantiate MyArray.
        MyArray = new int[5];

        // Define the individual array values.
        MyArray[0] = 0;
        MyArray[1] = 1;
        MyArray[2] = 2;
        MyArray[3] = 3;
        MyArray[4] = 4;

        // Use a for-each loop to display the values.
        for (int ThisValue : MyArray)
            System.out.println(ThisValue);
    }
}
```

The application begins by creating an `int[]` array named `MyArray`. It instantiates the array and then fills it with data. The `for-each` loop accesses each array element individually, fills the `int` variable — `ThisValue` — with that element's content, and then uses the `System.out.println()` method to display the information onscreen.

3. **Save the file to disk using the filename `SimpleArray.java`.**

4. **In your command prompt, type** javac SimpleArray.java **and press Enter.**

   The compiler compiles your application and creates a `.class` file from it.

5. **Type** java SimpleArray **and press Enter.**

   You see the expected output shown in Figure 10-1. Of course, you can easily fill the array elements with any `int` value.

EXTRA INFO

You can use a byte, short, int, or char variable to access array elements. However, it's illegal to use a long variable to access an array element, and the compiler will display an error if you try.

Create a ten element version of the SimpleArray application. Try filling the array elements with different types of data. How does the compiler react to the incorrect input? Finish this practice by filling the array elements with correct int values and then running it so that you can see the number of elements can change to whatever you need.

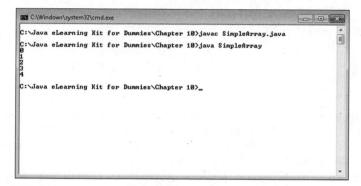

Figure 10-1

Determining the array characteristics

Arrays have specific characteristics, just as any other variable in Java does. In the following example, you perform some simple queries on an array and its associated elements. (In this context, a query is simply a question — you use methods to ask the array questions.)

Files needed: `ArrayProperties.java`

1. **Open the editor or IDE that you've chosen to use for this book.**

2. **Type the following code into the editor screen.**

```java
// Import the required API classes.
   import java.lang.Integer;

public class ArrayProperties
{
   public static void main(String[] args)
   {
      // Define and initialize an array of integer
      // values.
      int[] MyArray;
      MyArray = new int[5];
      MyArray[0] = 5;
      MyArray[1] = 10;
      MyArray[2] = 15;
      MyArray[3] = 20;
      MyArray[4] = 25;

      // Display the array properties.
      System.out.println("Length: " + MyArray.length);
      System.out.println("Class: " +
            MyArray.getClass().getCanonicalName());
```

```
        // Display the element properties.
        System.out.println("float Value: " +
            ((Integer)MyArray[4]).floatValue());
        System.out.println("Hexadecimal Value: "
            + Integer.toHexString(MyArray[4]));
    }
}
```

The application begins by creating an int [] array named MyArray and initializing it. A basic array provides access to its length through the length property. You can use the length property to iterate an array using a standard for loop. You can use the getClass(). getCanonicalName() method to obtain the kind of array from the instantiated object. The getClass() method actually returns an object with a number of properties and methods, but nothing other than the getCanonicalName() method returns a value by default.

After you access an array element using its index, you can perform the same sorts of tasks with it as you would the type in normal circumstances. For example, just as you can convert a primitive int type to a float type by using the floatValue() method, you can perform the same task by using an int array element. Likewise, you can coerce an element to box it as an object (see the "Automatic boxing and unboxing" section of Chapter 3 for a discussion of boxing) and then use the methods of the object type to work with it (Integer in this case).

3. **Save the file to disk using the filename ArrayProperties.java.**

4. **In your command prompt, type** javac ArrayProperties.java **and press Enter.**

   The compiler compiles your application and creates a .class file from it.

5. **Type** java ArrayProperties **and press Enter.**

   You see the expected output shown in Figure 10-2. Notice that the canonical name tells you the array type precisely.

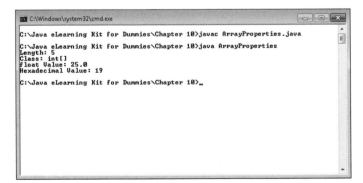

Figure 10-2

TIP

As with any other object type, you can't compare two arrays by using the equality (==) operator. You must instead use the `equals()` method. For example, if you want to check whether `Array1` is equal to `Array2`, you must use `Array1.equals(Array2)`.

Changing the array size

After you create an array in Java, the size is *immutable,* which means that it can't change. However, people need to change the size of things all the time. Sometimes you simply don't know how large something should be at the outset, and you don't want to create an array that wastes resources. Unfortunately, Java doesn't provide a simple method of resizing arrays. Most people create their own `resize()` method to make resizing arrays easier. (If you absolutely must have arrays that can change size, then you use the `ArrayList` object rather than a standard array, as described in the later "Developing variable-length arrays of arrays" section.)

One of the common tasks that Java developers must perform is resizing arrays. It's best if you create a separate method to perform the task. In the following example, you create a specialized method for resizing arrays. This is your first piece of truly generic code, and you can use it in any application you create.

> **LINGO**
>
> Any variable that can't change its value once you've instantiated and initialized it is considered **immutable.** For example, all constants are immutable because the value of a constant can never change. Likewise, arrays and many other objects are immutable, making it necessary to create a new instance of the object if you want to change certain characteristics. Arrays are containers, and the contents of that container — the elements — are **mutable** (changeable) as long as the type allows it.

Files needed: `ResizeArray.java`

1. **Open the editor or IDE that you've chosen to use for this book.**

2. **Type the following code into the editor screen.**

```java
// Import the required API classes.
import java.lang.reflect.Array;

public class ResizeArray
{
    public static void main(String[] args)
    {
        // Create and initialize an array.
        int[] MyArray = {0, 1, 2, 3, 4};

        // Display the original values and size.
        System.out.println("Original Size: " + MyArray.
            length);
        System.out.print("Original Content: ");
```

```
      for (int Value : MyArray)
         System.out.print(Value + " ");

      // Resize the array.
      MyArray = (int[])resize(MyArray, MyArray.length
         + 2);

      // Add two more values to the array.
      MyArray[5] = 5;
      MyArray[6] = 6;

      // Display the new values and size.
      System.out.println("\n\nNew Size: " + MyArray.
         length);
      System.out.print("New Content: ");
      for (int Value : MyArray)
         System.out.print(Value + " ");
   }

   public static Object resize(Object OldArray, int
         NewSize)
   {
      // Obtain the original size of the array.
      int OriginalSize = Array.getLength(OldArray);

      // Obtain the type of the original array.
      Class ArrayType = OldArray.getClass().
        getComponentType();

      // Create a new array of the same type.
      Object NewArray = Array.newInstance(ArrayType,
         NewSize);

      // Determine which array size is larger.
      int CopyLength = Math.min(OriginalSize,
        NewSize);

      // Make sure the user didn't pass in a zero
      // array size.
      if (CopyLength > 0)

         // Copy the contents of the old array to the
         // new array.
         System.arraycopy(OldArray, 0, NewArray, 0,
        CopyLength);

      // Return the new array.
      return NewArray;
   }
}
```

This version of the application uses a different technique for creating an initializing MyArray. In this case, the code performs the task in one step. Notice that the values appear within curly braces ({ }), which always defines a block in Java. The individual values in the block are separated by commas. You can use this technique for any array.

The code begins by displaying the original size and values contained in `MyArray`. (The new technique used to create `MyArray` emphasizes one reason that you might need to obtain the array length, even when using `for-each` loops to process array content.)

The `main()` method finishes by calling `resize()`. It then displays the new array length and element values.

The `resize()` method begins by obtaining the original array length. You might wonder why the code doesn't use the `length` property directly. The `resize()` method receives the old array as an `Object` type, not an `int []` type, so it can't easily access the native methods and properties. The reason you must use the `Object` type is that you have no way of knowing precisely what sort of array the user will pass into `resize()` for resizing. This example uses something called *reflection* to obtain the information about the array. Think of reflection as sort of examining a variable in a mirror. The mirror reflects the true content of the `Object`, which is an `int []`.

LINGO

Reflection is a programming technique that obtains the true content of an object, rather than relying on the base `Object` type. In many situations, it's necessary to use the `Object` type to create generic methods for processing data. However, the `Object` type has severe limits, which is where using reflection to determine the true nature of the object comes in handy.

The code also requires the type of the original array so it can create a new array of the same type. After the code determines the original array length and type, it uses the information to create the new array. The `Array.newInstance()` method creates a new array of the right type and with the new size requested by the caller.

Another potential problem with generic routines is that you can't easily determine whether the caller has requested to make the new array larger or smaller than the original. The code uses `Math.min()` to determine this information and place the smaller of the two array sizes in `CopyLength`. When `CopyLength` is larger than 0, the code copies the original array content to the new array by calling `System.arraycopy()`. If `CopyLength` equals 0, then there isn't anything to copy, and `resize()` returns an empty array.

3. **Save the file to disk using the filename `ResizeArray.java`.**

4. **In your command prompt, type** javac ResizeArray.java **and press Enter.**

   The compiler compiles your application and creates a `.class` file from it.

5. **Type** java ResizeArray **and press Enter.**

   The example outputs the original array information first and then the resized array information, as shown in Figure 10-3.

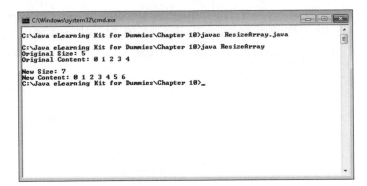

Figure 10-3

Sorting array data

At one time (long ago) programmers had to write their own routines for sorting data in arrays — an error-prone and difficult task. Java makes it easy to sort the content of arrays by using the methods in the `java.util.Arrays` class. In the following example, you use one such method to sort a `String[]`.

Files needed: `SortArray.java`

1. **Open the editor or IDE that you've chosen to use for this book.**

2. **Type the following code into the editor screen.**

```java
// Import the required API classes.
import java.util.Arrays;
import java.lang.String;

public class SortArray
{
    public static void main(String[] args)
    {
        // Create and initialize an array.
        String[] MyArray =
            {
                "Yellow",
                "Green",
                "Blue",
                "Red",
                "Orange",
                "Purple"
            };
```

```
        // Display the original content of MyArray.
        System.out.println("Original MyArray Order:");
        for (String Value : MyArray)
            System.out.println(Value);

        // Sort the array.
        Arrays.sort(MyArray);

        // Display the sorted content of MyArray.
        System.out.println("\nSorted MyArray Order:");
        for (String Value : MyArray)
            System.out.println(Value);
    }
}
```

The example begins by creating and initializing a `String[]`, `MyArray`. (Using `String` values can make the effects of a sort a little more noticeable.) The code then displays the original, unsorted contents of the array. It then calls `Arrays.sort()`, which sorts the content of the array. Finally, the code outputs the sorted array content.

3. **Save the file to disk using the filename** `SortArray.java`.

4. **In your command prompt, type** javac SortArray.java **and press Enter.**

   The compiler compiles your application and creates a `.class` file from it.

5. **Type** java SortArray **and press Enter.**

   The example outputs the original array information first and then the sorted array information, as shown in Figure 10-4.

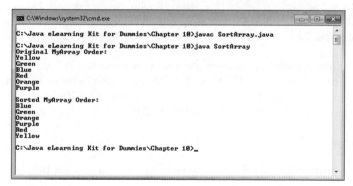

Figure 10-4

Try changing the case of some of the `String` entries. For example, try changing `Yellow` to `YELLOW` and `Red` to `red`. How does the sort order change? What does this tell you about the sorting mechanism that Java uses? Perform some more changes. Try several capitalizations of the same color, such as `Red`, `red`, `RED`, and `REd`. How does Java treat each of these capitalizations?

Creating Multidimensional Arrays

The arrays that you saw earlier in this chapter all have a single dimension, which means that they're a simple list. However, many people create lists that aren't so simple. For example, when you create a table, you're creating a *two-dimensional* list, indicated by the fact that tables use both rows and columns. Java lumps all arrays that have more than one dimension into a single category, multidimensional arrays. The following sections describe how to work with multidimensional arrays.

Defining a two-dimensional array

As previously mentioned, the easiest way to think about a two-dimensional array is as a table. However, two-dimensional arrays have many real-world representations. For example, you could use a two-dimensional array to keep track of the pieces on a chess board. A two-dimensional array could also represent something a little more abstract, such as the coordinates in a graph. No matter what you call the two dimensions, row and column or X and Y, a two-dimensional array requires two indices to access a specific element in the array.

In the following exercise, you create a two-dimensional array that contains the multiplication tables. That's right! You can use a two-dimensional array to hold this sort of information as well. By providing a multiplicand and a multiplier, you can obtain the product contained in the two-dimensional array.

Files needed: `TwoDimensions.java`

1. **Open the editor or IDE that you've chosen to use for this book.**

2. **Type the following code into the editor screen.**

```
// Import the required API classes.
import java.util.Scanner;

public class TwoDimensions
{
   public static void main(String[] args)
   {
      // Define the two-dimensional array.
      int[][] MathTable = new int[10][10];
```

```
// Fill the array with data.
for (int x = 1; x <= 10; x++)
    for (int y = 1; y <= 10; y++)
        MathTable[x - 1][y - 1] = x * y;

// Create the scanner.
Scanner GetNumber = new Scanner(System.in);

// Obtain the multiplicand.
System.out.print("Type a number between 1 and
    10: ");
int Multiplicand = GetNumber.nextInt();

// Obtain the multiplier.
System.out.print("Type a number between 1 and
    10: ");
int Multiplier = GetNumber.nextInt();

// Output the result.
System.out.print("The product is: " +
        MathTable[Multiplicand - 1][Multiplier -
    1]);
    }
}
```

The example begins by creating a two-dimensional int [] [] array, MathTable. Each dimension you want to create in an array requires another set of square brackets ([]). Because this is a two-dimensional array, it uses two sets of square brackets.

After the code creates the array, it fills the array with data. The values used to calculate the content of MathTable range from 1 through 10. However, remember that arrays always use a zero-based index. As a consequence, MathTable[2] [3] (the second row, third column) contains 3 * 4 or a value of 12. The for loops run from 1 to 10, but the indices run from 0 through 9, so the code must subtract 1 from both x and y to create the right index values.

At this point, MathTable contains a table of values that you can use to look up information, rather than recalculate it. Many applications rely on such *lookup tables* when they work with complex calculations. Rather than recalculate values every time they're needed, the application performs the task once, places the information in a table, and then looks up the information later. This technique makes your application run much faster.

To use `MathTable`, the application asks the user to supply two numbers. It then looks these values up in `MathTable` and outputs the result. Notice that the application looks up the product, but it doesn't recalculate it.

3. **Save the file to disk using the filename TwoDimensions.java.**

4. **In your command prompt, type** javac TwoDimensions.java **and press Enter.**

   The compiler compiles your application and creates a `.class` file from it.

5. **Type** java TwoDimensions **and press Enter.**

The application asks you to type a number between 1 and 10.

6. **Type** 2 **and press Enter.**

The application asks you to type another number between 1 and 10.

7. **Type** 8 **and press Enter.**

The example outputs the product of 2 * 8, as shown in Figure 10-5.

LINGO

Lookup tables store calculated information in an easy-to-access form. Many applications rely on lookup tables to store calculated data. Calculations take time, so recalculating the same information more than once wastes resources and can cause the application to run more slowly. The more complex the calculation, the more time an application can save by using a lookup table.

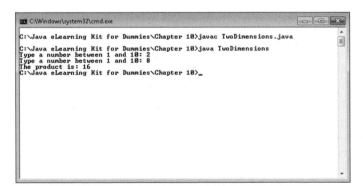

Figure 10-5

Obtaining the number of dimensions in an array

Sometimes you work with arrays where you don't know the number of dimensions or the array length at the outset. In some cases, these arrays may be *jagged arrays,* where each dimension has a different, fixed length. In the following example, you see how to create a jagged array and then use Java features to display the array content and determine the number of array dimensions.

Files needed: `ArrayDimensions.java`

1. **Open the editor or IDE that you've chosen to use for this book.**

2. **Type the following code into the editor screen.**

```java
public class ArrayDimensions
{
    public static void
        main(String[] args)
    {
        // Create a multidimensional array.
        int[][][] MultiArray =
            {
                {
                    {
                        1, 2, 3
                    }
                },
                {
                    {
                        4, 5, 6
                    },
                    {
                        7, 8, 9
                    }
                },
                {
                    {
                        10, 11
                    },
                    {
                        12, 13, 14
                    },
                    {
                        15, 16, 17, 18
                    }
                }
            };

        // Output the content of the array.
        for (int x = 0; x < MultiArray.length; x++)
            for (int y =0; y < MultiArray[x].length; y++)
                for(int z= 0; z < MultiArray[x][y].length;
                z++)
```

```
                System.out.format("Element %d, %d, %d =
                %d%n",
                        x, y, z, MultiArray[x][y][z]);

        // Obtain the number of dimensions.
        int Dimensions = GetDim(MultiArray);

        // When the code runs out of array elements,
        // output the result.

        System.out.println("The number of dimensions is:
            " + Dimensions);
    }

    public static int GetDim(Object Input)
    {
        // Define the starting number of dimensions.
        int Dimensions = 0;

        // Obtain the class of the input argument.
        Class ThisClass = Input.getClass();

        // Keep processing dimensions until done.
        while (ThisClass.isArray())
        {

            // Increment the output for each dimension.
            Dimensions++;

            // Obtain the class of the next array level.
            ThisClass = ThisClass.getComponentType();
        }

        // Return the number of dimensions.
        return Dimensions;
    }
}
```

A multidimensional array need not contain the same number of elements or child arrays per dimension. The example begins by creating MultiArray, a three-dimensional array with a varying number of child arrays and elements for each dimension. Notice how this example treats the multiple dimensions as arrays of arrays. This is a typical approach for creating a multidimensional jagged array.

Most people find it hard to see precisely how the dimensions work just from looking at the array code. So the first thing the example does is output the array elements. Notice how the output code lacks any sort of precise measurement of array dimension length. The `length` property always provides you with the `length` of a particular array in a given dimension.

It's also important to notice how the `length` property is accessed for each dimension. For example, when you use the `length` property with `MultiArray`, as in `MultiArray.length`, you access the length of the first dimension. To access the length of the second dimension, you must combine it with a specific element of the first dimension — the array within the array — using `MultiArray[x].length`. For example, to determine the length of the first array within the second dimension, you'd type **MultiArray[0].length** to access the first element of the first dimension.

The `GetDim()` method works by checking the class of each dimension. When it runs out of arrays, then it has run out of dimensions as well. Notice that the `GetDim()` method accepts an argument of type `Object`, `Input`. You use an `Object` type because you can't be sure that the caller will even supply an array. The first task is to determine whether `Input` contains an array. If it does, the array has at least one dimension, so the code increments `Dimensions` to match. The call to `ThisClass.getComponentType()` obtains the type of the next dimension. If this dimension is also an array, the `while` loop updates `Dimensions` again.

After `main()` calls `GetDim()`, it places the output value in `Dimensions`. It then displays the number of dimensions for the user. Notice that this part of the example uses the `println()` method because it's easier. However, the earlier output relied on the `format()` method to make it easier to present the information as nicely formatted output. Always remember to use the correct output method for a given situation.

LINGO

A **child array** is an array of elements or other child arrays that exists within a **parent array.** Think of each array as being a list. Sometimes you create a list of lists. The list contained within the list is the child array, while the parent array is the container that holds the child. A child array differs from an **element** in that an element is a single item, such as a number or a string. As an example, think of a library. An individual book is an element. All of the science fiction books are an array of books. When you place the science fiction book array, the cookbook array, and the horror classic array inside the library array, the library array becomes the parent and the science fiction book, the cookbook, and the horror classic arrays are child arrays.

3. **Save the file to disk using the filename `ArrayDimensions.java`.**

4. **In your command prompt, type** javac ArrayDimensions.java **and press Enter.**

   The compiler compiles your application and creates a `.class` file from it.

5. **Type** java ArrayDimensions **and press Enter.**

The example outputs the content of each element first, and then the number of dimensions, as shown in Figure 10-6. Notice that the example code handles the jagged array without any problem because it makes no assumptions about the array content or size. When writing array code of your own, you always need to consider that the caller could provide an array of any size or shape.

```
C:\Windows\system32\cmd.exe

C:\Java eLearning Kit for Dummies\Chapter 10>javac ArrayDimensions.java

C:\Java eLearning Kit for Dummies\Chapter 10>java ArrayDimensions
Element 0, 0, 0 = 1
Element 0, 0, 1 = 2
Element 0, 0, 2 = 3
Element 1, 0, 0 = 4
Element 1, 0, 1 = 5
Element 1, 0, 2 = 6
Element 1, 1, 0 = 7
Element 1, 1, 1 = 8
Element 1, 1, 2 = 9
Element 2, 0, 0 = 10
Element 2, 0, 1 = 11
Element 2, 1, 0 = 12
Element 2, 1, 1 = 13
Element 2, 1, 2 = 14
Element 2, 2, 0 = 15
Element 2, 2, 1 = 16
Element 2, 2, 2 = 17
Element 2, 2, 3 = 18
The number of dimensions is: 3

C:\Java eLearning Kit for Dummies\Chapter 10>
```

Figure 10-6

Change the number of entries and general shape of `MultiArray`. For example, try adding another child array immediately after the { 1, 2, 3 } array. Remember to add a comma between subarrays as shown for the other entries in the example. Run the application again. How does the new child array change the output?

Developing variable-length arrays of arrays

Standard arrays in Java are always a fixed size. There's nothing you can do with a basic Java array to resize it, except as shown in the "Changing the array size" section, earlier in this chapter. However, Java does come with an interesting class that reduces the work required to create and interact with highly flexible arrays — the `ArrayList`. Using an `ArrayList` doesn't remove the Java restrictions, but it does make it possible to circumvent them.

WARNING!

There's never a free ride with any technology, however, and the `ArrayList` is no exception. Yes, an `ArrayList` provides you significantly greater flexibility and reduces the work you need to perform when dealing with highly flexible arrays, which means you can be more productive. However, you can use only objects with the `ArrayList`, not primitive types. In addition, an `ArrayList` requires more memory and works more slowly than a standard array of the same type. To write great programs, you need to balance the pros of using an `ArrayList` with the cons and make a decision based on actual application requirements.

In the following example, you create an `ArrayList` that will accept any number of entries. All you need is a loop to keep accepting entries until the user types the correct value, which is –1 in this case. The example also provides some interesting new features, such as the use of a template. In addition, this example incorporates full error trapping.

Files needed: `VariableLengthArray.java`

1. **Open the editor or IDE that you've chosen to use for this book.**

2. **Type the following code into the editor screen.**

```java
// Import the required API classes.
import java.util.Scanner;
import java.util.ArrayList;
import java.lang.Integer;
import java.lang.String;
import java.util.InputMismatchException;

public class VariableLengthArray
{
    public static void main(String[] args)
    {
        // Define the variable length array.
        ArrayList<Integer> VarArray = new
          ArrayList<Integer>();

        // Create a variable to hold numbers.
        int Input = 0;

        // Create a variable to hold the output.
        String Output = "";

        // Create the scanner.
        Scanner GetNumber = new Scanner(System.in);

        while (Input >= 0)
        {
            try
```

```
      {
         // Obtain an Integer.
         System.out.print("Type a number between 1
         and 10 " +
                "or type -1 to end the program.");
         Input = GetNumber.nextInt();
      }
      catch (InputMismatchException e)
      {
         // Make sure Input has a correct value.
         Input = 0;

         // Clear the scanner.
         GetNumber.nextLine();

         // Display an error message and try again.
         System.out.println("Use numbers between 1
and 10!");
         continue;
      }

      // Check for a number outside the range.
      if ((Input > 10) || (Input == 0))
      {
         // Display an error message and try again.
         System.out.println("Use numbers between 1
         and 10!");
         continue;
      }

      // Check for an ending condition.
      if (Input < 0)
         break;

      // Add this number to the array.
      VarArray.add(Input);

      // Clear the old Output content.
      Output = "";

      // Check to make sure that VarArray contains
      // a value.
      if (!VarArray.isEmpty())
         for (Integer Item : VarArray)
            Output += Item + " ";

      // Display the result.
      System.out.println("Current Array Entries = "
      + Output);
   }
  }
 }
```

This example begins by creating an `ArrayList` object, `VarArray`. However, this example does something different from what you've seen in the past. There's a parameterized entry after `ArrayList`, `<Integer>`. Java lets developers create something called a *generic class* that you won't see demonstrated in this book, but which you'll encounter as you work with Java. A generic class acts as a template for specific object types. You can use the same code to create classes that work only with an `Integer` or a `String`. This is an advanced topic, but for now, all you need to know is that the parameter, `<Integer>`, takes the raw `ArrayList` and uses it to create a type-specific `ArrayList` that accepts only `Integer` values. Using strong typing when you can (a programming technique where the compiler specifically checks the type of each variable that goes into the `ArrayList`) will reduce the amount of errors in your application because the compiler is better aware of the intent of your code. In addition, strong typing reduces the amount of code you have to write.

LINGO

A **generic class** is one that provides a single implementation for any sort of object you want to work with. You tell Java the specific kind of object you want to use in a given instance by providing a parameter within angle brackets (`<>`) after the type declaration. For example, using `ArrayList` alone creates a raw object that can accept any input, while using `ArrayList<Integer>` creates an object that will accept only `Integer` values as input. There are situations where you use a raw type, such as when the `ArrayList` needs to accept objects of all types, and situations where you use the parameterized type, such as when the `ArrayList<Integer>` needs to accept only `Integer` objects.

This example relies on the user to provide input values in a specific range by using the `Input` argument. These values are collected for display in `String`, `Output`. A `Scanner`, `GetNumber`, provides the means for obtaining user input.

The `while` loop continues to collect input from the user until the user provides a value less than 0 as input — an incorrect input, in other words. The input prompt and associated `GetNumber.nextInt()` call appears in a `try. . .catch` structure to avoid any potential input problems from the user. This example shows one method of recovering from an input error that makes it possible for the loop to continue running.

When an application requires that the user provide only certain values, it must perform range checking. In this case, the `try. . .catch` structure has already excluded anything that isn't a number, so the range check looks for numbers between 1 and 10. When the user inputs a value outside that range, the code displays an error message and then lets the user try again. Notice that the way the range check is written allows the user to input the value of –1 required to end the application (the line that says `if (Input < 0)`).

The next `if` statement addresses the need to end the application. If the user inputs a negative number, the loop ends by executing the `break` clause.

After all these checks, the code finally calls `VarArray.add()` to add the number to the array. The application hasn't set the size of the array because it isn't necessary. An `ArrayList` can grow (using the `add()` method) or shrink (using the `remove()` method) as needed.

To see what `VarArray` contains, you need to build a string from its contents. The first step is to ensure `Output` doesn't contain anything. The code then checks `VarArray` to ensure it isn't empty by calling `isEmpty()`. A `for-each` loop makes it possible to add each item in `VarArray` to `Output`. The code then displays the content onscreen.

3. **Save the file to disk using the filename `VariableLengthArray.java`.**

4. **In your command prompt, type** javac VariableLengthArray.java **and press Enter.**

   The compiler compiles your application and creates a `.class` file from it.

5. **Type** java VariableLengthArray **and press Enter.**

   The application asks you to provide a numeric input between 1 and 10.

6. **Type** Hello **and press Enter.**

   The application displays a helpful message asking you to input a number between 1 and 10, as shown in Figure 10-7.

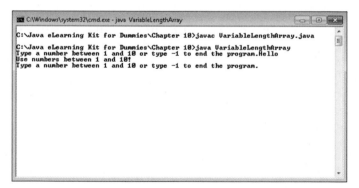

Figure 10-7

7. **Type** 99 **and press Enter.**

   The application isn't fooled this time either. It outputs the same helpful message, as shown in Figure 10-7.

8. Type 5 **and press Enter.**

You now see that the array contains one entry with a value of 5, as shown in Figure 10-8.

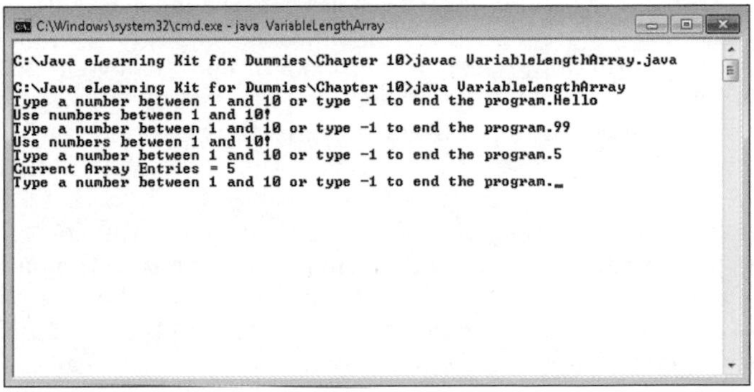

Figure 10-8

9. Type 8 **and press Enter.**

The application now has two entries of 5 and 8.

10. Type –1 **and press Enter.**

The example ends, as shown in Figure 10-9. Many application types rely on a looping mechanism like the one demonstrated in this application. A user continues to enter values until a preselected condition exists. At that point, the application ends.

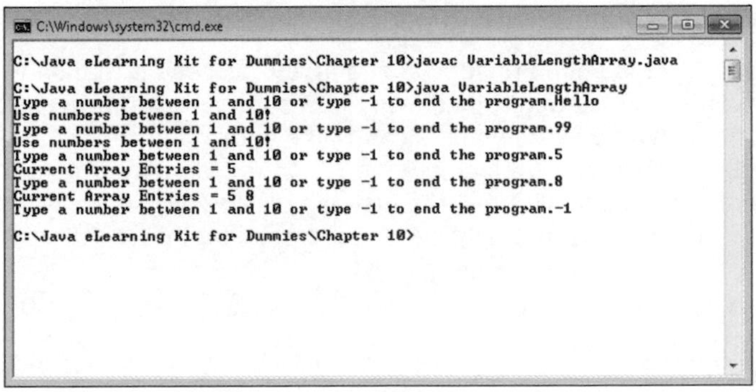

Figure 10-9

Interacting with Array-Like Structures

Arrays are open-ended structures that you can use to store all sorts of information. However, developers have found that specific array implementations are extremely useful. These array implementations perform specific tasks in applications, and developers use them so often that Java includes special classes to make working with them easier. This chapter helps you discover the four most important array-like structures that are actually special array implementations:

✔ **Stacks:** A stack works just like a pile of pancakes. You cook the pancakes and pile them one on top of the other. Then you take the pancakes to the table where you take the topmost pancake off the stack and give it to someone to eat. A stack is a Last In, First Out (LIFO) structure that's often used to store information between calls to other areas of an application or for other situations where you need to work backward through the list of items.

✔ **Queues:** A queue works just like a line at a bank. People arrive and stand at the back of the line. They work their way through the line and when they reach the front, a teller calls on them to address their needs. Many real-world situations require that an application process items in the order they're received. A queue is called a First In, First Out (FIFO) structure.

✔ **Deques:** A deque (pronounced *deck*) is a mixture of the stack and the queue. You use it when you need both behaviors in an application. There really are times when you need to process from either end of the list depending on the conditions. However, a deque never lets you cheat and obtain values from the middle of the list.

✔ **Lists:** A list is a kind of specialized array. You use it to gain the extra functionality needed to perform tasks such as combining lambda expressions with arrays. Using lists can make your code significantly shorter and easier to read than code using a standard array. You can access elements anywhere within a list, just as you do with an array, but lists provide far greater functionality. It's also possible to treat lists like a stack, queue, or deque as needed.

Using stacks

Stacks rely on some special functionality to work with the list member. In this example, you make it possible for users to *push* (add) values to the stack and *pop* (remove) values from the stack. The values are always removed in the opposite order in which you add them.

Files needed: `UsingStack.java`

1. **Open the editor or IDE that you've chosen to use for this book.**

2. **Type the following code into the editor screen.**

```java
// Import the required API classes.
import java.util.Scanner;
import java.util.Stack;
import java.lang.String;

public class UsingStack
{
    public static void main(String[] args)
    {
        // Create a stack that holds string values.
        Stack<String> PushAndPop = new Stack<String>();

        // Create a variable to hold the input.
        String Input = "";

        // Create a variable to hold the output.
        String Output = "";

        // Create the scanner.
        Scanner GetInput = new Scanner(System.in);

        // Continue processing entries until the user
        // types quit.
        while (!Input.toUpperCase().equals("QUIT"))
        {
            // Obtain a string for processing.
            System.out.print("Type any string you want,
                type POP " +
                    "to remove a value from the stack and
                    QUIT to " +
                    "end the program: ");
            Input = GetInput.nextLine();

            // Check for an exit command.
            if (Input.toUpperCase().equals("QUIT"))
                break;

            // Check for a POP command.
            if (Input.toUpperCase().equals("POP"))
                if (PushAndPop.isEmpty())
                {
                    System.out.println(
                        "The stack is empty, nothing to
                            pop.");
                    continue;
                }
```

```
                    else
                    {
                        System.out.println("Popping: " +
            PushAndPop.pop());
                        continue;
                    }

                    // If the user hasn't quit or popped an
                    // entry, push an entry onto the stack.

                    PushAndPop.add(Input);

                    // Display the contents of the stack.
                    Output = "";
                    for (String Item : PushAndPop)
                        Output += Item + " ";
                    System.out.println("The stack contains: " +
                        Output);
                }
            }
        }
```

The example begins by creating a parameterized Stack of type String named PushAndPop. It then creates the variables required to support the application and starts a processing loop using a while block. Notice that you must call toUpperCase() first, before calling equals() to perform the comparison with QUIT. As always, you must assume that the user can input the value in any case.

At this point, the example obtains input from the user, checks for QUIT and POP. When the user types QUIT, the program ends. When the user types POP, the application first checks to determine whether there's anything to pop from the stack by calling isEmpty(). If there is, the application pops the value from the stack by calling pop() and displays it onscreen. Otherwise, the application provides a helpful error message. In both cases, the processing loop continues.

When the user has typed something other than QUIT or POP, the application pushes the value onto the stack by calling add() and displays the stack content onscreen. Notice that you can iterate through a stack as you would any array.

3. Save the file to disk using the filename UsingStack.java.

4. In your command prompt, type javac UsingStack.java **and press Enter.**

The compiler compiles your application and creates a .class file from it.

5. **Type** java UsingStack **and press Enter.**

The application asks you to type any string you want and then provides special instructions for popping a value from the stack or ending the application. Notice that the instructions use uppercase for POP and QUIT for emphasis, even though the user doesn't have to type them in uppercase.

6. **Type** Hello **and press Enter.**

The application displays the content of the stack for you, as shown in Figure 10-10.

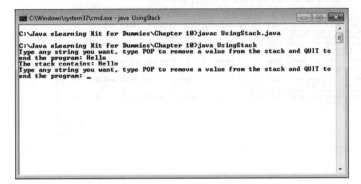

Figure 10-10

7. **Type** Goodbye **and press Enter.**

The application displays the content of the stack again. Notice that it now includes both Hello and Goodbye.

8. **Type** pop **and press Enter.**

The application removes a value from the stack. Notice that it removes Goodbye, the last item added, and not Hello, as shown in Figure 10-11.

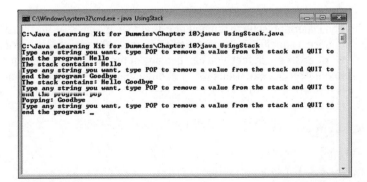

Figure 10-11

9. **Type** pop **and press Enter.**

   The application removes `Hello` from the stack.

10. **Type** pop **and press Enter again.**

    The application tells you that there's nothing more to pop from the stack, as shown in Figure 10-12.

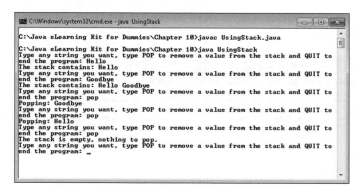

Figure 10-12

11. **Type** Quit **and press Enter.**

    The application ends.

Working with queues

Java sometimes gets a little confusing and working with the `Queue` is one of those situations. A `Queue`, unlike a `Stack`, is an interface and not an actual implementation. The "Creating an event listener interface" section in Chapter 9 describes interfaces to a degree.

> The important issue to remember is that to use a `Queue`, you must choose a specific implementation to partner with your `Queue`, such as a `LinkedList`. In fact, you can use any of these specific implementations to create a `Queue`. (Don't worry about how they differ at this point — this is the sort of information you start to understand as you work with Java more.)

- ✔ `AbstractQueue`
- ✔ `ArrayBlockingQueue`
- ✔ `ConcurrentLinkedQueue`

✔ DelayQueue

✔ LinkedBlockingQueue

✔ LinkedList

✔ PriorityBlockingQueue

✔ PriorityQueue

✔ SynchronousQueue

The odd part about working with these implementations is that they often work with more than one interface. For example, you can also use a LinkedList implementation to create a Deque (as you will in the "Employing deques" section, later in this chapter). The LinkedList is the implementation, while the interface, such as Queue, represents the behavior of that implementation.

In the following example, you create a Queue that's implemented by a LinkedList. The LinkedList implementation is the most commonly found form of Queue. This example uses code that's similar to the Stack example in the "Using stacks" section of the chapter.

Files needed: UsingQueue.java

1. Open the editor or IDE that you've chosen to use for this book.

2. Type the following code into the editor screen.

```
// Import the required API classes.
import java.util.Scanner;
import java.util.Queue;
import java.util.LinkedList;
import java.lang.String;

public class UsingQueue
{
    public static void main(String[] args)
    {
        // Create a queue that holds string values.
        Queue<String> MyQueue = new
            LinkedList<String>();

        // Create a variable to hold the input.
        String Input = "";

        // Create a variable to hold the output.
        String Output = "";

        // Create the scanner.
        Scanner GetInput = new Scanner(System.in);
```

```
// Continue processing entries until the user
// types quit.
while (!Input.toUpperCase().equals("QUIT"))
{
   // Obtain a string for processing.
   System.out.print("Type any string you want,
      type REMOVE " +
         "to remove a value from the queue and
         QUIT to " +
         "end the program: ");
   Input = GetInput.nextLine();

   // Check for an exit command.
   if (Input.toUpperCase().equals("QUIT"))
      break;

   // Check for a REMOVE command.
   if (Input.toUpperCase().equals("REMOVE"))
      if (MyQueue.isEmpty())
      {
         System.out.println(
               "The queue is empty, nothing to
remove.");
         continue;
      }
      else
      {
         System.out.println("Popping: " +
      MyQueue.poll());
         continue;
      }

   // If the user hasn't quit or popped an
   // entry, add an entry onto the queue.

   MyQueue.offer(Input);

   // Display the contents of the queue.
   Output = "";
   for (String Item : MyQueue)
      Output += Item + " ";
   System.out.println("The queue contains: " +
      Output);
   }
  }
 }
```

The code for this example is similar to the code for the UsingStack example on purpose. It's important to see how stacks and queues differ. The important changes are that you call `poll()` to remove an element from the queue in a way that won't cause an exception. Likewise, you call `offer()` to add an element to the queue in a way that won't cause an exception if the queue is size-constrained or whether there are other problems.

3. **Save the file to disk using the filename** UsingQueue.java.

4. **Type** javac UsingQueue.java **and press Enter.**

   The compiler compiles your application and creates a .class file from it.

5. **Type** java UsingQueue **and press Enter.**

   The application asks you to type any string you want and then provides special instructions for removing a value from the queue or ending the application.

6. **Type** Hello **and press Enter.**

   The application displays the content of the queue for you.

7. **Type** Goodbye **and press Enter.**

   The application displays the content of the queue again. Notice that it now includes both Hello and Goodbye.

8. **Type** remove **and press Enter.**

   The application removes a value from the queue. Notice that it removes Hello, the first item added, and not Goodbye, as shown in Figure 10-13. This behavior is precisely opposite of a stack.

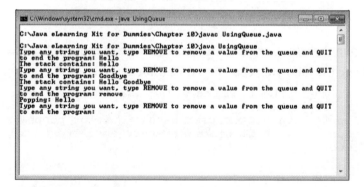

Figure 10-13

9. **Type** remove **and press Enter.**

   The application removes Goodbye from the queue.

10. **Type** remove **and press Enter again.**

    The application tells you that there's nothing more to remove from the queue.

11. **Type** Quit **and press Enter.**

    The application ends, as shown in Figure 10-14.

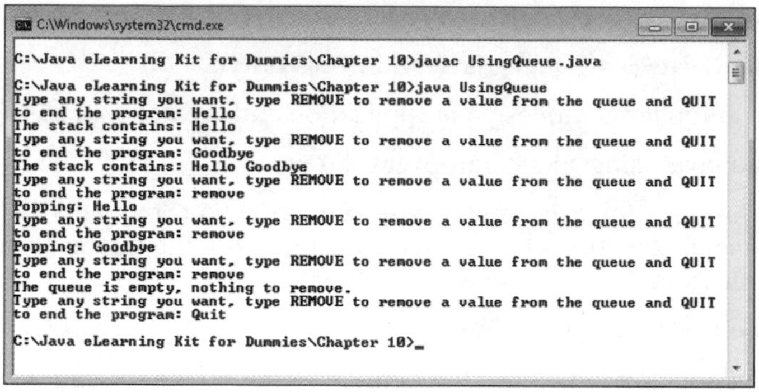

Figure 10-14

Employing deques

As previously mentioned, deques are a combination of a stack and a queue. You can work with either end of the deque as needed. In the following example, you create an expanded version of the UsingQueue example that demonstrates the capabilities of a deque.

Files needed: `UsingDeque.java`

1. **Open the editor or IDE that you've chosen to use for this book.**

2. **Type the following code into the editor screen.**

```java
// Import the required API classes.
import java.util.Scanner;
import java.util.Deque;
import java.util.LinkedList;
import java.lang.String;

public class UsingDeque
{
   public static void main(String[] args)
   {
      // Create a deque that holds string values.
      Deque<String> MyDeque = new
        LinkedList<String>();

      // Create a variable to hold the input.
      String Input = "";

      // Create a variable to hold the output.
      String Output = "";
```

```
// Create the scanner.
Scanner GetInput = new Scanner(System.in);

// Continue processing entries until the user
// types quit.
while (!Input.toUpperCase().equals("QUIT"))
{
   // Obtain a string for processing.
   System.out.print("Type any string you want,
      type FIRST" +
          " to remove a value from the front of
        the deque," +
          " LAST to remove a value from the end
        of the " +
          "deque, and QUIT to end the program:
        ");
   Input = GetInput.nextLine();

   // Check for an exit command.
   if (Input.toUpperCase().equals("QUIT"))
      break;

   // Check for a FIRST command.
   if (Input.toUpperCase().equals("FIRST"))
      if (MyDeque.isEmpty())
      {
         System.out.println(
               "The deque is empty, nothing to
remove.");
         continue;
      }
      else
      {
         System.out.println("Removing: " +
            MyDeque.pollFirst());
         continue;
      }

   // Check for a LAST command.
   if (Input.toUpperCase().equals("LAST"))
      if (MyDeque.isEmpty())
      {
         System.out.println(
               "The deque is empty, nothing to
remove.");
         continue;
      }
      else
```

```
        {
            System.out.println("Removing: " +
                MyDeque.pollLast());
            continue;
        }

        // If the user hasn't quit or removed an
        // entry, add an entry onto the deque.
        // However, add the entry to the beginning
        // when it's less than the current beginning
        // entry or to the end when it isn't.
        if (MyDeque.isEmpty())
            MyDeque.offer(Input);
        else
            if (MyDeque.peekFirst().compareTo(Input) >= 0)
                MyDeque.offerFirst(Input);
            else
                MyDeque.offerLast(Input);

        // Display the contents of the deque.
        Output = "";
        for (String Item : MyDeque)
            Output += Item + " ";
        System.out.println("The deque contains: " +
            Output);
    }
  }
}
```

This example works almost precisely the same as the UsingQueue
example. The difference is that this example can add or remove entries
at either end of the list, but not from the middle. When the user types
FIRST, the deque removes an entry from the front of the list. Likewise,
when the user types LAST, the deque removes an entry from the end of
the list. The example adds items either to the front or the back of the list
based on the contents of the list. When the new item has a value that is
less than the item that exists at the beginning of the list from a comparison perspective, the application adds that item to the front of the list.

3. **Save the file to disk using the filename** `UsingDeque.java`.

4. **In your command prompt, type** javac UsingDeque.java **and press Enter.**

   The compiler compiles your application and creates a `.class` file from it.

5. **Type** java UsingDeque **and press Enter.**

   The application asks you to type an entry. You can also type FIRST to
   remove an entry from the front of the list, LAST to remove an entry from
   the end of the list, or QUIT to end the program.

6. **Type** Red **and press Enter.**

The application adds a new entry to the list.

7. **Type** Yellow **and press Enter.**

Because a string with a value of Yellow is greater than a string with a value of Red (Y comes after R in the alphabet), the entry is added to the end of the list, rather than the beginning of the list.

8. **Type** Blue **and press Enter.**

Because Blue is less than Red, the entry is added to the beginning of the list. What you see now is that Red is bracketed by Blue and Yellow, as shown in Figure 10-15.

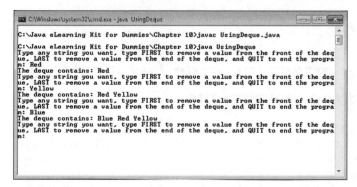

Figure 10-15

9. **Type** First **and press Enter.**

Notice that the application removes Blue from the list. That's because Blue is at the front of the list.

10. **Type** Last **and press Enter.**

The application removes Yellow from the list because Yellow is at the end of the list. Of course, Red is left alone at this point, so it doesn't matter whether you type FIRST or LAST to remove it.

11. **Type** Quit **and press Enter.**

The application ends, as shown in Figure 10-16.

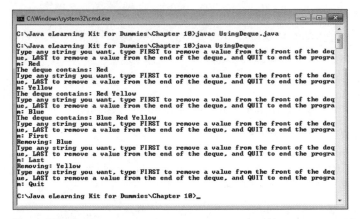

Figure 10-16

Iterating arrays by using List elements and lambda expressions

You can't easily use lambda expressions with standard arrays. However, you *can* use them with List elements, which provide all of the features of arrays, plus the ability to perform tasks such as resizing the array. Instantiating a List is considerably easier than using standard arrays a well. The example in this section shows how you can create, instantiate, and enumerate a List by using just two lines of code.

Files needed: `LambdaArray.java`

1. **Open the editor or IDE that you've chosen to use for this book.**

2. **Type the following code into the editor screen.**

```java
// Import the required API classes.
import java.util.List;
import java.util.Arrays;

public class LambdaArray
{
    public static void main(String[] args)
    {
        // Define an array of integer values.
        List<Integer> MyArray = Arrays.asList(0, 1, 2,
            3, 4);

        // Use a for-each loop to display the values.
        MyArray.forEach(ThisValue -> System.out.
            println(ThisValue));
    }
}
```

When creating a List, you must tell Java what type of List to create. In this case, you see an Integer list that contains numeric information. One of many ways to instantiate a List relies on a call to Arrays. asList(), where you supply the values you want the List to contain. When you compare this example to early examples in this chapter, you see that using a List is quite a bit faster and easier to understand.

Interacting with the List after you create it relies on special methods for the most part, such as forEach(). In this case, the method examines each List element in turn, passes the value to ThisValue, and then prints ThisValue on screen. Of course, your lambda expression can perform any task desired with the value — the example represents a simpler demonstration of what you can do.

3. **Save the file to disk using the filename LambdaArray.java.**

4. **In your command prompt, type** javac LambdaArray.java **and press Enter.**

   The compiler compiles your application and creates a .class file from it.

5. **Type** java LambdaArray **and press Enter.**

   You see the expected output shown in Figure 10-17. Of course, you can easily fill the array elements with any int value.

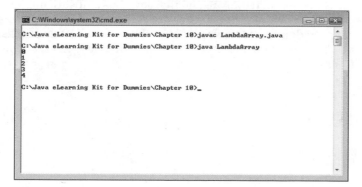

Figure 10-17

Using Maps to Create Collections

Arrays and the specialized lists described in the chapter so far make it possible to perform an amazing array of tasks with Java. However, there are situations where a Java application needs something that's more akin to a database, without actually having all the database baggage (such as having to buy a separate application). For example, you might want to be able to find a specific value in a list without having to look at every element individually.

The following sections describe a special sort of collection called a Map. The Map is an incredibly useful sort of storage container that makes many tasks easier.

Before you go any further though, always remember that every time you add functionality to a class, it causes an increase in class size. In addition, the class runs more slowly and can become harder to understand. If an array will serve the purpose in your application, use an array. Only use a Map when you need the specialized functionality that a Map provides.

Defining the map

The Map, like many basic container classes in Java, is actually an interface. A Map describes a class that provides a key and value pair for storing information. The key gives the data a unique name. No two entries can have the same key, which makes it possible to search for the key and always return a unique value. Any number of keys can have the same associated value.

As with any interface, you must create an implementation before you can use it. The Map is so incredibly useful that Java has a host of implementing classes associated with it. Here's the list of classes you can use to create a Map (again, you don't need to worry about the specifics of these classes for now — you'll begin to understand these differences as you create more Java applications):

✔ AbstractMap

✔ Attributes

✔ AuthProvider

✔ ConcurrentHashMap

✔ ConcurrentSkipListMap

✔ EnumMap

✔ HashMap

✔ Hashtable

✔ IdentityHashMap

✔ LinkedHashMap

✔ PrinterStateReasons

✔ Properties

✔ Provider

✔ RenderingHints

✔ SimpleBindings

✔ TabularDataSupport

✔ TreeMap

✔ UIDefaults

✔ WeakHashMap

A single section of a chapter can't even begin to discuss all these classes. You'll likely see a few more of these classes as the book progresses though. The important thing to remember is that all Map classes rely on a unique key to identify data and a value to hold the data.

Creating a map example

The example in this section defines a sorted list of people and the amount of money they owe. The example concentrates on getting you started with the Map interface — it won't demonstrate every feature that this class provides. In this case, you use a TreeMap class (one of the most useful classes for sorting data) to implement the Map interface.

Files needed: UsingMaps.java

1. **Open the editor or IDE that you've chosen to use for this book.**

2. **Type the following code into the editor screen.**

```java
// Import the required API classes.
import java.text.NumberFormat;
import java.util.Locale;
import java.util.Map;
import java.util.TreeMap;
import java.lang.String;
import java.math.BigDecimal;

public class UsingMaps
{
    public static void main(String[] args)
    {
        // Create a new Map object.
        Map<String, BigDecimal> MyMap =
                new TreeMap<String, BigDecimal>();
```

```
// Fill the Map with some entries.
MyMap.put("Jake", new BigDecimal(30.00));
MyMap.put("Ann", new BigDecimal(35.00));
MyMap.put("Sally", new BigDecimal(22.00));
MyMap.put("Adam", new BigDecimal(120.00));
MyMap.put("Zak", new BigDecimal(15.00));
MyMap.put("Jane", new BigDecimal(45.00));

// Create a formatter to use.
NumberFormat Currency =
      NumberFormat.getCurrencyInstance(Locale.
        US);

// Obtain each entry in order.
System.out.println("Displaying the inital
      entries:");
for (Map.Entry<String, BigDecimal> Item : MyMap.
      entrySet())
{
   // Display the entries.
   System.out.format("%s owes %s%n", Item.
     getKey(),
         Currency.format(Item.getValue()));
}

// Remove an entry.
MyMap.remove("Sally");

// Add another one.
MyMap.put("Toby", new BigDecimal(99.00));

// Display the values again.
System.out.println("\nDisplaying the updated
      entries:");
for (Map.Entry<String, BigDecimal> Item: MyMap.
      entrySet())
{
   // Display the entries.
   System.out.format("%s owes %s%n", Item.
  getKey(),
         Currency.format(Item.getValue()));
}
    }
  }
```

The example begins by creating a parameterized Map, MyMap. The key is of type String, and the value is of type BigDecimal. Notice how you separate the parameters with a comma. MyMap is a TreeMap, which means that it's automatically sorted for you. TreeMap also provides a number of useful methods, some of which you see in the code.

Because the new Map is empty, the application begins by adding some entries using the put() method. Every entry consists of a key and value pair. It doesn't matter what order you use to enter the data — MyMap will automatically sort it for you.

The values in this list are the amounts each person owes. Consequently, the code creates a NumberFormat object named Currency that relies on the formatting used in the U.S.

The next step is to use a for-each loop to list the contents of MyMap. Notice how you use the MyMap.Entry type to create a single entry, Item. To gain access to the entries, the code calls MyMap.entrySet(). Because this output is a little more complex, the application uses the format() method in place of println(). It displays how much each person in the list owes. The call to Currency.format() formats the numeric value in Item.getValue() as a dollar amount in a String.

To show how easy it is to manipulate the list, the code calls on MyMap.remove() to remove a specific entry using its key. It then adds another new entry and displays the result again. A Map makes it easy to change the list entries and find any entry you need.

3. **Save the file to disk using the filename UsingMaps.java.**

4. **In your command prompt, type** javac UsingMaps.java **and press Enter.**

   The compiler compiles your application and creates a .class file from it.

5. **Type** java UsingMaps **and press Enter.**

   The example outputs the original list information first and then the modified list information, as shown in Figure 10-18. Notice that in both cases, the list is always sorted. You don't have to do anything special to obtain this service.

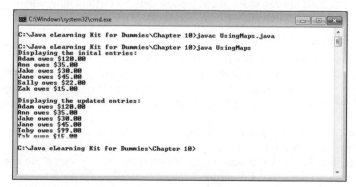

Figure 10-18

Working with Java Annotations

You've seen comments used in most of the examples in the book. The compiler ignores comments, so when you create a comment you can write anything that you feel will be helpful later in figuring out what the application can do. Comments document your code. However, there is another kind of documentation — the annotation. An annotation is a kind of documentation that the compiler also understands. When the compiler sees annotation in your code, it knows that it needs to do something special with the code that follows. Annotations are helpful in documenting your code in a functional way so that the compiler can help you enforce whatever documentation you provide.

Understanding annotations

The kinds and content of annotations, like comments, are limited only by your imagination. Yes, Java provides some predefined annotations, but you can also create annotations that describe program elements in any way you want. The idea is that you describe how an annotation should work, provide data for it, and the compiler takes care of the rest.

Annotations always begin with the @ (at) symbol. So, when you see @Documented, you know that you're seeing an annotation. The following sections tell you more about predefined and custom annotations.

Using predefined annotations

A predefined annotation is one that exists as part of Java. You find these annotations in the `java.lang.annotation` package. To use them, you add `import java.lang.annotation.*;` to the beginning of your application. The following list provides an overview of the predefined annotations:

✔ `@Deprecated`: Sometimes an *element* — a class, method, field, or other programming feature — is superseded by a newer element or is simply no longer needed. When this happens, you mark the element as deprecated so that developers know they need to update their code and stop using that particular element. Adding the `@Deprecated` annotation outputs the deprecated status of the element in the documentation generated by *Javadoc* (a utility that is used to create documentation automatically based on the content of your code files).

✔ @Documented: Any time you mark an element as documented, the Javadoc utility outputs it to the documentation file it creates based on the source file content.

✔ @FunctionalInterface: Specifies that the interface is a functional interface used for anonymous classes and lambda expressions, as described in Chapter 9.

✔ @Inherited: Classes can inherit characteristics from a parent class. By default, this includes functionality such as methods but doesn't include the parent class's annotations. Using the @Inherited annotation tells Java to apply the parent class annotations to the subclass as well.

✔ @Override: Specifies that a child class element is overriding a superclass (parent class) element. If this annotation is present and the superclass lacks an element of the same name, the compiler outputs an error so that you know something is wrong with the override.

✔ @Repeatable: Most annotations are applied only once to a particular element. However, in some cases you need to apply the annotation more than once. This annotation tells Java that it's acceptable to apply the annotation to a particular element more than one time.

✔ @Retention: An annotation can affect only the source code; the source code and compiler; or the source code, compiler, and JVM. This annotation defines what effect another annotation should have. For example, you may need only a documentation-specific annotation to affect the source code and compiler.

✔ @SafeVarargs: It's possible to perform operations that aren't safe on the arguments passed to a method or constructor. This annotation says that the code doesn't do anything unsafe and therefore doesn't require all the usual checks. Reducing the number of checks makes the application run faster.

✔ @SuppressWarnings: The Java compiler outputs a wealth of warnings to signal potential problems. For example, if you try to use a deprecated method in your code, the compiler outputs a warning message about it. This annotation tells the compiler not to output such warnings for the affected element.

✔ @Target: When you create your own annotations, it can be helpful to tell the compiler that these annotations should affect only a specific element type. For example, if you create an author block that is meant to appear only at the package level, then you can limit the annotation to just that element type by using the @Target annotation.

Creating new annotations

The set of predefined annotations that come with Java are relatively limited in use. To create really useful annotations, you have to design them yourself or get them as part of a third-party package. Creating a new annotation is a three-step process:

1. Add the appropriate `import` statement:

   ```
   import java.lang.annotation.*;
   ```

2. Define an interface that describes the annotation to the compiler:

   ```
   // Create an annotation description.
   @Documented
   @interface AuthorData
   {
       String Name();
       String Date();
       double Version() default 1.0;
   }
   ```

   In this case, the annotation will appear in the documentation created by Javadoc because it includes the `@Documented` annotation. Every annotation description starts with the `@interface` keyword followed by the name of the annotation type, which is `AuthorData` in this case.

   Within the curly braces, you see the fields used to define the annotation data. This example includes `Name`, `Date`, and `Version`. The `default` keyword provides a value for a particular field. This means the field will use the value if it isn't defined as part of the annotation in the application.

3. Use the annotation in the application:

   ```
   @AuthorData
   (
       Name = "John Smythe",
       Date = "04/01/2014"
   )
   ```

   The annotation appears before the element it affects, such as a class declaration. You must define each field that doesn't have a default value. Optionally, you also define fields that do have a default value. In this case, the name of the author is John Smythe, and the code was last updated on 04/01/2014.

Using annotations

Annotations can take several forms in an application. The intent is to provide some type of documentation and then react to that documentation in some way. For example, if you attempt to use a method that is documented as deprecated, the compiler should generate a warning message to tell you about it unless the call is marked with the @SuppressWarnings annotation. The following example shows various ways in which you can use annotations in your application.

Files needed: `Annotations.java`

1. **Open the editor or IDE that you've chosen to use for this book.**

2. **Type the following code into the editor screen.**

```
// Import the required API
// classes.
import java.lang.annotation.*;

// Create an annotation
// description.
@Documented
@interface AuthorData
{
    String Name();
    String Date();
    double Version() default 1.0;
}

// Use the annotation description.
@AuthorData
(
    Name = "John Smythe",
    Date = "04/01/2014"
)
public class Annotations
{
    @SuppressWarnings("deprecation")
    public static void main(String[] args)
```

GO ONLINE

Annotations are an incredibly powerful new feature in that they can help others interact with your code with considerably fewer errors. In addition, annotations can help you document your code more clearly and even provide special functionality. With this in mind, some developers are creating annotation plugins that you'll be able to use with prepackaged annotations. One of the more important existing plugins is the Checker Framework found at `http://types.cs.washington.edu/checker-framework/`. This framework provides access to type checking annotations, such as @NonNull, which ensures an object has a non-null value and @ReadOnly, which creates static objects that others can't change. You can read more about these plugins at `http://docs.oracle.com/javase/tutorial/java/annotations/type_annotations.html`.

```
{
    // Call on the deprecated method.
    SayHello("Hello There!");
}

// Define a deprecated method.
@Deprecated
static void SayHello(String value)
{
    System.out.println(value);
}
}
```

In this case, the code begins by creating a new annotation named AuthorData. You can read about this process in the "Creating new annotations" section of this chapter. Your custom annotations will normally appear in a separate package, but this one is shown as part of the application code for the sake of simplicity.

The next step is to use the @AuthorData annotation to document the Annotations class declaration. The annotation will actually appear in the Javadoc output as part of the class information.

This example contains a deprecated method, SayHello(). Of course, using that method will generate an error unless you also tell the compiler that it's acceptable to use it in particular cases. You can see the use of both the @Deprecated and @SuppressWarnings predefined annotations in this example.

3. **Save the file to disk by using the filename** `Annotations.java`.

4. **In your command prompt, type** javac Annotations.java **and press Enter.**

   The compiler compiles your application and creates a `.class` file from it. Notice that the compiler doesn't generate any warnings for the deprecated SayHello() method.

5. **Type** java Annotations **and press Enter.**

   You see a simple output message from the application.

 *Summing Up*

Here are the key points you learned about in this chapter:

✔ An array is a list of like items that you can access one element at a time.

✔ Arrays provide methods and properties that describe the array object. In addition, you can access element methods and properties just as you would the base type.

✔ Any array you create is immutable, which means that you must create a new array to resize an existing array.

✔ Each array dimension requires a set of square brackets ([]) to define it. So a two-dimensional array requires two sets ([] []).

✔ Stacks implement a LIFO structure that removes the last item added to the list first.

✔ Queues implement a FIFO structure that removes the first item added to the list.

✔ Deques provides a combination of the capabilities found in both stacks and queues.

✔ Lists make it possible to combine array-like structures with lambda expressions to create a more flexible whole that also requires considerably less code to use.

✔ A Map is a kind of interface that you use to create complex lists that rely on key and value pairs.

✔ Type annotations make it possible to document a code element in a way that the compiler understands, such as indicating that an element is deprecated.

Try-it-yourself lab

For more practice with the features covered in this chapter, try the following exercise on your own:

1. **Open the TwoDimensions.java file supplied with the source code for this book.**

2. **Save the file as ThreeDimensions.java.**

3. **Change the class name to ThreeDimensions.**

   The class name must always match the filename. Otherwise, Java won't compile the file for you.

4. **Add a third dimension to MathTable and fill the table with x, y, and z data.**

5. **Add a third numeric input statement with its associated prompt.**

   This code relies on the Scanner. So, you'd have a line such as int ZAxis = GetNumber.nextInt(); in your code. Make sure you include a prompt for the information.

6. **Compile the application.**

7. **Run the application.**

8. **Provide the three inputs required by the prompts.**

   Does the application output the correct results? For example, does 2 * 3 * 4 actually display an output of 24?

Know this tech talk

annotation: A method of adding documentation to application source code where the compiler can see and interact with the document. This is contrasted to a *comment,* which is documentation that the compiler can't see.

array: The simplest type of list that Java supports. You can add, access, and remove array elements in any order.

array element: An individually accessible item within the list of items stored in an array. The elements are numbered from 0 through the end of the array. Each element is accessed using its unique number.

deque: A double-ended queue — one in which you can add or remove items from either end of the list, but not from the middle of the list. The term deque is pronounced as *deck.*

generic class: A class that relies on a template to create objects of a specific type using generic code that applies equally to all types. The developer provides a parameter that specifies the kind of object the generic class should create. For example, `ArrayList<Integer>` takes a raw `ArrayList` that accepts any object and turns it into a parameterized `ArrayList` that accepts only `Integer` data.

immutable: A variable that can't change its characteristics once you create it.

jagged array: An array in which the dimensions aren't of equal length. The dimension sizes remain fixed after declaration, but the array lacks a precise number of elements per dimension. This type of array is helpful in real-world situations where objects have a differing number of data points.

lambda expression: An anonymous class that contains just one functional interface and one method. Normally, a lambda expression is designed to perform a task using the shortest possible code.

lookup table: An array that's used to hold calculated information that an application uses relatively often. Calculating the information once and storing it in a table makes the application run faster.

map: An intelligent array of items that provides database-like capabilities for data management. A map creates an ordered collection of data that makes it possible to perform complex analysis with less work than an array would require.

parameterized type: A data type that creates container objects that can hold objects of a specific type. The parameter appears within angle brackets (`<>`) after the type declaration and defines specifically which type the container will hold. For example, `ArrayList<Integer>` declares an `ArrayList` object that will hold only `Integer` values. By declaring a specific type, the container can perform type-checking and raise an exception when the application tries to place the wrong type within the container object. The advantages are that the developer obtains additional error-checking, there's less code to write, and the code typically runs faster because the variable type is known during compile type. However, these advantages come at a loss of flexibility, so sometimes the right choice is to use a raw type in place of the parameterized type.

queue: A method of creating an array-like structure where items are removed in the order they are added. This is a First In, First Out (FIFO) structure. When visualizing a queue, think of a line at the bank or grocery store where people enter the queue and wait until it's their turn to receive service.

raw type: A data type that creates container objects that can hold objects of any type. For example, both the `Type` class and the `Array List` class are container types that you can use as a raw type to hold objects of any sort.

stack: A method of creating an array-like structure where the last item added is the first item removed from the list. This is a Last In, First Out (LIFO) structure. When visualizing a stack, think of a stack of pancakes, where the last pancake added is the first one you'd eat.

Chapter 11

Performing Advanced String Manipulation

- ✔ Create strings from other sorts of data and create other sorts of data from strings by *using the conversion methods supplied as part of the Java API.*

- ✔ Locate specific data in strings by *using searches, comparison, and substrings.*

- ✔ Perform string modifications by *replacing string content, extracting characters, and splitting strings.*

- ✔ Create the perfect output for your application by *relying on a wealth of formatting techniques.*

Most applications make heavy use of strings because strings are a data form that humans understand easily. In addition, strings offer flexibility that other data types don't offer. For example, when working with a string, you can mix numbers and text together. A string can contain any sort of information you like. In addition, a string can even include escape characters to make the string's content appear in a way that you like. In short, humans understand strings, and strings are incredibly flexible, making them a popular way to store data.

Unfortunately, the computer doesn't understand string content nearly as well as you do. For example, if you want to perform math-related tasks in your application, you must convert numbers in string format to an actual numeric primitive or object type. Otherwise, the computer will have no idea of how to interact with the data. Fortunately, Java makes the task of converting to and from strings easy.

Strings can become quite long. When they become long enough, you may need to search them in various ways. In addition to looking for specific characters, words, and phrases, you may need to find control characters or perform other tasks that relate to just part of the string. When working with Java, you can search for information at the beginning or end of the string. You can also compare two strings to determine which one contains the sort of information you need. Finally, you can work with substrings, which are parts of strings — a string broken into pieces.

The ability to manipulate strings is also essential. For example, you might want to replace every occurrence of *Jack* with *Jane* in a sentence. You can also extract specific characters (such as escape characters) from a sentence or split the string into smaller pieces by using a *separator character* (a special kind of character that separates one part of the string from another part). Manipulating strings also includes formatting them. You've already performed formatting by using escape characters, as described in the section on escape sequences in Chapter 4. This chapter tells you about a few additional tricks you can use to format strings and make them look nice onscreen.

Converting Data to and from Strings

Data conversion is an essential part of Java programming. Humans understand strings far better than they understand the abstractions of other data types that Java uses. In addition, strings let you combine disparate types such as numbers and Boolean values together. However, you can't use strings to perform computations or assess the truth value of an expression. In short, you need some way to convert between data types.

The most common conversion between `String` and another data type is numbers. In some cases, it's simply easier to manipulate numeric values as strings. However, the following example shows one clear benefit to using a `String` for user input and then converting the data to an `int` — error handling. The following example demonstrates a technique for ensuring accurate numeric input from the user.

LINGO

Data conversion defines a method for changing data from one type to a completely different type. For example, using data conversion, you can change a string into a number. You use data conversion when working with different types, which contrasts with casting, where you convert between similar types, such as between `int` and `byte`. You saw the first example of casting in the section on bytes in Chapter 3.

Files needed: `ConvertIntAndString.java`

> 1. **Open the editor or IDE that you've chosen to use for this book.**
>
> 2. **Type the following code into the editor screen.**

EXTRA INFO

Java 8 makes it possible to use unsigned integer and long values. Normally an integer value ranges between –2,147,483,648 to 2,147,483,647. Likewise, a standard long ranges in value from –9,223,372,036,854,775,808 to 9,223,372,036,854,775,807. However, when working with unsigned values, an integer ranges from 0 to 4,294,967,295, and a long ranges from 0 to 18,446,744,073,709,551,615. This extended positive range can make it possible to perform all sorts of tasks that wouldn't be possible with signed integers and longs, but you can't use negative numbers. To make unsigned values work, you need to use unsigned methods such as `parseUnsignedInt()`, `toUnsignedLong()`, `toUnsignedString()`, and `parseUnsignedLong()` for data conversion. Even though addition, subtraction, and multiplication work the same, division also requires the special `divideUnsigned()` and `remainderUnsigned()` methods. You can read more about the special unsigned methods at `http://download.java.net/jdk8/docs/api/java/lang/Integer.html` and `http://download.java.net/jdk8/docs/api/java/lang/Long.html`.

```java
// Import the required API classes.
import java.util.Scanner;
import java.lang.String;
import java.lang.Integer;

public class ConvertIntAndString
{
    public static void main(String[] args)
    {
        // Create a variable to hold the input.
        String Input = "";

        // Create an intermediate variable.
        int Convert = 0;

        // Create a variable to hold the output.
        String Output = "";

        // Create the scanner.
        Scanner GetInput = new Scanner(System.in);

        // Obtain a string for processing.
        System.out.print("Type any numeric value: ");
        Input = GetInput.nextLine();

        try
        {
            // Convert the String to an int.
            Convert = Integer.parseInt(Input);
        }
        catch (NumberFormatException e)
        {
            // The user input an incorrect value.
            System.out.println("Type an integer value.\n" +
                e.getMessage());

            // Exit the program.
            return;
        }

        // Change the value of the input.
        Convert += 5;

        // Check for a number that's too large
        if (Convert < Integer.parseInt(Input))
        {
            System.out.println("The input number is too
                large!");
            return;
        }
```

```
        // Convert the int to a String.
        Output = String.valueOf(Convert);

        // Display the result.
        System.out.printf("%s + 5 = %s%n", Input,
            Output);
    }
}
```

The application begins by creating three variables: `Input` of type `String`, `Convert` of type `int`, and `Output` of type `String`. The user is then asked to provide an integer input. Of course, the user can type any value. That's why the call to `Integer.parseInt()` is placed in a `try. . .catch` structure. The only exception that this call generates is the `NumberFormatException`. When this occurs, it means that the user has input something other than an integer value.

At this point, the code has access to a known good `int`, so it performs a math operation with it. One of the problems with primitive types in Java is that they don't throw an exception when an overflow occurs (when the application places more information in the variable than it can hold), so this example includes specific code to check for the condition. When the condition occurs, the application outputs an error message and exits.

When the math operation succeeds, the code converts the numeric value in `Convert` to a `String`. At this point, you could easily format the value to provide a pleasing appearance onscreen, but the example leaves that task for the "Formatting String Output" section of the chapter.

LINGO

When converting from a string to a numeric type, the code will **parse** the string looking for data of the right type. Parsing is the act of dividing the string into pieces and then looking through each piece for specific information called a **token.** The string is normally split at spaces, so "This is a String!" becomes four tokens: "This", "is", "a", and "String!" When the right token is found, the code then converts the value of that token into the correct numeric type.

3. **Save the file to disk using the filename `ConvertIntAndString.java`.**

4. **In your command prompt, type** `javac ConvertIntAndString.java` **and press Enter.**

   The compiler compiles your application and creates a `.class` file from it.

5. **Type** `java ConvertIntAndString` **and press Enter.**

   The application asks the user to provide a numeric input.

6. **Type** Hello **and press Enter.**

The application displays the expected error message of "Type an integer value."

7. **Perform Steps 5 and 6 using** 5.5 **as an input value.**

The application correctly detects that this is a floating point number and not an integer, so it displays the error message yet again.

8. **Perform Steps 5 and 6 using** 2147483648 **as an input value.**

This is an integer value, but it's one more than the value an `int` can hold, so the application displays an error message.

9. **Perform Steps 5 and 6 using** 2147483647 **as an input value.**

This value will fit in an `int`, but it causes an overflow, so the application displays an error message.

10. **Perform Steps 5 and 6 using** 1,555 **as an input value.**

This is one case where the application could provide additional handling to allow the user to enter the value. The "Extracting characters" section of the chapter tells you how to work around this particular issue. For now, the application should work with a value of 1,555, but it doesn't because of the comma in the input.

11. **Perform Steps 5 and 6 using** 15 **as an input value.**

You see the expected output shown in Figure 11-1. The use of a string prevents all sorts of incorrect entries. Additional error handling also prevents overflows, but the focus here is that the `String` to `int` and `int` to `String` data conversion serves a useful purpose.

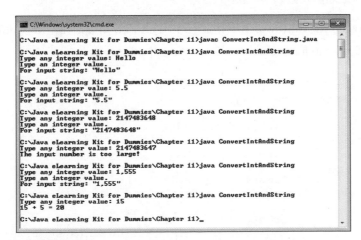

Figure 11-1

Change all the data conversion calls from `parseInt()` to `parse UnsignedInt()`. In addition, you must change `String.valueOf (Convert)` to read `Integer.toUnsignedString(Convert)`. Perform Steps 3 through 10 again to see how the behavior of the application changes. Try inputting a negative number to see what happens.

Finding Information in Strings

Strings are extremely flexible and can contain a lot of information. That makes working with the `String` type different from other data types you use because a `String` can actually contain so much information that it can be hard to find exactly the bit of information you want. Fortunately, the `String` data type also comes with a wealth of methods you can use to locate specific bits of information. The following sections describe these methods and show you how to use them.

Looking at the beginning or end of the string

Sometimes it's helpful to look at the beginning or end of a string for specific information. You may not care what the center of the string contains; only that it starts (or ends) the right way. In the following example, you see how to look for specific information at the beginning and end of a string.

Files needed: `StartAndEnd.java`

1. **Open the editor or IDE that you've chosen to use for this book.**

2. **Type the following code into the editor screen.**

```java
// Import the required API classes.
import java.util.Scanner;
import java.lang.String;

public class StartAndEnd
{
    public static void main(String[] args)
    {
        // Create a variable to hold the input.
        String Input = "";

        // Create the scanner.
        Scanner GetInput = new Scanner(System.in);

        // Obtain a string for processing.
        System.out.print("Type the secret string: ");
        Input = GetInput.nextLine();
```

```
    // Check the beginning and end of the string.
    if ((Input.toUpperCase().startsWith("HELLO"))
        && (Input.toUpperCase().endsWith("WORLD")))
        System.out.println("You typed the secret
            string!");
    else
        System.out.println("Try again.");
    }
}
```

The example asks for an input string from the user. It then converts this string to uppercase and looks at both the beginning and the end of the string for a specific value. In this case, the beginning of the string must contain the word HELLO, and the end of the string must contain WORLD. Using the `toUpperCase()` method ensures that the user can type the input in any case and still succeed. When the input doesn't match, the application outputs an error message.

3. **Save the file to disk using the filename StartAndEnd.java.**

4. **In your command prompt, type** javac StartAndEnd.java **and press Enter.**

   The compiler compiles your application and creates a `.class` file from it.

5. **Type** java StartAndEnd **and press Enter.**

   The application asks the user to provide a string.

6. **Type** Some String **and press Enter.**

   The application displays the expected error message.

7. **Perform Steps 5 and 6 using** Hello Beautiful World **as an input value.**

   You see the success message, as shown in Figure 11-2. As you can see, the center of the string doesn't matter.

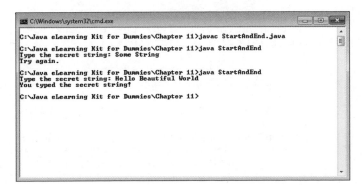

Figure 11-2

Working with substrings

Substrings are parts of a string. You choose a section of string at the beginning, middle, or end of a string and use it as a separate entity. Developers use substrings for all sorts of tasks. For example, many sorting routines are based on substrings, as are many search techniques. The following example shows a simple use of substrings.

Files needed: `Substrings.java`

1. **Open the editor or IDE that you've chosen to use for this book.**

2. **Type the following code into the editor screen.**

```java
// Import the required API
// classes.
import java.util.Scanner;
import java.lang.String;

public class Substrings
{
   public static void main(String[] args)
   {
      // Create a variable to hold the input.
      String Input = "";

      // Create the scanner.
      Scanner GetInput = new Scanner(System.in);

      // Obtain a string for processing.
      System.out.print("Type the secret string: ");
      Input = GetInput.nextLine();

      // Look for the search string.
      int Start = Input.toUpperCase().indexOf("HELLO");

      // Determine whether the string exists.
      if (Start != -1)
         System.out.println(
               "The string contains " +
               Input.substring(Start, Start + 5) +
               " at position: " + Start);
      else
         System.out.println("The string doesn't
            contain HELLO.");
   }
}
```

LINGO

A **substring** is any set of contiguous characters found in a larger string. An application can take a series of contiguous characters out of the beginning, middle, or end of a string and use it as a substring. The characters in a substring are always contiguous — you can't take a character here and a character there and call it a substring. For example, in the string "Hello World," one potential substring is the word *Hello*.

The example asks for an input string from the user. It then converts this string to uppercase and looks for the word HELLO anywhere in the string. The indexOf() method returns a number that specifies the location of HELLO in the string. If HELLO doesn't appear in the string, then indexOf() returns a value of –1. The if statement detects this value and provides the required output.

When the user has entered the word HELLO somewhere in the string, the application uses the substring() method to extract the word from Input. This example uses both a starting and an ending index. You can also call the substring() method with just a starting index, which returns the entire string from that point on.

3. Save the file to disk using the filename Substrings.java.

4. In your command prompt, type javac Substrings.java **and press Enter.**

The compiler compiles your application and creates a .class file from it.

5. Type java Substrings **and press Enter.**

The application asks the user to provide a string.

6. Type Hello World **and press Enter.**

The application displays the expected success message.

7. Perform Steps 5 and 6 using Yellow Hello Goodbye **as an input value.**

You see the success message again as shown in Figure 11-3. As you can see, the position of HELLO in the string doesn't matter.

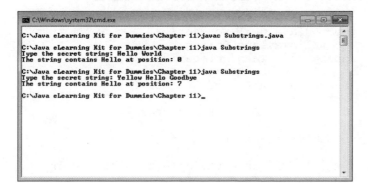

Figure 11-3

Modifying String Content

In many cases, you need to change the content of a string in some way. For example, you might want to replace every occurrence of the letter *T* with a letter *U*. It's also possible to remove characters and to split strings into pieces as needed. Some of these techniques see a lot of use in applications because they're so handy. For example, you'll find that sometimes you must split a path to a file on disk into its component parts in order to actually locate the file. The following sections explain how to modify string content.

Extracting characters

Users can input data in a range of formats. In some cases, you can prevent an error by extracting excess characters from the string. For example, when a user types 1,555 in place of 1555, the application can simply remove the comma (,) before it processes the input. The following example builds on the ConvertIntAndString example shown in the "Converting Data to and from Strings" section of the chapter to demonstrate character extraction techniques.

Files needed: `ExtractCharacter.java`

1. **Open the editor or IDE that you've chosen to use for this book.**

2. **Type the following code into the editor screen.**

```java
// Import the required API classes.
import java.util.Scanner;
import java.lang.String;
import java.lang.Integer;
import java.text.DecimalFormatSymbols;
import java.util.Locale;

public class ExtractCharacter
{
    public static void main(String[] args)
    {
        // Create a variable to hold the input.
        String Input = "";

        // Create an intermediate variable.
        int Convert = 0;

        // Create a variable to hold the output.
        String Output = "";
```

```
// Create the scanner.
Scanner GetInput = new Scanner(System.in);

// Obtain a string for processing.
System.out.print("Type any integer value: ");
Input = GetInput.nextLine();

// Obtain the thousands separator for the
// current locale.

DecimalFormatSymbols DFS =

    DecimalFormatSymbols.getInstance(Locale.
      getDefault());
char Thousands = DFS.getGroupingSeparator();

// Remove the thousands separator from the
// string.
String TempString = "";
for (int Index = 0; Index < Input.length();
  Index++)
    if (Input.charAt(Index) != Thousands)
      TempString += Input.charAt(Index);

// Place the remainder in Input.
Input = TempString;

try
{
    // Convert the String to an int.
    Convert = Integer.parseInt(Input);
}
catch (NumberFormatException e)
{
    // The user input an incorrect value.
    System.out.println("Type an integer value.\n" +
        e.getMessage());

    // Exit the program.
    return;
}

// Change the value of the input.
Convert += 5;

// Check for a number that's too large.
if (Convert < Integer.parseInt(Input))
{
    System.out.println("The input number is too
      large!");
    return;
}
```

```
            // Convert the int to a String.
            Output = String.valueOf(Convert);

            // Display the result.
            System.out.printf("%s + 5 = %s%n", Input,
               Output);
        }
    }
```

This example works much the same as the ConvertIntAndString example. However, notice that after the application obtains input from the user, it begins a process of checking for the thousands separator that the user could have added between groups of numbers. The DFS, of type DecimalFormatSymbols, provides access to a number of formatting symbols, including the thousands separator obtained with a call to getGroupingSeparator().

Whenever you work with potentially regional information, such as a thousands separator, make sure you obtain the correct information for the desired locale. In this case, the application obtains the default locale for the system by calling Locale.getDefault(). However, you can also obtain specific locales as needed by accessing other members of the Locale class.

Now that the application knows which character represents a thousands separator, it uses a for loop to remove this character from Input. The code relies on a temporary String, TempString to aid in the task. The actual character extraction is performed using the Input.charAt() method, which allows the loop to examine one character at a time in the string. Whenever the current character doesn't equal the value in Thousands (in other words, it isn't a thousands character), it gets added to TempString. Of course, you could use the same method to perform any sort of extraction.

3. **Save the file to disk using the filename ExtractCharacter.java.**

4. **In your command prompt, type** javac ExtractCharacter.java **and press Enter.**

   The compiler compiles your application and creates a .class file from it.

5. **Type** java ExtractCharacter **and press Enter.**

   The application asks the user to provide a numeric input.

6. **Type** 1,555,212 **and press Enter.**

   You see the expected output shown in Figure 11-4.

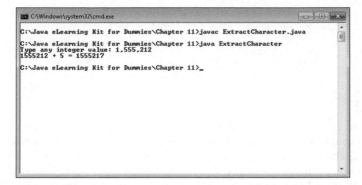

Figure 11-4

Splitting strings

Splitting strings using a particular separator character, such as a space or a slash, is a common practice in Java programming. Developers often receive strings that contain a number of pieces of information that are combined in some way. Using splitting techniques lets the developer work with individual string pieces to coax the information needed by the application out of the string. The following example demonstrates how to use string splitting.

Files needed: `Splitter.java`

1. **Open the editor or IDE that you've chosen to use for this book.**

2. **Type the following code into the editor screen.**

```java
// Import the required API classes.
import java.util.Scanner;
import java.lang.String;

public class Splitter
{
    public static void main(String[] args)
    {
        // Create a variable to hold the input.
        String Input = "";

        // Create the scanner.
        Scanner GetInput = new Scanner(System.in);

        // Obtain a string for processing.
        System.out.print("Type a series of words: ");
        Input = GetInput.nextLine();
```

```
        // Split the string into pieces.
        String[] Output = Input.split(" ");

        // Display the strings on screen.
        for (String Item : Output)
            System.out.println(Item);
    }
}
```

The example begins by obtaining a series of words from the user. Actually, any series of characters of any type separated by spaces will do. The code then calls the split() method to divide the individual words in the string into a String array, Output. At this point, the code can output the separate words using a for-each loop.

3. **Save the file to disk using the filename Splitter.java.**

4. **In your command prompt, type** javac Splitter.java **and press Enter.**

   The compiler compiles your application and creates a .class file from it.

5. **Type** java Splitter **and press Enter.**

   The application asks the user to provide a string.

6. **Type** This is a string to split. **and press Enter.**

   You see the string split into separate words, as shown in Figure 11-5.

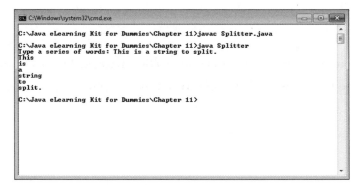

Figure 11-5

Formatting String Output

The ConvertIntAndString example discussed in the "Converting Data to and from Strings" section of the chapter lacked some features. The ExtractCharacter example added the ability to type numbers that included thousands separators. The following example completes the application by providing nicely formatted output.

Files needed: `FormatNumbers.java`

1. **Open the editor or IDE that you've chosen to use for this book.**

2. **Type the following code into the editor screen.**

```java
// Import the required API classes.
import java.util.Scanner;
import java.lang.String;
import java.lang.Integer;
import java.text.DecimalFormatSymbols;
import java.util.Locale;

public class FormatNumbers
{
    public static void main(String[] args)
    {
        // Create a variable to hold the input.
        String Input = "";

        // Create an intermediate variable.
        int Convert = 0;

        // Create a variable to hold the output.
        String Output = "";

        // Create the scanner.
        Scanner GetInput = new Scanner(System.in);

        // Obtain a string for processing.
        System.out.print("Type any integer value: ");
        Input = GetInput.nextLine();

        // Obtain the thousands separator for the
        // current locale.

        DecimalFormatSymbols DFS =

                DecimalFormatSymbols.getInstance(Locale.
                getDefault());
        char Thousands = DFS.getGroupingSeparator();

        // Remove the thousands separator from the
        // string.
        String TempString = "";
        for (int Index = 0; Index < Input.length();
          Index++)
            if (Input.charAt(Index) != Thousands)
                TempString += Input.charAt(Index);

        // Place the remainder in Input.
        Input = TempString;

        try
        {
```

```
        // Convert the String to an int.
        Convert = Integer.parseInt(Input);
    }
    catch (NumberFormatException e)
    {
        // The user input an incorrect value.
        System.out.println("Type an integer value.\n" +
            e.getMessage());

        // Exit the program.
        return;
    }

    // Change the value of the input.
    Convert += 5;

    // Check for a number that's too large.
    if (Convert < Integer.parseInt(Input))
    {
        System.out.println("The input number is too
            large!");
        return;
    }

    // Convert the int to a String.
    Output = String.valueOf(Convert);

    // Add the thousands separators to Input.
    int Compare = (Input.length() - 1) % 3;
    TempString = "";
    for (int Index = Input.length() - 1; Index >= 0;
      Index--)
        if (((Index % 3) == Compare) && (Index !=
      Input.length() - 1))
            TempString = Input.charAt(Index) +
                String.valueOf(Thousands) + TempString;
        else
            TempString = Input.charAt(Index) +
            TempString;
    Input = TempString;

    // Add the thousands separators to Output.
    Compare = (Output.length() - 1) % 3;
    TempString = "";
    for (int Index = Output.length() - 1; Index >= 0;
        Index--)
        if (((Index % 3) == Compare) && (Index !=
            Output.length() - 1))
            TempString = Output.charAt(Index) +
```

```
                       String.valueOf(Thousands) + TempString;
             else
                 TempString = Output.charAt(Index) +
                 TempString;
         Output = TempString;

         // Display the result.
         System.out.printf("%s + 5 = %s%n", Input,
            Output);
     }
}
```

This example adds on to the ExtractCharacter example. In order to provide formatted output, you need to know which thousands separator character to use. Early in the code, the application uses the `DecimalFormatSymbols` object, `DFS`, to store the thousands separator in the `char` variable, `Thousands`, by calling `getGroupingSeparator()`.

The code used to format a string with thousands separators appears near the end of the code. It begins by creating an `int` variable named `Compare` that holds a comparison value. This variable tells Java when to place a comma in the output string. Notice that this is one of the times when you must use the modulus operator (`%`). Suppose that the user types four characters as numbers, which would make the output of `Input.length()` 4. Subtract 1 from this value, and the value is now 3. When you divide that value by 3, the remainder is 0, which is what's stored in `Compare`.

Formatting a string this way means working backward through the string. Some formatting simply works that way. You count off three numbers from the right and add a comma before you start the next series of three numbers, working right to left as you go. It helps to think about how you perform this specific task. In this case, the `for` loop begins at the right end of the string and progresses toward the left end, just as you'd perform the task.

Every time the `for` loop processes another character, it must make a decision about inserting a thousands separator. If the code is already looking at the right end of the string, there isn't any reason to add a thousands separator, which is what the (`Index != Input.length() - 1`) part of the if statement is all about.

Figuring out when you're at the third character from the right is a little harder. `Index` starts at the length of the string minus 1. So, when you have a string with four characters, `Index` starts with a value of 3. Dividing 3 by a value of 3 leaves a remainder of 0, which is the same number that was placed in `Compare`. Only the second part of the `if` statement makes this first pass through the for loop `false`. Three characters later, `Index` has a value of 0, which, when divided by 3, produces a remainder of 0, which again equals Compare. This time the code adds a thousands separator because the code isn't looking at the right end of the string.

There's one last quirk to notice in this example. Instead of using Thousands directly, the code uses String.valueOf(Thousands). Remember that Thousands is a char and so is the output of Input. charAt(Index). If you add these two values together, Java will add their values, rather than concatenate them as strings.

The loop for processing Output is the same as the loop for processing Input. Consequently, you could create a method from this code and call it from main() as needed. The example uses this approach for the sake of clarity.

3. **Save the file to disk using the filename FormatNumbers.java.**

4. **In your command prompt, type** javac FormatNumbers.java **and press Enter.**

   The compiler compiles your application and creates a .class file from it.

5. **Type** java FormatNumbers **and press Enter.**

   The application asks the user to provide a numeric input.

6. **Type** 1,555,212 **and press Enter.**

   You see the expected output shown in Figure 11-6.

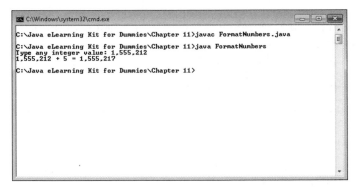

Figure 11-6

 ## Summing Up

Here are the key points you learned about in this chapter:

- Converting data from one type to another means changing the actual presentation and storage of the data, rather than casting it as a larger form of the same type.

- The `String` type provides a number of ways to find information, including looking at a particular part of the string, comparing two strings, and working with substrings.

- Modifying a `String` includes replacing string elements, extracting characters from the string, and splitting the string into pieces.

- Formatting a `String` makes it more presentable to the user and also makes your application friendlier by displaying data in a form the user understands.

Try-it-yourself lab

For more practice with the features covered in this chapter, try the following exercise on your own.

1. **Open the `FormatNumbers.java` file supplied with the source code for this book.**

2. **Save the file as `FormatNumbers2.java`.**

3. **Change the class name to `FormatNumbers2`.**

   The class name must always match the filename. Otherwise, Java won't compile the file for you.

4. **Create a method called `FormatThousands()`.**

5. **Create a generic form of the code used to add the thousands separators to the Input and Output strings.**

   This step means adding input arguments and adding a return value to the `FormatThousands()` method.

6. **Remove the specific code used to add the thousands separators from the example.**

7. **Add calls to the `FormatThousands()` method as needed.**

8. **Compile the application.**

9. **Run the application.**

10. **Provide the input required by the prompt.**

Does the application output the correct results? Does using the `FormatThousands()` method make the code easier to understand?

Know this tech talk

data conversion: A method of converting data between unlike types, such as `String` and `int`. When performing data conversion, Java must actually change the representation of the data so that it fits into the new type.

locale: The characteristics of application output that define a particular language. For example, some languages use a period for the decimal marker, while others use a comma. Formatting data with locale in mind makes it easier for people who speak other languages to use it.

parse: The act of breaking up a string into pieces called tokens, normally at spaces, and then analyzing each token for specific information. For example, "Java is a great language." has five tokens, "Java", "is", "a", "great", and "language."

substring: A string of characters taken from the beginning, middle, or end of a string and used as a separate entity in an application.

token: A single identifiable piece of information within a string. Generally, the sentence is separated by spaces into tokens, so the sentence "Sunny days are nice!" has four tokens in it, "Sunny", "days", "are", and "nice!".

Chapter 12

Interacting with Files

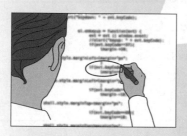

- ✔ Locate and interact with files and directories on a hard drive by *using the features of the* `java.io.File` *class.*

- ✔ Open files so that you can *read file content and interact with it.*

- ✔ Write data to files as needed to *update the file content and create new files.*

- ✔ Use temporary files as needed to *write data to disk while the application runs and then remove it when the application ends.*

All of the applications in this book to date rely on computer memory to perform tasks. Computer memory is a kind of temporary storage. When you turn the computer off, the memory is gone. However, another sort of memory exists — files on disk. These files are more permanent in nature. If you don't specifically delete a file (or the system deletes it for you), the file continues to exist on disk (with the exception of some major calamity such as a disk crash). The permanent memory provided by files lets applications pick up where they left off between computer sessions. Files also hold the data you want to work with in some way.

This chapter helps you discover the techniques used to locate, read, and write files on the hard drive. By knowing these techniques, you can move forward in learning how to locate, read, and write files from other data sources, such as the network. Working with files is a first step into entering a new world of data that this book hasn't previously discussed.

Interacting with the File System

It doesn't matter whether you're using a Macintosh, Linux, or Windows computer — every operating system has some sort of file system associated with it. Yes, differences between file systems exist, but even so, the basic concepts are the same. A file is stored in a specific location on the drive, and if you know that location, you can read and write the file.

LINGO

A **file** is a storage container for data. Files can use a number of methods to hold and organize the data. Some of these organizational methods are easily readable by humans (such as text files), but others aren't (such as graphics files).

Most operating systems rely on a hierarchical storage structure that relies on directories of files. Essentially, a *directory* is simply a container used to store files and other directories.

The location of the directory on disk is called the *path*. A path normally begins at the upper-most point of the drive hierarchy, called the *root node* in most operating systems, and works its way down. For example, a path of C:\ would be the root node on the C drive. The Temp directory located within the root node would have a path of C:\Temp.

Some operating systems allow the use of relative paths. A relative path describes the location of a directory or file based on the current location. Using relative paths can be tricky and won't be explored in this chapter.

A final path designation is the current path — the current location within the hierarchy. Most Java applications rely on the application directory as the current path (sometimes also called the *default* path). Most of the applications in this chapter rely on the current location in the interest of simplicity. In addition, using the current location means that the applications will work equally well on Linux, Macintosh, and Windows systems, which is one of the goals for this book.

The following sections describe some of the ways in which you can access directories and paths using Java. You'll also discover techniques for getting more info about these objects in the file system, such as whether or not a file is hidden.

LINGO

A **directory** is a storage container for both directories (called subdi-rectories) and files. The directory is associated with the operating system's file structure. It's usually hierarchical.

LINGO

A **path** is a description of the loca-tion of a particular directory or file on the hard drive. An absolute path starts with the drive and the root node of the drive and then works its way down to the spe-cific directory or file. Most operat-ing systems also support relative paths that define the location of a directory or file based on the cur-rent location in the directory hier-archy. The "Accessing the Java executables" section of Chapter 1 describes how to create paths on various platforms (Macintosh, Linux, Solaris, and Windows), so you can see how paths differ on various systems.

GO ONLINE

File systems vary among the operating systems. In addition, learning absolutely everything about a file system could require an entire book. Most applications you write using Java can rely on an absolute path or the current path. However, you'll want to know as much as possible about the file system.

Macintosh users have a variety of sources at their disposal. For hardcore technical information, you can rely on the Apple documentation on sites, such as `http://support.apple.com/kb/TA27115`. If you just want to know how paths work, check out the much easier tutorial at `http://www.westwind.com/reference/OS-X/paths.html`. You can also find an interesting comparison of Macintosh and Windows paths at `http://www.zeusprod.com/technote/filepath.html`.

The Macintosh and Linux operating systems are both strongly based on UNIX principles. Consequently, it won't surprise you to discover that once you know how the Macintosh file system works, you also have considerable knowledge about the Linux file system. You can find a good description of the Linux file system and how it contrasts with Windows at `http://www.freeos.com/node/36`. A more technical description of the Linux file system appears at `http://tldp.org/LDP/Linux-Filesystem-Hierarchy/html`.

There are many misconceptions about the Windows file system. The only one of importance for this book is that you must use the backslash when working with Windows paths. It turns out that the forward slash works just as well in most cases (with some exceptions) because Windows, like the Macintosh and Linux file systems, has some basis in UNIX. Part of the problem with Windows is that it has had many file systems over the years, including File Allocation Table (FAT); New Technology File System (NTFS), which is covered at `http://technet.microsoft.com/library/cc766145.aspx`; and now, in Windows 8, the Resilient File System (ReFS), explained at `http://blogs.msdn.com/b/b8/archive/2012/01/16/building-the-next-generation-file-system-for-windows-refs.aspx`. All these file systems work essentially the same way at the command line, which is where you'll be working with applications in this particular chapter. You can find a good resource for Windows developers at `http://www.westga.edu/its/index_5327.php`.

Managing directory information

As previously mentioned, a *directory* is a kind of container used to hold files and other directories. A directory within the current directory is always called a *subdirectory*. The directory that holds the files and subdirectories is called the *parent* directory. The following example demonstrates a technique for listing the content of a directory so you know what files and subdirectories it contains.

Files needed: `ListContent.java`

1. **If necessary, create the directory you plan to use for this example.**

   When working with the downloadable source code, you can find this example in the Chapter 12 directory.

2. **Using a technique appropriate for your operating system, change directories to the example directory.**

3. **Using a technique appropriate for your operating system, create two directories in the current application directory: Test1 and Test2.**

   The downloadable source code already includes this addition.

4. **Using a technique appropriate for your operating system, create a text file: `MyText.txt`. Make sure `MyText.txt` contains some content.**

   The downloadable source code already includes this addition, which contains the string `"Content from a file!"`

5. **Open the editor or IDE that you've chosen to use for this book.**

6. **Type the following code into the editor screen.**

```java
// Import the required API classes.
import java.io.File;

public class ListContent
{
    public static void main(String[] args)
    {
        // Create an object that holds the current
        // directory.
        File Dir = new File(".");

        // Obtain a list of child entries in the
        // directory.
        String[] Children = Dir.list();

        // List the name of each child.
        for (String Child : Children)
            System.out.println(Child);
    }
}
```

The example begins by creating a `File` object, `Dir`. Even though it's counterintuitive, the `File` object can refer to either a file or a directory. Later examples will demonstrate how to detect the difference. For now, all you need to know is that a `File` object can contain either object type.

When working with a `File` object, you must define the location of the file or the directory. Providing an input string that has only a period (`.`) tells Java to use the current directory. This is a similarity in all three operating systems used for this book — a period always tells the operating system that you want to use the current directory.

The next step is to call the `list()` method, which returns a `String[]`, `Children`, that contains one string for each file or directory in the current location. In this case, the example relies on a `for-each` loop to display the name of each `Child` in `Children`.

7. **Save the file to disk using the filename `ListContent.java`.**

8. **In your command prompt, type** javac ListContent.java **and press Enter.**

   The compiler compiles your application and creates a `.class` file from it.

9. **Type** java ListContent **and press Enter.**

   The application displays the content of the current directory, as shown in Figure 12-1. Notice that the output contains the `ListContent` source file, `ListContent.java`, the `ListContent.class` file, and the three additions you made earlier. (If you're using the downloadable source rather than creating the files from scratch, your listing will contain all of the files and directories for the chapter.)

```
C:\Windows\system32\cmd.exe

C:\Java eLearning Kit for Dummies\Chapter 12>javac ListContent.java

C:\Java eLearning Kit for Dummies\Chapter 12>java ListContent
ListContent.class
ListContent.java
MyText.txt
Test1
Test2

C:\Java eLearning Kit for Dummies\Chapter 12>_
```

Figure 12-1

Interacting with files

Files act as containers for data. In most cases, you search directories for the particular file that contains the data needed by an application. After the search is complete, you interact with the files in various ways to use and modify the data the files contain. In the following example, you create an application that ignores other directory entries (doesn't print them) and prints the names of the files contained in the current directory.

Files needed: `ShowFiles.java`

1. **Open the editor or IDE that you've chosen to use for this book.**

2. **Type the following code into the editor screen.**

```java
// Import the required API classes.
import java.io.File;

public class ShowFiles
{
    public static void main(String[] args)
    {
        // Create an object that holds the current
        // directory.
        File Dir = new File(".");

        // Obtain a list of child entries in the
        // directory.
        String[] Children = Dir.list();

        // Check each entry for a filename.
        for (String Child : Children)
        {
            // Create a File object for the child.
            File ChildFile = new File(Child);

            // Determine whether the child is a file.
            if (ChildFile.isFile())
            {
                // Display the filename.
                System.out.println(ChildFile.getName());
            }
        }
    }
}
```

This example is an extension of the ListContent application. It begins by creating the `File` object, `Dir`, to interact with entries in the current directory. However, in this case, instead of listing every `Child` in `Children`, the code uses `Child` to create a `File` object, `ChildFile`.

When you create a `File` object that uses just a filename for the argument, Java looks in the current directory for that file. If you want to look for a file in a different location, you must provide a path to find the file.

To determine whether `ChildFile` refers to a file, the code calls the `isFile()` method. This method returns `true` when the `File` object contains a file. When `ChildFile` does refer to a file, the example calls `ChildFile.getName()` to obtain the name of the file and display it onscreen.

3. **Save the file to disk using the filename** ShowFiles.java.

4. **In your command prompt, type** javac ShowFiles.java **and press Enter.**

   The compiler compiles your application and creates a .class file from it.

5. **Type** java ShowFiles **and press Enter.**

   The application displays only the files in the current directory, as shown in Figure 12-2. (If you're using the downloadable source rather than creating the files from scratch, your listing will contain all of the files for the chapter.)

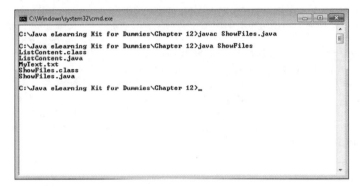

Figure 12-2

Java 8 provides new functionality for working with file listings. The Files.list(), Files.walk(), and Files.find() methods (all part of the java.nio.file.Files package) all return Stream objects (part of the java.util.stream package) that you can use to learn more about the file system. Use the list() method to obtain a listing of the specified directory, the walk() method to obtain information about the file system starting at a specific point in the listing, and the find() method to locate files that match the specification you provide. You can read more about these functions at http://download.java.net/jdk8/docs/api/java/nio/file/Files.html. The Stream object documentation appears at http://download.java.net/jdk8/docs/api/java/util/stream/BaseStream.html.

Defining file and directory attributes

Both files and directories have attributes. One of these attributes determines whether the object is a file or a directory — the ShowFiles example demonstrates how to use this attribute to separate files from directories in the list of entries (by calling `isFile()`). There's a similar `isDirectory()` method you can use to detect directories. However, files and directories provide a wealth of other attributes that help you determine how to interact with them.

By using the file and directory attributes carefully, you can create robust applications that don't suffer from the file and directory problems found in some applications you use (such as listing entries the user can't access). In the following example, you create an application that prints separate lists of directories and files, along with a number of useful attributes for each entry.

LINGO

File systems rely on **attributes** to determine how to interact with files and directories. For example, an attribute can determine whether a file is readable, writeable, or both. Special attributes can tell you when a file or directory was last modified. In short, attributes help you understand file and directory entries better.

Files needed: `GetAttributes.java`

1. **Open the editor or IDE that you've chosen to use for this book.**

2. **Type the following code into the editor screen.**

```
// Import the required API classes.
import java.io.File;
import java.util.Calendar;

public class GetAttributes
{
    public static void main(String[] args)
    {
        // Create an object that holds the current
        // directory.
        File Dir = new File(".");

        // Obtain a list of child entries in the
        // directory.
        String[] Children = Dir.list();

        // Check each entry for a directory.
        System.out.println("Directories:");
        for (String Child : Children)
        {
            // Create a File object for the child.
            File ChildDir = new File(Child);
```

```java
            // Determine whether the child is a file.
            if (ChildDir.isDirectory())
            {
                // Display the attributes.
                ShowAttributes(ChildDir);
            }
        }

        // Check each entry for a filename.
        System.out.println("\nFiles:");
        for (String Child : Children)
        {
            // Create a File object for the child.
            File ChildFile = new File(Child);

            // Determine whether the child is a file.
            if (ChildFile.isFile())
            {
                // Display the attributes.
                ShowAttributes(ChildFile);
            }
        }
    }

    public static void ShowAttributes(File Entry)
    {
        // Display the filename.
        System.out.println(Entry.getName());

        // Display the attributes.
        System.out.print("\tHidden? " + Entry.isHidden());
        System.out.print("\tExecutable? " +
                Entry.canExecute());
        System.out.print("\tReadable? " + Entry.
                canRead());
        System.out.println("\tWriteable? " +
                Entry.canWrite());

        // Display the statistics.
        Calendar FileDate = Calendar.getInstance();
        FileDate.setTimeInMillis(Entry.lastModified());
        System.out.format("\tLast Modified: %te %tB %tY",
                FileDate, FileDate, FileDate);
        System.out.println("\tSize: " + Entry.length());
    }
}
```

The example begins in the `main()` method. As with previous examples in this chapter, the code begins by obtaining a list of entries in the current directory. It then processes each of the entries by looking first for directories and then for files, using the same technique as used in the ShowFiles example.

In this case, instead of printing the directory or filename, the code calls `ShowAttributes()` with the `File` object, `ChildDir` or `ChildFile`. The `ShowAttributes()` method begins by displaying the entry name (file or directory).

Displaying attributes, such as hidden, executable, readable, and writeable, requires only that you call the required method. When working with a production application, you'd use these attributes to determine what you can do with the entry. For example, before you write data to a file, you should ensure that the file supports writing.

Files and directories also have statistics associated with them, such as size and date of last modification. Java doesn't support all of the statistics supported by all of the file systems for each of the platforms. Instead, it focuses on common statistics. In this case, the example shows how to print the date that the file or directory was last modified and the size of the directory or file.

The date you receive is the number of milliseconds since January 1st, 1970, which isn't particularly useful. The example shows how to convert that value into a usable date by creating a `Calendar` object, `FileDate`, and then calling `setTimeInMillis()` with the date and time contained in `Entry.lastModified()`. The example then uses the same code shown in the `DisplayDateTime` example from Chapter 4 to display the date.

3. **Save the file to disk using the filename `GetAttributes.java`.**

4. **In your command prompt, type** javac GetAttributes.java **and press Enter.**

   The compiler compiles your application and creates a `.class` file from it.

5. **Type** java GetAttributes **and press Enter.**

   The application displays the attributes for both files and directories contained in

EXTRA INFO

The new date and time API provided with Java 8 (described in the "Using the New Date and Time API" section of Chapter 3) can shorten the code for obtaining a file date a little. Instead of the two-step process shown in the example, you can substitute a single line of code: `Date FileDate = new Date(Entry.lastModified());`. To make this bit of code work, you must also add `import java.util.Date;` to the beginning of the listing. However, the difference in executable size and application speed is negligible, and the technique shown works with older versions of Java.

the current directory, as shown in Figure 12-3. Notice that the directory entries show 0 for the size statistic. That's because directories are containers and don't contain any data. Files generally contain data, so they have a size. (If you're using the downloadable source rather than creating the files from scratch, your listing will contain the attributes for all of the files and directories for the chapter.)

```
C:\Windows\system32\cmd.exe

C:\Java eLearning Kit for Dummies\Chapter 12>javac GetAttributes.java

C:\Java eLearning Kit for Dummies\Chapter 12>java GetAttributes
Directories:
Test1
        Hidden? false    Executable? true        Readable? true  Writeable? true
        Last Modified: 22 March 2012    Size: 0
Test2
        Hidden? false    Executable? true        Readable? true  Writeable? true
        Last Modified: 22 March 2012    Size: 0

Files:
GetAttributes.class
        Hidden? false    Executable? true        Readable? true  Writeable? true
        Last Modified: 23 March 2012    Size: 1852
GetAttributes.java
        Hidden? false    Executable? true        Readable? true  Writeable? true
        Last Modified: 23 March 2012    Size: 2012
ListContent.class
        Hidden? false    Executable? true        Readable? true  Writeable? true
        Last Modified: 22 March 2012    Size: 621
ListContent.java
        Hidden? false    Executable? true        Readable? true  Writeable? true
        Last Modified: 22 March 2012    Size: 469
MyText.txt
        Hidden? false    Executable? true        Readable? true  Writeable? true
        Last Modified: 23 March 2012    Size: 20
ShowFiles.class
        Hidden? false    Executable? true        Readable? true  Writeable? true
        Last Modified: 22 March 2012    Size: 716
ShowFiles.java
        Hidden? false    Executable? true        Readable? true  Writeable? true
        Last Modified: 22 March 2012    Size: 772

C:\Java eLearning Kit for Dummies\Chapter 12>_
```

Figure 12-3

REMEMBER

Just because a file or directory has a certain attribute, it doesn't mean that it makes sense to perform the associated task on the file or directory. For example, even if a directory returns true when you make the `canExecute()` method call, it doesn't mean you can actually execute a directory. In fact, you can execute only files that contain the right kind of code. Likewise, even if an executable file has the `writeable` attribute set to `true`, it doesn't mean that you should write anything to the file. Attributes specify what you can do, not what you should do.

Manipulating path data

A path describes a location. Absolute paths always begin at the root directory of a drive and work toward the directory or file in question. Relative paths describe the location of a file or directory in relation to the current directory. The current directory is always described using a single period (.), while the parent directory is described using two periods (..). The use of one or two periods to describe a location is a kind of relative path. In the following example, you discover the absolute and relative paths of directories and files.

Files needed: ShowPaths.java

1. Open the editor or IDE that you've chosen to use for this book.

2. Type the following code into the editor screen.

```
// Import the required API classes.
import java.io.File;

public class ShowPaths
{
    public static void main(String[] args)
    {
        // Create an object that holds the current
        // directory.
        File Dir = new File(".");

        // Obtain a list of child entries in the
        // directory.
        String[] Children = Dir.list();

        // Check each entry for a filename.
        for (String Child : Children)
        {
            // Create a File object for the child.
            File ChildFile = new File(Child);

            // Display the relative path.
            System.out.println(ChildFile.getPath());

            // Display the absolute path.
            System.out.println(ChildFile.
                getAbsolutePath());
        }
    }
}
```

In this example, the application begins by getting the list of directories and files in the current directory. It then processes each of these entries one at a time. The call to getPath() displays the relative path, which is simply the name of the directory or file in this case. On the other hand, the call to getAbsolutePath() provides a precise location for this file or directory on disk.

3. Save the file to disk using the filename ShowPaths.java.

4. In your command prompt, type javac ShowPaths.java **and press Enter.**

The compiler compiles your application and creates a .class file from it.

5. Type java ShowPaths **and press Enter.**

The application displays the path information for each of the files and directories in the current location. The precise information you see in Figure 12-4 will vary by your operating system. Each operating system provides a unique way to display path information. The output you see in Figure 12-4 is for the Windows operating system. (If you're using the downloadable source rather than creating the files from scratch, your listing will contain the path information for all of the files and directories for the chapter.)

```
C:\Windows\system32\cmd.exe

C:\Java eLearning Kit for Dummies\Chapter 12>javac ShowPaths.java

C:\Java eLearning Kit for Dummies\Chapter 12>java ShowPaths
GetAttributes.class
C:\Java eLearning Kit for Dummies\Chapter 12\GetAttributes.class
GetAttributes.java
C:\Java eLearning Kit for Dummies\Chapter 12\GetAttributes.java
ListContent.class
C:\Java eLearning Kit for Dummies\Chapter 12\ListContent.class
ListContent.java
C:\Java eLearning Kit for Dummies\Chapter 12\ListContent.java
MyText.txt
C:\Java eLearning Kit for Dummies\Chapter 12\MyText.txt
ShowFiles.class
C:\Java eLearning Kit for Dummies\Chapter 12\ShowFiles.class
ShowFiles.java
C:\Java eLearning Kit for Dummies\Chapter 12\ShowFiles.java
ShowPaths.class
C:\Java eLearning Kit for Dummies\Chapter 12\ShowPaths.class
ShowPaths.java
C:\Java eLearning Kit for Dummies\Chapter 12\ShowPaths.java
Test1
C:\Java eLearning Kit for Dummies\Chapter 12\Test1
Test2
C:\Java eLearning Kit for Dummies\Chapter 12\Test2

C:\Java eLearning Kit for Dummies\Chapter 12>_
```

Figure 12-4

Opening Files for Reading

Files aren't very useful unless you can access the information they contain. For this example, you access the information in the MyText.txt file you created in the "Managing directory information" section of the chapter. However, file access largely works the same way no matter what sort of file you open. In the following example, you open a file, read its content, and display the content onscreen.

Files needed: ReadData.java

1. **Open the editor or IDE that you've chosen to use for this book.**

2. **Type the following code into the editor screen.**

```java
// Import the required API classes.
import java.io.FileInputStream;
import java.io.FileNotFoundException;
import java.io.IOException;
import java.util.Scanner;

public class ReadData
{
    public static void main(String[] args)
    {
        // Create the file input stream.
        FileInputStream Input = null;
        try
        {
            Input = new FileInputStream("MyText.txt");
        }
        catch (FileNotFoundException e)
        {
            // Display an error message if the file is
            // missing.
            System.out.println("The file doesn't
                exist!\n" + e.getMessage());

            // Exit without doing anything more.
            return;
        }

        // Define an object to read from the stream.
        Scanner Reader = new Scanner(Input);

        // Read each line in turn and display it.
        while (Reader.hasNextLine())
            System.out.println(Reader.nextLine());

        // Close the file when you're done.
        try
        {
            Input.close();
        }
        catch (IOException e)
        {
            // Generate an error message when necessary.
            System.out.println("Couldn't close the
                file!/n" + e.getMessage());
        }
    }
}
```

Reading a file begins with the `FileInputStream`, `Input`. Think of the `FileInputStream` as a kind of conduit that transfers data from disk to your application. The `FileInputStream` requires you to provide the name of the file as a minimum. When the file is outside of the current directory, you must also provide the complete path to that file. Notice that you must enclose this code within a `try. . .catch` block, just in case the file doesn't exist. If the file doesn't exist, the application displays an informational message and exits because there isn't anything to process.

There are a number of ways to request information from the `FileInputStream`. This example shows the easiest method, using a `Scanner` object, `Reader`. You use precisely the same technique for reading from a text file as you do from the keyboard. However, the data file represents pre-recorded input, so the example calls `hasNextLine()` to determine whether there's any more input to process. When there's input to process, the code calls `nextLine()` to obtain the input as a string.

Whenever you read or write from a file, you must always close the file when you're done using it. There are many potential problems that occur when you fail to close the file. At a minimum, the application could cause a memory leak in the underlying operating system, which would make the memory inaccessible to other applications and could possibly cause system instability. In addition, failure to close the file could cause damage to the data the file contains. Because there are situations where closing the file might not work, such as the user deleting the file before it gets closed, you must also encase the `Input.close()` call in a `try. . .catch` block.

3. **Save the file to disk using the filename `ReadData.java`.**

4. **In your command prompt, type** javac ReadData.java **and press Enter.**

    The compiler compiles your application and creates a `.class` file from it.

5. **Type** java ReadData **and press Enter.**

    The application displays the content of the `MyText.txt` data file, as shown in Figure 12-5. The output from your example will vary from that shown in Figure 12-5 if you've modified the content of `MyText.txt`.

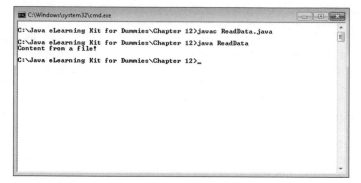

Figure 12-5

Writing to Files

Writing to a file saves the data you write for later use. Data can take any form that you normally create with your computer. Of course, the `MyText.txt` file contains textual information. However, the same techniques used to write text data can apply to other sorts of data. The actual implementation can vary a little, but the idea is the same. In the following example, you create an application that can write data to a file.

Files needed: `WriteData.java`

1. **Open the editor or IDE that you've chosen to use for this book.**

2. **Type the following code into the editor screen.**

```java
// Import the required API classes.
import java.io.FileNotFoundException;
import java.io.FileOutputStream;
import java.io.OutputStreamWriter;
import java.io.IOException;
import java.util.Scanner;
import java.lang.String;

public class WriteData
{
    public static void main(String[] args)
    {
        // Create the file output stream.
        FileOutputStream Output = null;
        try
        {
            Output = new FileOutputStream("MyText.txt");
        }
        catch (FileNotFoundException e)
        {
            System.out.println("The file doesn't
              exist!\n" + e.getMessage());
        }

        // Define an object to write to the stream.
        OutputStreamWriter Writer =
                new OutputStreamWriter(Output);

        // Create a string for input data.
        String Data = "";

        // Define a means for inputting from the
        // keyboard.
        Scanner GetData = new Scanner(System.in);

        // Keep processing data until told otherwise.
        while (Data.toUpperCase().compareTo("DONE") != 0)
        {

            // Get some input from the user.
            System.out.print(
                    "Type something to write to the file or
              DONE to exit: ");
            Data = GetData.nextLine();

            // Write each line in turn.
            try
            {
                Writer.write(Data + "\n");
            }
```

```
                        catch (IOException e)
                        {
                           // Display an error message.
                           System.out.println("Couldn't write to the
                           file!/n" +
                                   e.getMessage());
                        }

                        // Display what was written.
                        System.out.println("Writing: " + Data);
                     }

                  // Close the file when you're done.
                  try
                  {
                     Writer.close();
                  }
                  catch (IOException e)
                  {
                     // Generate an error message when necessary.
                     System.out.println("Couldn't close the
                      file!/n" + e.getMessage());
                  }
               }
            }
```

Compare the code in this example with the ReadData example and you see that there are many similarities. What has changed is that instead of reading data, you're outputting data. In sum, the direction of information flow has changed. With this in mind, the application creates a `FileOutputStream`, `Output`, and uses it to create an `OutputStreamWriter`, `Writer`.

In order to make this example a bit more realistic, the application creates a `Scanner`, `GetData`, and uses it to obtain input from the user. When the user types a new value and presses Enter, the application outputs it to the data file and also writes it onscreen. To end the application, the user types Done (in any case) and presses Enter.

As with reading data, you must close the file when the application ends. Otherwise, it's almost certain that you'll experience data loss. The same sorts of exceptions occur with this application as when you read data.

3. **Save the file to disk using the filename `WriteData.java`.**

4. **In your command prompt, type** javac WriteData.java **and press Enter.**

   The compiler compiles your application and creates a `.class` file from it.

5. **Type** java WriteData **and press Enter.**

   The application asks you to provide some input data to write to the file.

6. **Type** Hello **and press Enter.**

   The application tells you that it has written the data to disk.

7. **Type** Done **and press Enter.**

   The application ends. Of course, you don't really know whether the application has worked — it could tell you anything! This is one situation where you can check the functionality of one example by using another example.

8. **Type** java ReadData **and press Enter.**

   You see the strings that you previously typed as shown in Figure 12-6. Notice that the original string is overwritten with the new data.

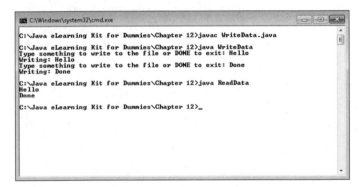

Figure 12-6

Creating and Using Temporary Files

As their name implies, temporary files are used to temporarily store information on disk. Applications use temporary files for a lot of different tasks — everything from making a backup of a data file before writing information to it to using the disk in place of memory as a scratchpad for information. In the following example, you create, write, and read a temporary file on disk.

Files needed: UseTempFiles.java

1. **Open the editor or IDE that you've chosen to use for this book.**

2. **Type the following code into the editor screen.**

```java
// Import the required API classes.
import java.io.File;
import java.io.FileInputStream;
import java.io.FileNotFoundException;
import java.io.FileOutputStream;
import java.io.OutputStreamWriter;
import java.io.IOException;
import java.util.Scanner;
import java.lang.String;

public class UseTempFiles
{
    public static void main(String[] args)
    {
        // Create a temporary file.
        File Temp = null;
        try
        {
            Temp = File.createTempFile("MyTemp", ".txt");
        }
        catch (IOException e)
        {
            // Generate an error message when necessary.
            System.out.println("Couldn't create the
                file!/n" + e.getMessage());

            // Exit the application.
            return;
        }

        // Configure the file for automatic deletion
        // when the application ends.
        Temp.deleteOnExit();

        // Write data to the file.
        WriteData(Temp);

        // Pause to look at the file.
        System.out.print(
            "Check the temporary file and then press
                Enter.");
        Scanner GetEnter = new Scanner(System.in);
        GetEnter.nextLine();

        // Read data from the file.
        ReadData(Temp);
    }
```

```
    // Write data to the temporary file.
    public static void WriteData(File Temp)
    {
        // Create the file output stream.
FileOutputStream Output = null;
        try
        {
            Output = new FileOutputStream(Temp);
        }
        catch (FileNotFoundException e)
        {
            System.out.println("The file doesn't
                exist!\n" + e.getMessage());
        }

        // Define an object to write to the stream.
        OutputStreamWriter Writer =
                new OutputStreamWriter(Output);

        // Write some data to the file.
        try
        {
            Writer.write("This is a temporary file!");
        }
        catch (IOException e)
        {
            // Display an error message.
            System.out.println("Couldn't write to the
                file!/n" + e.getMessage());
        }

        // Display what was written.
        System.out.println("Writing Data.");

        // Close the file when you're done.
        try
        {
            Writer.close();
        }
        catch (IOException e)
        {
            // Generate an error message when necessary.
            System.out.println("Couldn't close the
                file!/n" + e.getMessage());
        }
    }
```

```
// Read the data back from the temporary file.
public static void ReadData(File Temp)
{
   // Create the file input stream.
   FileInputStream Input = null;
   try
   {
      Input = new FileInputStream(Temp);
   }
   catch (FileNotFoundException e)
   {
      // Display an error message if the file is
      // missing.
      System.out.println("The file doesn't
         exist!\n" + e.getMessage());

      // Exit without doing anything more.
      return;
   }

   // Define an object to read from the stream.
   Scanner Reader = new Scanner(Input);

   // Read each line in turn and display it.
   while (Reader.hasNextLine())
      System.out.println(Reader.nextLine());

   // Close the file when you're done.
   try
   {
      Input.close();
   }
   catch (IOException e)
   {
      // Generate an error message when necessary.
      System.out.println("Couldn't close the
         file!/n" + e.getMessage());
   }
}
}
```

This looks like a lot of code, but you already know how most of it works because you've already seen it in action. The WriteData() and ReadData() methods work just like the ReadData and WriteData examples in this chapter. The only difference is that instead of using a String to define the name of the file, this version uses the File object, Temp, to define it.

The main() method begins by creating a temporary File, Temp. This file has a filename that begins with MyTemp and has a file extension of .txt. The filename also includes a random number to make it unique. Consequently, you can use the same call to create as many temporary files as needed for your application. The application could always experience an error, such as a lack of hard drive space to create the temporary file, so you must encase this call in a try. . .catch block.

An important part of using temporary files is making sure they actually are temporary. If you look at the location used to hold temporary files on your hard drive, it almost certainly contains a wealth of temporary files that didn't get deleted by the application that created them. This is an extremely poor way to write application code. To tell Java that you want to delete this file automatically, the application calls deleteOnExit().

At this point, the File object is used like any other File object to read and write data. The difference is that this data is temporary.

3. **Save the file to disk using the filename UseTempFiles.java.**

4. **In your command prompt, type** javac UseTempFiles.java **and press Enter.**

   The compiler compiles your application and creates a .class file from it.

5. **Type** java UseTempFiles **and press Enter.**

   The application writes data to the temporary file and tells you to find the temporary file on your system. Of course, the question is whether this temporary file actually exists and where you can find it on disk. The temporary file is real and you'll see it in action in the next step. The location depends on your operating system. When working with a Macintosh or Linux system, you'll likely find the file in your /tmp directory. In most cases, you can find the folder by executing the echo $TMPDIR command. Windows users will typically find the temporary files in their C:\Users*UserName*\AppData\Local\Temp directory, where UserName is the user's name. You can also obtain this information by executing the echo %Temp% command. In my case, the temporary files are found in the C:\Users\John\AppData\Local\Temp directory.

6. **Locate the temporary file on your drive system.**

   You see a file similar to the one shown in Figure 12-7. The filename will contain MyTemp at the beginning and use the .txt extension, just as expected. In this case, the filename is MyTemp8399517910498436675. txt. The numbers in the middle are arbitrary. When you open this file, you see the text that the application wrote to it.

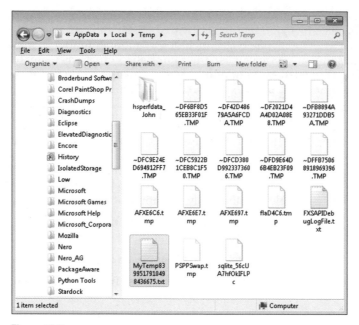

Figure 12-7

7. **Press Enter at the command prompt you used to run your application.**

The application displays the temporary information as shown in Figure 12-8.

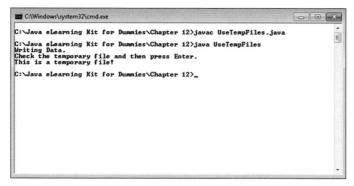

Figure 12-8

8. **Look at the temporary directory again.**

Notice that the application has automatically deleted the file and cleaned up after itself. This is how your application should always work with temporary files.

Summing Up

Here are the key points you learned about in this chapter:

- ✔ Files store data in specific locations on your hard drive.
- ✔ Directories act as containers to hold both directories and files.
- ✔ A path describes the precise location of a file or directory on disk.
- ✔ Attributes make it possible to determine specifics about a file or directory, such as whether you can read or write it.
- ✔ An absolute path begins at the root directory of the host drive and contains every subdirectory between it and the location of the desired directory or file.
- ✔ A relative path begins at the current location and describes how to access the desired directory or file from that point.
- ✔ The single period (.) represents the current directory, while the double period (..) represents the parent directory.
- ✔ Reading and writing files involves the use of streams that act as conduits between the hard drive and the user application.
- ✔ Whenever you finish reading from or writing to a data file, you must close it or the file could become damaged.
- ✔ Temporary files are useful for creating backups of files while you write to them or acting as a scratchpad for your application.

Try-it-yourself lab

For more practice with the features covered in this chapter, try the following exercise on your own.

1. **Open the `ReadData.java` file supplied with the source code for this book.**

2. **Save the file as `ReadData2.java`.**

3. **Change the class name to `ReadData2`.**

   The class name must always match the filename. Otherwise, Java won't compile the file for you.

4. **Create a file named `MyInt.txt` and fill it with the numbers 1 through 5, separated by spaces.**

   The numbers should appear as 1 2 3 4 5. The space helps Java recognize individual integer values.

5. **Change the Input line to use the new file by changing the `FileInputStream` constructor.**

   You change this text to read `FileInputStream("MyInt.txt")`.

6. **Change the `Reader` loop so it handles `int` values rather than strings.**

   Your code will look similar to this:

   ```
   while (Reader.hasNextInt())
       System.out.println(Reader.nextInt());
   ```

7. **Compile and run the application.**

   Does the application output the correct results? How could you change this application to work with `char` values instead?

Know this tech talk

attribute: An indicator of the configuration or status of a file or directory on disk. One attribute describes whether the entry is a file or a directory. Other attributes describe whether the entry is readable, writeable, or hidden. There are also statistics associated with the entries, such as the date of last modification and the size of a file.

directory: A container used to store files or other directories on disk. Directories help organize the disk content and make it easier to find.

file: A permanent storage container on disk for data. A file can contain both textual and binary data.

path: A string that can start with a volume letter or name, a list of directory entries, and sometimes ending with a filename that describes the location of a directory or file on disk. Paths can take a number of forms. An absolute path always starts at the root directory of the disk and moves down through the directory hierarchy toward the directory or file in question. Relative paths describe the location of a file or directory in relation to the current location on disk.

stream: A connection between an application and a data source used to transfer data to or from the application. Streams normally flow in one direction: either input or output. If you want to read data from a data source, you use an input stream. On the other hand, if you want to write data to a data source, you use an output stream.

Chapter 13

Manipulating XML Data

- ✔ Use Java to *read, write, and manipulate XML data* as part of your application strategy.

- ✔ Read XML from disk to *create data displays onscreen.*

- ✔ Write XML to disk to *save data in an organized manner without loss of context.*

1. **How can I use XML data in my Java applications?**

Java provides full access to standardized XML data files so you can save both data and its context, save user settings using the same method across platforms, and access information in other locations such as web services. You can get an overview of this technology beginning on page

2. **Is it possible to read XML data from disk and use it without a lot of hassle?**

It's relatively easy to read XML data from disk and use the information in a consistent way to present information, as described on page

3. **Will I have to do a lot for formatting to write my XML data to disk?**

Creating XML output is relatively straightforward in Java — you worry about the data, Java worries about the formatting, as shown on page

You have many different ways to store your data, but the majority of them are either unique to a particular platform or are implemented inconsistently across platforms. In the past, developers often had to use text files to transfer data between platforms, but text files suffer from a loss of context. The data is there, but what the data means is missing. The eXtensible Markup Language (XML), one of the better innovations when it comes to data storage, was developed in order to address this issue. XML provides the means to describe data in a way that none of the context or meaning is lost. This Chapter builds on what you discovered in Chapter 12 to provide a basic overview of XML usage in Java.

Understanding How XML and Java Interact

It's important not to become overwhelmed by XML before you even get started using it. At its core, XML is simply a fancy sort of text file. So, when you read XML into your application, the underlying technology is simply reading a text file — just as you've already done in Chapter 12. The difference is in the way the text is interpreted. XML relies on *tags* — information between angle brackets (`<>`) — to describe the data contained within the text file. So, on top of reading the file into the application as text, Java must also provide a means to interpret the data in order to obtain the meaning that the text contains. For example, an entry such as `<Name>John</Name>` could mean that the user's name is John.

Java follows all the standards-based rules regarding XML. In addition, it implements these standards in the same way across all platforms that Java supports. Consequently, when you write an application that uses XML on your PC, the same code works in the same way on a Macintosh or a Linux system. It's this ability to move data anywhere and yet maintain the data context and meaning that makes XML such a great choice for data storage.

Even though this chapter discusses only Java's use of XML with disk-based files, XML is used in a considerable number of environments. For example, you can use XML to request information from other people or vendors using any of the methods that the other person or vendor supports (such as REpresentational State Transfer or REST for web services). XML is so useful that any book on Java has to at least tell you that the technology exists and that it's relatively straightforward to use, as this book has done.

GO ONLINE

This book doesn't offer a tutorial on XML — it assumes that you have at least a basic knowledge of XML already. However, if you don't know anything about XML, be sure to investigate some of the many well-written online tutorials about XML. Of all the available tutorials, the one on the w3schools. com site at `http://www.w3schools.com/xml` is probably the easiest to understand and provides the best examples. As your knowledge increases, try the tutorial on the XMLFiles.com site at `http://www.xmlfiles.com/xml`. When you have the basics down, try the Java-specific tutorial at `http://docs.oracle.com/javase/tutorial_intro.html`.

Reading XML Data from Files

To work with XML, you must read the data from some source. Keep in mind that, no matter what source you use, the XML data follows the same convention. So, whether you get the data from your local disk drive or from a website, the essential process is the same. You read the data from the source and then use code to interpret the information it contains.

This chapter uses a simple XML file for demonstration purposes named, `MyData.xml`. This file contains a few bits of interesting information in a particular format. Here's the content of that file:

```xml
<?xml version="1.0" encoding="UTF-8" standalone="no"?>
  <Root>
    <Name>Sally</Name>
    <Fruits>
       <Fruit>Apple</Fruit>
       <Fruit>Pear</Fruit>
    </Fruits>
    <Color>Blue</Color>
  </Root>
```

The first line is the processing instruction found in every fully formed XML document. Every XML document also has a *root* node that defines the beginning and end of the document content. The three *child* nodes define the name of the person involved, a list of favorite fruits, and her favorite color. The list of fruits consists of <Fruit> nodes, each of which contains a single fruit. Most XML files are more complicated than this one, but this serves as a good starting point.

The following example demonstrates how to read this file and display its content onscreen.

Files needed: ReadXML.java, MyData.xml

1. **Open the editor or IDE that you've chosen to use for this book.**

2. **Type the following code into the editor screen.**

```java
// Import the required API classes.
import java.io.File;
import javax.xml.parsers.DocumentBuilderFactory;
import javax.xml.parsers.DocumentBuilder;
import javax.xml.parsers.ParserConfigurationException;
import org.w3c.dom.Document;
import org.xml.sax.SAXException;
import java.io.IOException;
import org.w3c.dom.Node;
import org.w3c.dom.NodeList;
import org.w3c.dom.Element;

public class ReadXML
{
    public static void main(String[] args)
    {
        // Create a File object to access the file on disk.
        File InputFile = new File("MyData.xml");

        // Create a factory for building an XML document.
        DocumentBuilderFactory Factory =
                DocumentBuilderFactory.newInstance();

        // Create an object to build a document.
        DocumentBuilder Builder = null;
        try
        {
            Builder = Factory.newDocumentBuilder();
        }
        catch (ParserConfigurationException e)
        {
```

```java
            // Display an error message and exit.
            System.out.println("Could not create document builder!"
                + e.getMessage());
            return;
        }

        // Use the factory to build an XML document based
        // on the file content.
        Document XMLDoc = null;
        try
        {
            XMLDoc = Builder.parse(InputFile);
        }
        catch (SAXException e)
        {
            // Display an error message and exit.
            System.out.println("Could not parse the file!"
                + e.getMessage());
            return;
        }
        catch (IOException e)
        {
            // Display an error message and exit.
            System.out.println("Could not access the file!"
                + e.getMessage());
            return;
        }

        // Obtain the root node and process it, along with all of
        // the child nodes it contains.
        Element Root = XMLDoc.getDocumentElement();
        ProcessElements(Root, 0);
    }

    public static void ProcessElements(Element ThisElement,
                                       int Level)
    {
        // Display the current level.
        System.out.print(Level);

        // Add tabs to the output.
        for (int Count = 0; Count <= Level; Count++)
            System.out.print("\t");

        // Display the node name.
        System.out.print(ThisElement.getNodeName());
```

```
        // If the child node is a value, then print it as well.
        if (ThisElement.hasChildNodes())
            if (ThisElement.getFirstChild().getNodeType() ==
                Node.TEXT_NODE)

                System.out.print("\t" +
                    ThisElement.getFirstChild().getNodeValue());

        // End this line of output.
        System.out.println();

        // Check for child nodes.
        if (ThisElement.hasChildNodes())
        {
            // Obtain a list of the nodes contained in this element.
            NodeList ChildNodes = ThisElement.getChildNodes();

            // Process each of the nodes.
            for (int Index = 0; Index < ChildNodes.getLength();
                Index++)
            {
                if (ChildNodes.item(Index).getNodeType() ==
                    Node.ELEMENT_NODE)
                {
                    Element ChildElement =
                        (Element)ChildNodes.item(Index);
                    ProcessElements(ChildElement, Level + 1);
                }
            }
        }
    }
}
```

This is one of the most complex examples in the book, so it requires a substantial number of imports. Normally, you'd start to use the wildcard character for this number of imports. For example, instead of using `import javax.xml.parsers.DocumentBuilderFactory;`, you'd type `import javax.xml.parsers.*;` instead so that you don't need to individually type the classes from the package. The reason the example uses this approach is so that you can see precisely which classes to import. The imports also appear in the order in which they're used in the example code.

The example begins by creating a `File` object, `InputFile`, to access the XML file on disk. This file contains XML *data;* it doesn't contain an XML *document*. The difference between the two is that the XML data is simply text that contains information in a specific format. An XML document adds intelligence to that data so that you can tell the difference between a color and a fruit.

To create an XML document, you begin by creating a `Document Builder Factory` — `Factory`, in this case. Think of `Factory` as a special object that outputs a kind of product, which turns out to be a `DocumentBuilder` named `Builder`. You can use `Builder` to create an XML document based on the content in `MyData.xml`. To do this, `Builder` must read the content of `MyData.xml` and interpret it in a process called *parsing*. The output of the `Builder.parse()` method call is an XML `Document` object, `XMLDoc`.

At this point, you have access to an XML document that contains a number of elements, beginning with the processing instruction and the topmost element, `<Root>`. The next step is to process this information to provide useful output. Calling `ProcessElements()` with the `Root Element` and the current document level (0) starts the process.

The `ProcessElements()` method shows how to use recursion in Java. *Recursion* is a special programming technique where a method calls itself to perform work. The idea is to divide a complex task consisting of multiple subtasks into a really simple single task and then use the result from that task to work upward into more complex parts of the task. You use recursion when you can't be sure how many levels a complex task will contain.

LINGO

The act of **parsing** any kind of data involves reading and interpreting the data to create a particular kind of object output. When working with XML data, the act of parsing interprets the special symbols within the text document and uses them to create a `Document` object that has intelligence about the design of the XML data. The result is that you can request information from the `Document` about the content of the XML document in context. A `<Color>` node becomes different from a `<Fruit>` node.

The `ProcessElements()` method begins by displaying the current level. It then adds a number of tabs to indent the information at higher levels to a greater degree. The method displays the element name next and then displays the value contained within that element, if any. Notice how the code uses the `getNodeType()` method to obtain the type of the current node and compare it against a known node type, which is `Node.TEXT_NODE` for an element value.

At this point, the code must ask whether there are any child nodes to process. For example, the `<Root>` element will have child nodes, but the `<Fruit>` element doesn't. When there are child elements to process, the code creates a `NodeList` object, `ChildNodes`, to access them. It then processes each node in turn. When the node type is `Node.ELEMENT_NODE`, the method *coerces* the type (changes it, essentially) into an Element, `ChildElement`, and uses `ChildElement` to recursively call `ProcessElements()`. Notice that performing this recursive call increases the `Level` value.

LINGO

You use **recursion** to break tasks down into simple pieces in Java. A recursive method keeps breaking down the task until only a simple task is left. It then uses the result of that task to make higher-level tasks easier to manage and perform. Recursive routines are an elegant way to handle situations where you don't know how complex the task will become at the outset. For example, there isn't any way to know how many elements an XML file will contain, so using recursion provides one method for dealing with that complexity.

Any time you use recursion, you must provide a method for the recursive routine to stop. In this case, recursion continues only as long as there are nodes of type `Node.ELEMENT_NODE` to process. When the code runs out of these nodes to process, the application automatically stops calling the `ProcessElements()` method recursively. If you don't provide an escape mechanism, the code will continue to run infinitely, and the system will eventually run out of memory (causing a system crash).

3. **Type** javac ReadXML.java **and press Enter.**

   The compiler compiles your application and creates a `.class` file from it.

4. **Type** java ReadXML **and press Enter.**

   The application displays a hierarchical list of the nodes within the XML file, as shown in Figure 13-1. Notice how the level numbering and the indentation show precisely how the data is organized within the file.

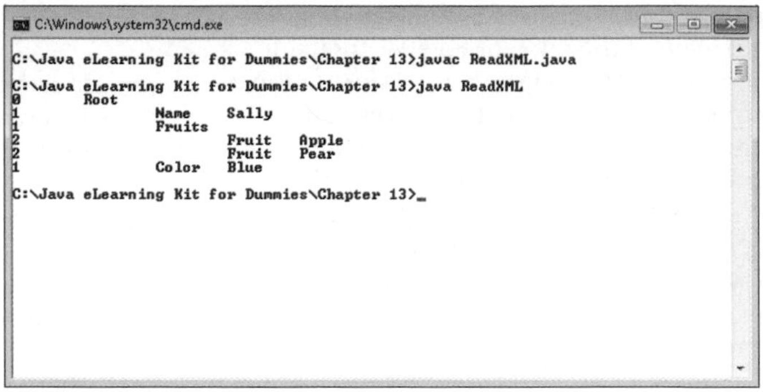

Figure 13-1

Writing XML Data to Disk

Reading XML data and creating a document that is stored in memory from it is only half the process. If you want to use XML to permanently store information on disk, you must also know how to write it.

The following example demonstrates how to create the XML document used in the ReadXML example, MyData.xml. The example will then add some information to the XML document stored in memory and write the data to disk as an XML file.

Files needed: WriteXML.java

1. **Open the editor or IDE that you've chosen to use for this book.**

2. **Type the following code into the editor screen.**

```java
// Import the required API classes.
import javax.xml.parsers.DocumentBuilderFactory;
import javax.xml.parsers.DocumentBuilder;
import javax.xml.parsers.ParserConfigurationException;
import org.w3c.dom.Document;
import org.w3c.dom.Element;
import org.w3c.dom.Text;
import javax.xml.transform.TransformerConfigurationException;
import javax.xml.transform.TransformerException;
import javax.xml.transform.TransformerFactory;
import javax.xml.transform.Transformer;
import javax.xml.transform.dom.DOMSource;
```

```java
import java.io.File;
import javax.xml.transform.stream.StreamResult;

public class WriteXML
{
    public static void main(String[] args)
    {
        // Create a factory for building an XML document.
        DocumentBuilderFactory Factory =
                DocumentBuilderFactory.newInstance();

        // Create an object to build a document.
        DocumentBuilder Builder = null;
        try
        {
            Builder = Factory.newDocumentBuilder();
        }
        catch (ParserConfigurationException e)
        {
            // Display an error message and exit.
            System.out.println("Could not create document builder!"
                    + e.getMessage());
            return;
        }

        // Create a document using the document builder.
        Document XMLDoc = Builder.newDocument();

        // Every XML document must have a root element.
        Element Root = XMLDoc.createElement("Root");

        // Add the root element to the document.
        XMLDoc.appendChild(Root);

        // Add a name element to the root.
        Element Child = XMLDoc.createElement("Name");
        Text ChildData = XMLDoc.createTextNode("Sally");
        Child.appendChild(ChildData);
        Root.appendChild(Child);

        // Create a favorite fruits list.
        Element Fruits = XMLDoc.createElement("Fruits");
        Root.appendChild(Fruits);

        // Add a favorite fruit element to Fruits.
        Child = XMLDoc.createElement("Fruit");
        ChildData = XMLDoc.createTextNode("Apple");
        Child.appendChild(ChildData);
        Fruits.appendChild(Child);
```

```java
      // Add a favorite fruit element to Fruits.
      Child = XMLDoc.createElement("Fruit");
      ChildData = XMLDoc.createTextNode("Pear");
      Child.appendChild(ChildData);
      Fruits.appendChild(Child);

      // Add a favorite color element to the root.
      Child = XMLDoc.createElement("Color");
      ChildData = XMLDoc.createTextNode("Blue");
      Child.appendChild(ChildData);
      Root.appendChild(Child);

      // Create a factory for transforming the memory
      // representation of the XML document into an
      // actual XML document.
      TransformerFactory TFactory =
            TransformerFactory.newInstance();

      // Create a transformer to perform the work.
      Transformer CreateResult = null;
      try
      {
         CreateResult = TFactory.newTransformer();
      }
      catch (TransformerConfigurationException e)
      {
         // Display an error message and exit.
         System.out.println("Could not create transformer!"
              + e.getMessage());
         return;
      }

      // Define a Document Object Model source used as a
      // basis for the output document.
      DOMSource Source = new DOMSource(XMLDoc);

      // Define a file to receive the XML document.
      File OutputFile = new File("MyData.xml");

      // Define a stream to transfer the file.
      StreamResult Result = new StreamResult(OutputFile);

      // Perform the transformation required to output
      // the document to disk.
      try
      {
         CreateResult.transform(Source, Result);
      }
      catch (TransformerException e)
      {
```

```
        // Display an error message and exit.
        System.out.println("Could not save XML document!"
            + e.getMessage());
    }

    // Display a success message.
    System.out.println("Document successfully saved!");
    }
}
```

As with the ReadXML example, this example requires a relatively large number of imports that are listed in the order in which they're used. The application begins with the same process used for reading an XML file: creating a `DocumentBuilderFactory`, using the `Factory` to create a `DocumentBuilder`, and then calling on `Builder` to create a new XML document, `XMLDoc`. This same process occurs in just about every XML application you create.

Every XML document starts with a `Root Element` that the code creates using `createElement()`. The code appends `Root` to `XMLDoc` to begin building the XML document.

When working with an `Element` — `Child`, in this case — that contains a value, the value is contained within a `Text` object — `ChildData` here. The code appends `ChildData` to `Child` (the element contains the value) and then appends `Child` to `Root` (the root-element contains all of the top level elements). Each top-level element follows the same process.

Second-level elements are appended to first-level elements. For example, `Fruits` is a first-level element. It contains two second-level `Fruit` elements, one with a value of `Apple` and another with a value of `Pear`. Notice how the code appends the `Child` elements to the appropriate parent.

At some point, the code has created an XML document. This isn't XML data suitable for writing to disk because it's in a form that's more useful for working with the data in memory. The code creates a `TransformerFactory`, `TFactory`, to create a `Transformer` object, `CreateResult`, that transforms the XML document into XML data that the application can then write to disk.

The code creates a `DOMSource`, `Source`, to provide access to the information in `XMLDoc`. It also creates a `File` object, `OutputFile`, to hold the data on disk. To send data to `OutputFile`, the application must also create a `StreamResult` object, `Result`. At this

GO ONLINE

Several standards exist for creating XML data stored in files. This example uses the Document Object Model (DOM). Discussing the precise differences between the XML storage techniques is well outside the scope of this book. The best place to learn about DOM is `http://www.w3.org/DOM`. You can find a DOM tutorial at `http://www.w3schools.com/htmldom/default.asp`.

point, the code transforms the data found in XMLDoc by accessing it through Source. It then sends the transformed result through Result to OutputFile for storage as text.

3. **Type** javac WriteXML.java **and press Enter.**

   The compiler compiles your application and creates a .class file from it.

4. **Type** java WriteXML **and press Enter.**

   The application displays a success message. Of course, you have no idea whether or not the application output something useful.

5. **Open** MyData.xml **using your favorite XML viewer (most browsers can perform this task).**

   You see the final XML document, as shown in Figure 13-2. Your output may vary a little from that shown in the screenshot — this output is for Internet Explorer.

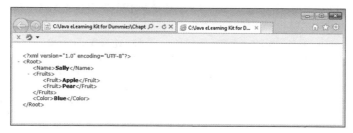

Figure 13-2

Summing Up

Here are the key points you learned about in this chapter:

- ✔ Reading an XML file from disk provides data to your application.

- ✔ Your application must parse an XML file in order to convert it from text to an actual document.

- ✔ The process for creating an XML document begins with a factory that creates an XML document builder, which is used to build the XML document.

- ✔ To create an XML document, you must build it out of component objects such as Element and Text.

- ✔ Each node in an XML document is appended to its parent, including element values, which are actually Text objects.

- ✔ Saving an XML document as XML data means transforming it and then sending it to a file on disk.

Try-it-yourself lab

For more practice with the features covered in this chapter, try the following exercise on your own:

1. **Open the `MyData.xml` file supplied with the source code for this book.**

2. **Add more nodes to the file so that it includes additional data to process. Use the following code additions (in bold) as an example.**

```
<?xml version="1.0" encoding="UTF-8" standalone="no"?>
<Root>
    <Name>Sally</Name>
    <Fruits>
        <Fruit>Apple</Fruit>
        <Fruit>Pear</Fruit>
    </Fruits>
    <Color>Blue</Color>
    <Likes>
        <Movies>
            <Movie>Princess Bride</Movie>
            <Movie>Sleeping Beauty</Movie>
        </Movies>
    </Likes>
</Root>
```

3. **Type** java ReadXML **and press Enter.**

   The application displays a hierarchical list of the nodes within the XML file. How does the output from the application change with the change in the data file? How many levels does the output include now?

Know this tech talk

element: A major division of data within an XML document. It consists of a start tag, an end tag, and everything between. An element commonly contains attributes, other elements, and a single value. However, an element can contain a wealth of other data types.

eXtensible Markup Language (XML): A markup language specifically designed to make it easy to transfer data between applications and disparate computer platforms. Even though XML relies on text as an underlying storage technology, it actually conveys considerable information about the context and properties of the data it transports.

node: Any discrete object within an XML document.

parse: The act of reading information from a source, interpreting it, and creating a new object from it as output. Parsing is one way to convert information from one type to another. In many cases, parsers read data in text format and create an intelligent object from it that can use the textual information in unique ways.

recursion: A programming technique where a method calls itself to break a complex task down into simpler pieces. The result of the simple task is then used to make completing the complex task possible. A recursive method must always include some means of escape so that the routine will exit once the task is simple enough.

value: The single text value between the start tag and end tag of an element that defines the content of that element. For example, when looking at `<Name>Sally</Name>`, the value is `Sally`.

Index

U

V

Notes

Notes

Notes

Notes

About the Author

John Mueller is a freelance author and technical editor. He has writing in his blood, having produced 93 books and over 300 articles to date. The topics range from networking to artificial intelligence and from database management to heads-down programming. Some of his current books include a Windows command-line reference, books on VBA and Visio 2007, a C# design and development manual, and an IronPython programmer's guide. His technical editing skills have helped over more than 63 authors refine the content of their manuscripts. John has provided technical editing services to both *Data Based Advisor* and *Coast Compute* magazines. He has also contributed articles to magazines such as *Software Quality Connection, DevSource, InformIT, SQL Server Professional, Visual C++ Developer, Hard Core Visual Basic, asp.netPRO, Software Test and Performance,* and *Visual Basic Developer.* Be sure to read John's blog at http://blog.johnmuellerbooks.com/.

Dedication

This book is dedicated to my wonderful wife and best friend, Rebecca, whose smile can warm the coldest day.

Author's Acknowledgments

Thanks to my wife, Rebecca, for working with me to get this book completed. I really don't know what I would have done without her help in researching and compiling some of the information that appears in this book. She also did a fine job of proofreading my rough draft. Rebecca keeps the house running while I'm buried in work.

Russ Mullen deserves thanks for his technical edit of this book. He greatly added to the accuracy and depth of the material you see here. Matt Wagner, my agent, deserves credit for helping me get the contract in the first place and taking care of all the details that most authors don't really consider. I always appreciate his assistance. It's good to know that someone wants to help.

A number of people read all or part of this book to help me refine the approach, test the coding examples, and generally provide input that all readers wish they could have. These unpaid volunteers helped in ways too numerous to mention here. I especially appreciate the efforts of Eva Beattie, Glenn A. Russell, Hamid Ramazani, William Bridges, and Osvaldo Téllez Almirall, who provided general input, read the entire book, and selflessly devoted themselves to this project.

Finally, I would like to thank Connie Santisteban, Paul Levesque, Virginia Sanders, and the rest of the editorial and production staff at Wiley for their assistance in bringing this book to print. It's always nice to work with such a great group of professionals.

Publisher's Acknowledgments

Acquisitions Editor: Constance Santisteban

Senior Project Editor: Paul Levesque

Copy Editor: Virginia Sanders

Technical Editor: Russ Mullen

Editorial Assistant: Annie Sullivan

Sr. Editorial Assistant: Cherie Case

Project Coordinator: Patrick Redmond

Cover Image: ©olaser/iStockphoto.com

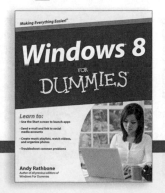

Math & Science

Algebra I For Dummies,
2nd Edition
978-0-470-55964-2

Anatomy and Physiology
For Dummies, 2nd Edition
978-0-470-92326-9

Astronomy For Dummies,
3rd Edition
978-1-118-37697-3

Biology For Dummies,
2nd Edition
978-0-470-59875-7

Chemistry For Dummies,
2nd Edition
978-1-118-00730-3

1001 Algebra II Practice
Problems For Dummies
978-1-118-44662-1

Microsoft Office

Excel 2013 For Dummies
978-1-118-51012-4

Office 2013 All-in-One
For Dummies
978-1-118-51636-2

PowerPoint 2013
For Dummies
978-1-118-50253-2

Word 2013 For Dummies
978-1-118-49123-2

Music

Blues Harmonica
For Dummies
978-1-118-25269-7

Guitar For Dummies,
3rd Edition
978-1-118-11554-1

iPod & iTunes
For Dummies, 10th Edition
978-1-118-50864-0

Programming

Beginning Programming
with C For Dummies
978-1-118-73763-7

Excel VBA Programming
For Dummies, 3rd Edition
978-1-118-49037-2

Java For Dummies,
6th Edition
978-1-118-40780-6

Religion & Inspiration

The Bible For Dummies
978-0-7645-5296-0

Buddhism For Dummies,
2nd Edition
978-1-118-02379-2

Catholicism For Dummies,
2nd Edition
978-1-118-07778-8

Self-Help & Relationships

Beating Sugar Addiction
For Dummies
978-1-118-54645-1

Meditation For Dummies,
3rd Edition
978-1-118-29144-3

Seniors

Laptops For Seniors
For Dummies, 3rd Edition
978-1-118-71105-7

Computers For Seniors
For Dummies, 3rd Edition
978-1-118-11553-4

iPad For Seniors
For Dummies, 6th Edition
978-1-118-72826-0

Social Security
For Dummies
978-1-118-20573-0

Smartphones & Tablets

Android Phones
For Dummies, 2nd Edition
978-1-118-72030-1

Nexus Tablets
For Dummies
978-1-118-77243-0

Samsung Galaxy S 4
For Dummies
978-1-118-64222-1

Samsung Galaxy Tabs
For Dummies
978-1-118-77294-2

Test Prep

ACT For Dummies,
5th Edition
978-1-118-01259-8

ASVAB For Dummies,
3rd Edition
978-0-470-63760-9

GRE For Dummies,
7th Edition
978-0-470-88921-3

Officer Candidate Tests
For Dummies
978-0-470-59876-4

Physician's Assistant Exam
For Dummies
978-1-118-11556-5

Series 7 Exam For Dummies
978-0-470-09932-2

Windows 8

Windows 8.1 All-in-One
For Dummies
978-1-118-82087-2

Windows 8.1 For Dummies
978-1-118-82121-3

Windows 8.1 For Dummies
Book + DVD Bundle
978-1-118-82107-7

ℯ Available in print and e-book formats.

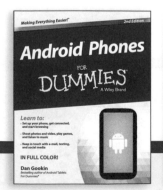

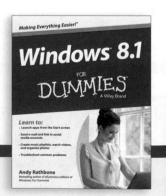

Available wherever books are sold. **For more information or to order direct visit www.dummies.com**

Take Dummies with you everywhere you go!

Whether you are excited about e-books, want more from the web, must have your mobile apps, or are swept up in social media, Dummies makes everything easier.

Leverage the Power

For Dummies is the global leader in the reference category and one of the most trusted and highly regarded brands in the world. No longer just focused on books, customers now have access to the For Dummies content they need in the format they want. Let us help you develop a solution that will fit your brand and help you connect with your customers.

Advertising & Sponsorships

Connect with an engaged audience on a powerful multimedia site, and position your message alongside expert how-to content.

Targeted ads • Video • Email marketing • Microsites • Sweepstakes sponsorship

21 Million Monthly Page Views & 13 Million Unique Visitors